PRAISE FOR *THE AMATEUR*

'This fascinating, beautifully written book opens up a whole new world. It's about colonial amateur readers, readers from Africa, the Caribbean, and South Asia, who loved literature from the far-reaches of empire and who often struggled to come to terms with what their love of canonical white literature meant to them and others. Funnily enough that is now a struggle even those of us who love literature closer to the centre share: why do we love these classics so much, remote as they are from most of those around us and indeed from the world we actually live in? A book, then, that anyone interested in great literature can learn from.'

Simon During, Honorary Professor of Culture and
Communication, The University of Melbourne, Australia

'In gorgeous prose, Saikat Majumdar conjures up scenes of autodidacts and amateur readers in the colonies, describing their idiosyncratic, haphazard, and ambivalent encounters with books. These encounters, he shows, have much to teach scholars of literature. A brilliant and groundbreaking contribution to postcolonial studies as well as to debates about the aims, methods, and value of reading.'

Rita Felski, John Stewart Bryan Professor of English,
University of Virginia, USA

'In an age of hyper-professionalism, *The Amateur* shows the possibilities, pleasures, and productive potential of amateur reading, even – perhaps especially – when undertaken in colonial and postcolonial settings. Majumdar's deft history of amateur reading and criticism doubles up as a history of literary humanities across the reaches of the British empire, including India, South Africa, and the Caribbean. Scholarly and erudite, but also playful and engaging, this is an important book that should be read by all those interested in English literature, colonial, and postcolonial studies.'

Sanjay Seth, Professor of Politics, Goldsmiths,
University of London, UK

'By offering subtly surprising readings of readings, *The Amateur* celebrates the power of the autodidact amateurs' literary creativity. An unusual and innovative work, it returns to read a long line of colonial readers who blossom into writers – in India, Africa, and the

Caribbean – and who miraculously turn the pleasure of the colonized at reading the colonizers' literature into an improbable vehicle for their personal and at times collective means of imaginative liberation. By subtle displacements – both deliberate and unintended – these authors turn English writing into a vehicle of meaningful, at times rebellious alterity. In this beautifully written book, the delicacy of Majumdar's readings discovers improbable personal and collective rebellions inside the heart of what is generally regarded as literary imitation.'

Supdita Kaviraj, Professor of Indian Politics and
Intellectual History, Columbia University, USA

THE AMATEUR

Self-Making and the Humanities in the Postcolony

Saikat Majumdar

BLOOMSBURY ACADEMIC

NEW YORK • LONDON • OXFORD • NEW DELHI • SYDNEY

BLOOMSBURY ACADEMIC
Bloomsbury Publishing Inc
1385 Broadway, New York, NY 10018, USA
50 Bedford Square, London, WC1B 3DP, UK
29 Earlsfort Terrace, Dublin 2, Ireland

BLOOMSBURY, BLOOMSBURY ACADEMIC and the Diana logo
are trademarks of Bloomsbury Publishing Plc

First published in the United States of America 2024

Cover design by Eleanor Rose
Cover images: (top) Man reading in bookstore © HamZa Nouasria / Unsplash;
(bottom) Woman reading on phone © Tom Levold / Flickr

Library of Congress Cataloging-in-Publication Data

Names: Majumdar, Saikat, author.
Title: The amateur : self-making and the humanities in the postcolony / Saikat Majumdar.
Description: New York : Bloomsbury Academic, 2024. |
Includes bibliographical references and index.
Identifiers: LCCN 2023053406 (print) | LCCN 2023053407 (ebook) | ISBN 9781501399879
(paperback) | ISBN 9781501399862 (hardback) | ISBN 9781501399886 (ebook) |
ISBN 9781501399893 (pdf)
Subjects: LCSH: Literature–Study and teaching. | Humanities–Study and teaching. |
Criticism–Study and teaching. | Learning and scholarship. | Amateurism. |
South Asia–Intellectual life. | Caribbean Area–Intellectual life. | Africa–Intellectual life.
Classification: LCC PN61 .M35 2024 (print) | LCC PN61 (ebook) |
DDC 820.9–dc23/eng/20240206
LC record available at https://lccn.loc.gov/2023053406
LC ebook record available at https://lccn.loc.gov/2023053407

ISBN: HB: 978-1-5013-9986-2
    PB: 978-1-5013-9987-9
    ePDF: 978-1-5013-9989-3
    eBook: 978-1-5013-9988-6

Typeset by Integra Software Services Pvt. Ltd.
Printed and bound in Great Britain

To find out more about our authors and books visit www.bloomsbury.com
and sign up for our newsletters.

For Anjali Prabhu and Rita Felski
Thank you for your faith in this amateur

CONTENTS

ACKNOWLEDGEMENTS

Some books have a moment of birth that one can recall with clarity. Other books live in you for a long time, raising drowsy heads and going back to sleep. They become parts of you that you don't see any more till they suddenly become adults and demand their way out. Was the amateur that wandering college student who was both irritated and strangely excited by the inevitability of examinations and the memorization of answers, turning to a secret life with books that was also a shirking of studies? Or did it come to pointed life when chatting about the idea of the literary intellectual, Terry Castle handed me a copy of Marjorie Garber's *Academic Instincts*, a book that had more serious fun with the figure of the amateur than I'd seen anywhere till then?

As someone with multiple bad habits of writing different things that at the end of the day become one large cloud of obsession, I've always felt the impossible tension between amateur and the professional as pervasive and inescapable. It was a tension that survived graduate degrees in literature and writing and lived within a working life that sustained that obsession. I just didn't know it yet. Others stepped in, asking me to take that tension seriously. Reading some of my early writing on this, Rita Felski shared her excitement, suggesting that I write something for the journal *New Literary History*. The article 'The Critic as Amateur' appeared in *NLH* in 2017, carrying in it the seeds of this book. Aarthi Vadde, another thinker on critical amateurism, joined hands with me to co-edit a collection of essays of that same title; Haaris Naqvi and Amy Williams brought it to life in 2019. I learned much from the contributors to that volume that spanned the UK, South Africa, India, Australia, and the United States, which happily included Derek Attridge, who has encouraged all my idiosyncrasies since graduate school, from boredom to amateurism and beyond. I'm also grateful to Simon Gikandi for publishing an article from this book in *PMLA* under his editorship.

Most of the writing that made this book was done with the support of two institutions: my employer, Ashoka University, who gave me a generous sabbatical leave for the academic year 2022–3, and The Stellenbosch Institute of Advanced Study, who hosted me as a Fellow from January to June 2023, not only giving me access to resources and experts in South Africa that I couldn't have reached otherwise, but also placing me in a community of brilliant and supportive fellows drawn from all disciplines in the humanities, social and natural sciences. Beyond the deeply generous staff at the Institute, this project has benefitted from the particular suggestions of Sharad Chari, Charne Lavery, Regenia Gagnier, Bronwen Morgan, Scott Nethersole, John Dupré, and Robert Vosloo.

Apart from the detailed and deeply helpful anonymous reports for Bloomsbury – both on the proposal and on the final manuscript – a few people read the draft at different stages and offered genuinely helpful comments. I'm grateful to David Attwell, Rosinka Chaudhuri, Simon During, and Sanjay Seth not only for these comments but for their groundbreaking scholarship that has nourished this book in ways only these pages can tell. Fellow South Africanist Sohinee Roy pointed me to many roads I wouldn't have taken otherwise and helped me get some hard-to-get material. My librarian at Ashoka University, Bibhuti Nath Jha, has also procured rare and out-of-print books essential to this project with remarkable agility and speed, and for that I'm grateful.

Several lectures allowed me to air some of these ideas at various stages of the writing process. Apart from the Fellows' Seminar at the Stellenbosch Institute, I'm thankful to Amit Chaudhuri for inviting me to speak about the amateur at the annual Literary Activism Symposium, organized by the University of East Anglia and Presidency University, to Olerato Mogomotsi and Divine Fuh for asking me to give a lecture as part of the African Epistemologies Advanced Seminar Series at the Institute for Humanities in Africa, the University of Cape Town, to Geetanjali Chawla for inviting me to deliver the inaugural Professor Prem Kumari Srivastava Memorial Annual Lecture at Maharaja Agrasen College, the University of Delhi, to my colleague, Jonathan Gil Harris, for sharing my *NLH* article, 'The Critic as Amateur' for the English Proseminar at Ashoka University, and discussing elements of this work there.

A shoutout to Haaris Naqvi for supporting this book, all the way from early idea to publication, and the Hali Han for keeping me on my toes about deadlines and duties on my end.

All sing in a chorus
There's room for all
Let not the mean
Or learned dean
Restrict the books
T' a favoured few
We've Books for all.
Books for the rich
And Books for the poor
Books for the man
And Books for the dame.
Books for the sick
And Books for the fit
Books for the blind
And Books for the dumb.
Books for the bungler
And Books for the wrangler
Books for the burgher
And Books for the cotter
Books for the lettered
And Books for the fettered
We've Books for all
For one and all

— S.R. Ranganathan, The Five Laws of Library Science,
quoted in J. Daniel Elam, World Literature for
the Wretched of the Earth

Chapter 1

THE COLONIAL MAP OF MISREADING

Cramming half-heartedly for the Scholarship,
I looked up from the red-jacketed Williamson's
History of the British Empire, towards
the barrack's plumed, imperial hillsides
where canon-bursts of bamboo sprayed the ridge,
riding to Khartoum, Rorke's Drift,
through dervishes of dust,
behind the chevroned jalousies
I butchered fellaheen, thuggees, Mamelukes, wogs
> — Derek Walcott, *Another Life*, quoted in
> Abdulrazak Gurnah, 'Learning to Read'

The imagination of the modern high school or college classroom across the historical stretch of the British Empire is incomplete without a certain student right at the back of the lecture hall. They are perpetually distracted, immersed in their own unruly imagination; they shirk homework and fail at examinations. But they are scandalous in a special way. Their failure is both a rebellion and a creation, a glazed indifference to an instrumental system of education whose colonial character – often long past decolonization – is hinted rather than directly established. Rabindranath Tagore's short story, 'Tota Kahini', translated as 'The Bird's Tale', is iconic in this indictment. In this allegorical story, a bird is captured by the order of the king. Infuriated by its wild and unrestrained singing, the king hands the bird over to pundits who train it day and night, drowning it in tables and grammar, till the bird eventually becomes a lifeless body, silent at last, brought to the king, who squeezes its corpse stuffed with paper and nods with satisfaction at the death of its wild song.

Rabindranath's legendary impatience with institutionalized education of the kind he saw in existence ranged from his own shirking of school as a boy to his establishment of Visva-Bharati as a university of alternative education. The vastness of his critique of traditional education is not my subject here. I wish rather to return to the figure of that scandalous student who variously articulates failure, frustration, and disappointment in their institutional experience of colonially derived curricular education that has, for instance, taken on a particularly pervasive form in India, all the way to our postcolonial present. Recalling his education at the University of Calcutta sometime in the second decade of the twentieth century, the Bengali memoirist and essayist Nirad C. Chaudhuri had this to say about all but a few exceptions among his professors: 'I paid no attention whatever to what they said and sat on one of the back-benches, either reading a book of my choice, or scribbling, or thinking my own thoughts.'[1] Shirking lectures, loafing off in the back benches, he however turned to another institution, the library, to which he credits 'nearly all my higher education'. Nearly forty years later, writing about his undergraduate education at the University of Allahabad in 1964, the poet Arvind Krishna Mehrotra recalls the pettily strategic character of his curricular study, comprising of subjects that were 'scoring', the frenzy of note-taking and rote-learning, and efforts to game the examination system by guessing possible questions from test-papers of previous years and decades – all the while privately growing as a poet and a thinker entirely outside this institutional space. And a another twenty years later, remembering his newly minted college degree from 1988, also at the University of Allahabad, Pankaj Mishra describes it as 'three idle bookish years at a provincial university in a decaying old provincial town' that had left him with stodgy but patchy learning in a dated colonial fashion but ironically with the desire to fill this large lacunae as hungrily as possible.

Debates around Western education in the British colonies are now vast enough to make up their own subfield. I return to some of its key contours later in this book. But long before I became familiar with these ceaselessly evolving debates, and long past my own stumbling familiarity with them, I cannot overcome my own memory of the slow, tedious violence of the apparatus of test-papers and note-taking and cheat sheets that were our sole weapons to deal with the giant demon of examinations that tested how well we knew the periodic tables of literary history and style taxonomies of authors – even in the last years of the previous century. But why did we feel this violence? And what was this strange force behind the urge to defy it? Perhaps it was the anxiety of being irresponsible young people in a developing nation where the responsible chose careers in medicine and engineering. Perhaps it was urgency for a kind of cosmopolitanism only attainable from books in the pre-digital age; perhaps a kind of bohemeana that only eclectic reading could read and support.

In the end, it was not something purely definable by any of these forces, significant as they all were. But my dream in this book has been to show that a certain kind of reader was inspired to seek their own eclectic, often confused and misdirected adventures with books – particularly books from the metropolitan west that were divorced from their own immediate reality. Perversely, their inspiration was powered by frustration with patterns of the strategic instrumentalism, sometimes of an exclusionary kind, that Western humanistic education came to constitute in the colony and the postcolony. The reasons behind them vary according to history and geography, and yet certain unifying patterns are discernible across the stretch of the historical British Empire (which occasionally overlapped with other forms of domination). The ironic centrality of British colonial education to the making of these adventurous autodidacts makes the English language my natural and primary archive, but this is in no way to suggest that that was the only language in which these figures conducted their reading lives. While Nirad C. Chaudhuri read and wrote just as much in Bengali as in English, Toru Dutt's connection with French literature was possibly deeper than her connection with English, along with the reading she did in Bengali and rudimentary Sanskrit. Peter Abrahams memorably chronicles his rich and troubling relation with Afrikaans literature as trapped between a beloved teacher and a history of racist nationalism, and Sindiwe Magona recollects early tremors of movement between Xhosa and English, and describes her later classroom challenges while teaching Afrikaans. The unique history of the Black and Brown diaspora in the Caribbean has left most writers there only with European languages and their creolized variations, and for the figures I read from that part of the world, English accounts for their primary reading and writing lives. Historically however, the global identity of the British Empire has been richly multilingual and deeply polyphonic. My focus on English in this book is, to a great extent, a gesture of offering unity to a large cultural and territorial expanse through my own scholarly expertise on world English. But the logic and reality of British colonial education in the humanities and the future writing lives of these figures also point to English as the natural archive of this study.

Most people would agree that autodidactism is vital to any form of aesthetic education, even when institutions and systems are fulfilling to students. Recent trends in critique and postcritique have also established the amateur reader to be more central to criticism than it might have been assumed in the decades of high professionalization of literary study in the twentieth century. But there is a unique urgency and aspiration in the amateur self-making of the literary subject in a structure of peripheral colonial education, distant from the imperial metropolis of power and culture that claims special attention. No doubt that my own memory of this desolate aspiration is one of the contexts of my interest in this process. But this small personal inspiration aside, my journey through the memorable accounts of reading and self-making left by a group of exceptional thinkers across the stretch of the British Empire across three continents has revealed to me the enabling idiosyncrasies of aesthetic education when self-willed in isolation, amidst conditions far from ideal for it.

This, then, is a book about aesthetic education that is at odds with itself. It is an education that takes place through a ceaseless conflict with its archive. Both this education and the choice of this archive are governed by structures of imperial power. What were the governing principles behind the education to which these colonial and postcolonial readers were subjected? Was this education driven by traditional liberal humanist conceptions of learning and development that acknowledged the humanity of these subjects? Or was it organized according to the scaffolding of imperialism, serving the visible and invisible, long- and short-term needs of empire? Recent inquiries into the colonial history of the humanities and the imaginative social sciences have moved beyond a simplistic opposition between these two. They have offered multiple other possibilities, including some that are hard to categorize. I will discuss some of them below, and in greater detail in relevant chapters following this one. But it remains important to remember that modern critical theory has read understood education significantly as a repressive process seeking to incorporate subjects into dominant systems. Louis Althusser's celebrated essay 'Ideology and Ideological State Apparatuses' remains a canonical text here, reading education, particularly primary and secondary education (along with church and family) as a mechanism through which human beings are incorporated to the needs and roles of the capitalist state, emerging, in the process as subjects under the delusion of independent selfhood.[2] Postcolonial writers, activists, and scholars have long revealed the ideological objectives of colonial education, in the making of colonial subjects whose legacy has lasted long past decolonization.

'The night of the bullet was followed by the morning of the chalk and blackboard,' Ngũgĩ wa Thiong'o wrote memorably, identifying the soft power of education as bolstering the hard military power of imperialism.[3] It has been established worldwide – through the machinations of post-Renaissance European colonialism as well as through twentieth-century models of economic neocolonialism – that the hard power of neither weaponry nor capitalism is quite sustainable in the long run without the softer powers of culture, of which religion and education have remained key, often coming together in the edifice of missionary education. Scholars such as Gauri Viswanathan, Chris Baldick, Rosinka Chaudhuri, and Sanjay Seth, to whose work I will extensively return in subsequent chapters, have convincingly put forward the complex nature of imperially structured education in the colony, and its various points of conflict with indigenous subjectivities.[4] At the same time, major thinkers have also celebrated various pedagogies of the oppressed and the disenfranchised, notably by Paolo Freire, bell hooks, and Gayatri Chakravarty Spivak.[5] The key question that I ask is this: what happens when those who are variously oppressed or excluded seek out texts to read, primarily from Western humanities, particularly when the aspiration for an enlightened and cosmopolitan subjecthood driving this reading is structured within the ideology and infrastructure of imperialism?

The complex hug and battle with colonial education and its roster of texts that this aspiration creates has been articulated memorably by many postcolonial writers. 'The Western literary canon may be an abstraction elsewhere,' writes Ankhi Mukherjee at the opening of her book *What Is a Classic? Postcolonial Rewriting and Invention of the Canon*, 'but in the postcolony it is a key prop in an all-too-familiar scene involving a shelf of European books and a "provincial" writer who dreams of arriving at the hubs of world literature.'[6] This imaginative and intellectual tension is one of the most significant points of origin of postcolonial literatures written in European languages. A defining feature of this torn relation is the striking disjuncture between the immediate sensory experience of the colonized/decolonized subject, and the reality contained within their reading. The literature, for instance, that played a formative role in the literary *Bildung* of V.S. Naipaul embodied this very paradox. 'There was, for instance,' he wrote, 'Wordsworth's notorious poem about the daffodil. A pretty little flower, no doubt; but we had never seen it. Could the poem have any meaning for us?'[7] Daffodils and snow and strawberries – could they ever become part of the indigenous subjectivity, literary or otherwise, in hot tropical climes where they arrived textually, often with the authority of the educational canon? And conversely, did sandy tropical beaches and palm trees stand the danger of becoming 'exotic', given the nature of their description in these texts, notwithstanding their tangible physicality in the immediate reality surrounding these readers? Abdulrazak Gurnah reflects on the strange desolation of the imperial gaze in Western literature directed at the native as captured in Derek Walcott's poem, 'Another Life': 'Cramming half-heartedly for the Scholarship,/I looked up from my red-jacketed Williamson's', only to see 'behind the chevroned jalousies/I butchered fellaheen, thuggees, Mamelukes, wogs'.[8] The poem, from which I have quoted at length as an epigraph to this chapter, appears to be required reading for some competitive scholarship, as was common in the British colonies. Walcott's narrator recognizes that the racial disdain and sense of alienness in the book they are reading, directed at people very much like themselves – 'fellaheen, thuggees, Mamelukes, wogs', much like Chinua Achebe would feel while reading Joseph Conrad's *Heart of Darkness*. And Gurnah realizes it in his own reading of the poem: 'I recognize this sense of seeing oneself through the eyes of another culture, and one which is used to despising you.' Reading this was a kind of a decentring of one's subjectivity, a kind of an othering of one's self, which, though a disturbing experience, was a productive kind for the novelist of the future: 'And before I could learn to read these texts and see what was there, I first had to learn to look at myself through different eyes, to imagine myself differently as a consumer of these narratives.'[9]

These have been well-known and severely felt questions for generations of postcolonial writers and thinkers. They have found canonical moments of articulation in texts like Ngũgĩ's *Decolonising the Mind,* with its arguments about colonial education cutting off native children from local myths and folktales and alienizing, even exoticizing African figures and realities through imperial constructions of Africa. Both Ngũgĩ and Gurnah talk about the splitting of the colonized consciousness into the spaces of the private and the instrumental-professional, between the local vernacular and English; for Gurnah, it would be some time before English would gain 'any narrative utility' beyond the relationship he had with the language, which was 'casual and instrumental', that of just 'a subject at school'.[10] And in J.M. Coetzee's 'The Novel in Africa', the fictitious Nigerian novelist and speaker Emmanuel Egudu, makes the argument that the reading of novels itself does not make sense in Africa, the solipsism and interiority of the act being out of place in the communal and performative culture of the land.[11] It is a claim, while framed as provocative and suspicious within the behavioural dynamics of the characters in Coetzee's text, nevertheless must give us some pause. But here's the disturbing yet unavoidable reality: notwithstanding the contrarian or adversarial nature of this relationship between the text and the reader, such acts of reading are often carried out with passion. What happens, therefore, when a colonial or postcolonial subject gets 'hooked' to such texts, to use Rita Felski's term for intense readerly attachment?[12] Does that attachment then lead to what Lauren Berlant has called in a different context, 'cruel optimism', desire for objects, ideas, or reality that actually hinder one's own happiness and prosperity?[13]

There is much contention here. But contention, when carried out with passion and sincerity, always creates value, if of unexpected or even accidental kinds. Here, the struggle with archive and institution creates, before anything else, lasting moments of misreading that are simultaneously idiosyncratic and symptomatic of a larger colonial alienation. A colonial education brings with it an archive that is as human as it is alien – texts of literature, history, and social life that is far removed from the immediate experience of the local reader. But this distance is much more than merely physical or ethnographic; it becomes formal, generic, and even spiritual, outlining forms of life inconceivable to readers in the colony. Ankhi Mukherjee points to the primacy of the global novel in the bookcase of Amitav Ghosh's grandfather, in Ghosh's essay 'The March of the Novel Through History: The Testimony of My Grandfather's Bookcase', all in English but translated from European languages, including the Russian giants, the great nineteenth-century realists, as well as a whole shelf of forgotten Nobel Prize winners. In his essay, Ghosh remembers the distinct criteria of admission to this bookcase, shaped by exclusion as much as by inclusion: 'textbooks and schoolbooks were never allowed; nor were books of a technical or professional nature – nothing to do with engineering, or medicine or law, or indeed any of the callings that afforded my uncles their livings'.[14] While the bookcase had a few works of psychology and anthropology that had entered the literary consciousness of the time, such as *The Golden Bough*, works of Freud, Marx and Engels, Havelock Ellis and Malinowski, the bulk of the books were novels that signified the notion of a cosmopolitan canon of high world literature. Ghosh did not recall seeing a bookshelf with a similar aspiration during his student days in England in the 1970s and the 1980s. He only encountered iterations of such reading and archives in other locations of the Global South, such as in the lives of the Burmese novelist Mya Than Tint, or the Indonesian novelist, Pramoedya Ananta Toer. The presence of the Western novel in such native archive of reading reveals an enthusiasm that is, however, scarcely able to bridge the socio-historical distance with which this genre of European modernity arrives in the postcolony – be it for the fictitious Egudu or the real Naipaul or Ghosh or Pankaj Mishra, all of whom negotiate with the genre in the different ways required by their respective generations. The consequent mistakes, anxieties, and misreadings reveal vast cracks of knowledge, often entire abysses about the socio-historical contexts of texts, institutional norms about reading practice, and perhaps most crucially, the metropolitan relation to Western literature that tend to shape reading practices institutionalized by the discipline.

This brings me to the title of this book, and the amateur in it. In his influential book, *Cultural Capital: The Problem of Literary Canon Formation*, John Guillory argued that the main function of canon formation, be it conservative or politically disruptive, was the consolidation of cultural capital, which unites the traditionally liberal humanist with queer, feminist, or decolonial approaches to literary study.[15] To engage effectively in any of these was to successfully participate in the production of cultural capital. That the colony can be just as eager for the ownership of such cultural capital is revealed by Amitav Ghosh in the essay above, when he quotes Nirad C. Chaudhuri writing about Calcutta in the 1920s and 1930s: 'Not to be able to show at least one book by a Nobel Laureate was regarded almost as being illiterate.'[16] To inquire into the very possibility of reading in the absence (or minimal presence) of such cultural capital, therefore, is to carry out a deeply fallible project, as among other things, cultural capital starts to build up the moment one initiates a functional reading process. Likewise, I recognize the dangers of describing critical amateurism as lacking cultural capital. Such amateurism, sometimes identified as the performance of the dilettante or a virtuoso – or even the older figure of the (inevitably gendered) man-of-letters – has historically been invested with significant socio-economic privilege. But the idea and even the historical practice of the amateur reader has a doubleness, indeed, multiplicity to it, that requires closer attention.

Reading unschooled

What does it mean to be an amateur when it comes to reading, thinking, and writing – particularly about the process of engaging with literature and articulating the experience of that engagement? In her provocative book, *Academic Instincts*, Marjorie Garber has raised the tantalizing question about the fields where the amateurism is shunned, and those where they are actually seen as desirable, values which also seem to change with history.[17] At least during certain periods, in some cases including our present, amateurism is seen as desirable in politics worldwide, implying the 'unsullied' outsider free of the usual corruption and the inertia of power that is seen as defining the seasoned politician. Both the 2016 election of Donald Trump as the US president and Brexit, the popular British vote to exit the European Union have been read as at least partly driven by a popular suspicion of experts and intellectuals – howsoever the consequence of these decisions have turned out to be. Another space where the amateur–professional duality has prospered for a long time is sports, where a certain implication of class superiority has sometimes shaped the idea of the amateur, who plays for love, as opposed to the upwardly mobile (and therefore lower-class) professional who has pointed social and economic objectives to achieve through their performance – and hence, is 'less pure' in their pursuit. But such examples scarcely offer the complete picture. 'We don't,' writes Garber, 'so much value amateur surgeons, for example, or amateur lawyers. We live in a world of professionals and professionalization, from big league sports to massage therapy.'[18] Amateur detectives have their esteem primarily in fiction, ranging from Auguste Dupin to Hercules Poirot to Miss Marple and Sherlock Holmes, charismatic amateurs all. What does this mean for discussion of literary texts? Is there a way of reading literature that illustrates institutional training? I don't mean scholarly ways of reading, or methods valued by the academic profession at different points in history, questions that I will address in the next chapter. The methods of professional scholarship remain far out of the reach of these (post)colonial amateurs, who draw far more deeply on sources of individual imagination than on disciplinary models established at any point, even within cultural contexts available to them. But it remains crucial to evaluate the impact of institutional education as might be available to a successful product of such institutions.

Stepping aside from the question of cultural capital as articulated by John Guillory, which shapes the socio-political identity of professional academics, one can ask more basic questions about what a college education in literature may achieve for a graduate. What is the skill or set of skills that can be accumulated through several years of systematic study in an institutional setting under a pre-set curriculum that is recognized by the state and the free market (howsoever indifferent that recognition might be) as a valid certification? The answers are many, and yet the skill that many of these non-metropolitan readers lack most emphatically vis-à-vis their encounter with Western texts is what I would call a knowledge of a larger whole. This knowledge is the unique gift of a literary-historical training, supposed to enrich rather than negate, the idiosyncratic pleasure of reading a single text, or the singularity of that experience. It stems from the realization that literary works, whatever their pleasures and challenges, do not exist in isolation, that they can be located not only in an author's life but in entire traditions of literature, art, and thought, in a larger community of ideas that is not generally available without scholarly training.

Of course, every reader of a literary work brings some context to her reading. No mind is a blank slate, and by the time we are old enough to read, we bring with us knowledges of various worlds of our own, worlds from which literary works are themselves crafted. It can be any kind of knowledge – that of childrearing, sports, furniture design, nature, banking, or for that matter, the affective knowledge of love, grief, or boredom. In fact, it is the recognition of worlds known from the non-literary realm that forms the ground for empathy, a vital element of engagement with the literary work. If literature is woven from life, no one alive does not bring some knowledge of the collective whole from which a work of literature is crafted, as that collective whole is founded in life itself. Non-metropolitan readers lacking proper literary education have often brought peculiar forms of local knowledge to Western texts about whose cultural contexts they were ignorant, often to the production of a wholly different kind of meaning. But professional training in literary study gives us the specific literary context of a particular work, whether its relationship to questions of craft, genre, or technique, or a particular national or regional tradition of writing, or the material contexts of its production. And then there are larger historical, political, and economic contexts within which the works emerge and are read – we can adjust the scale of our reading as narrowly or as widely as it suits our methodology, or for that matter, our ideology.

The professionally trained reader of literature comes from an organized community that has institutionalized elements and traditions of knowledge held to be integrally allied to its archive of study. Such alliances include the material–historical and the formal–aesthetic, and even if there are debates about the relative importance of specific elements, the community is held together by a broad consensus about the overall relevance of this apparatus of knowledge to the literary text – a consensus, which, it goes without saying, shifts with the passage of time. The reader who lacks this professional training comes from no such community and hence lacks not only expertise in these forms of knowledge, but the means to access them, and moreover, a full sense of the importance of this very apparatus. And yet, if the text is linguistically available to her, it is essentially open to reading, and in this reading she brings to the text the knowledge of life as she possesses it, regardless of the relation of such knowledge to institutionalized scholarship.

The two modes of reading are separated not merely by quantitative differences in 'expertise' – in fact, both the notion of 'expertise' and its quantifiability must remain open to question if we are to move beyond the disciplinary ideology of literary study. There exists, rather, a clear qualitative difference between them – that which stems from the divergence between the critic and the scholar. In this, the critic is more closely allied to the poet or the fiction writer than to the scholar. The provincial amateur, who charts their own relationship to a text without access to community, institution, or essential archive, can aspire to be a critic but rarely to be a scholar. It is also inevitably the difference between the work of a subjective (usually but not necessarily idiosyncratic) agency and that of an organized community. It is the difference, in the end, between self and archive.

The two modes, that of criticism and scholarship approximate two kinds of relationship to the literary text as they have been traditionally understood. They remain ontologically entwined – scholarship must be critical in spirit, and there is much criticism that is deeply scholarly – but I would argue that they are epistemologically separable. In his provocative recent book on literary study as a profession, *Professing Criticism*, John Guillory has pointed to the historical struggle between scholarship and criticism exactly as literary study was seeking professional integration as an academic discipline within the university. The attempt was to 'reconcile criticism, as a discourse of opinion, with scholarship, as a discourse of knowledge'.[19] Literary criticism traded its amateur status for a professional identity by successfully resolving its tension with scholarship, and according to Guillory, its way of doing so 'was to organize the disorganized discourses of philology, literary history, and belletristic appreciation into the one discipline of literary criticism'.[20] The intriguing consequence was that criticism thus became an academic profession before it became a discipline.

Joseph North's ambitious argument in *Literary Criticism: A Political History* charts a comparable struggle between criticism and scholarship that leads to the almost complete disappearance of the function of the critic and the ascendency, and finally, the complete dominance of the figure of the scholar over academic literary studies in the Anglo-American academy since the 1980s.[21] It is significant that North reads criticism as a 'program of aesthetic education' that had its ascendancy with the Leavises and I.A. Richards in England, while scholarship entails reading literary texts diagnostically, to reveal social and historical knowledge surrounding the production of a text. My interpretation of the figure of the scholar and that of the critic is closely related to what North suggests, though I approach the figures from a slightly different angle. The way I see it, the scholar is defined by their commitment to their archive of study. Their sense of self is subordinated to (though not effaced by) this commitment. The critic, on the other hand, celebrates and foregrounds their subjectivity; the archive, in their case, is subordinated to the self, through which it is processed and presented, the very personal colour of that refraction remaining the most cherished element of the process.

What, then, has been the relation between literary study and professionalism? Has the latter been historically central to the former? Has the consolidation of literary study as an academic discipline made the two synonymous? In *Professing Criticism*, Guillory provides a sustained analysis of the emergence of literary study as a professionalized discipline and its embeddedness in the profession of teaching. He reads the discipline's centralization professionalism as indicating 'an ambivalent relation to its amateur past, its earlier identity as criticism'.[22] This ambivalence, according to him, has never really been closed, and 'literary study attempts to resolve this ambivalence by professing criticism'.[23] Even though literary study was an old practice in the west, the nineteenth century brought radical uncertainties about its proper object, which felt divided between language and literature. It was F.R. Leavis who integrated it as a practice with scientific credentials, but according to Guillory, Leavis did not necessarily see it becoming a profession. But his followers were more intent on professionalization.

This account of the professionalization of literary criticism allows Guillory to arrive at the most radical claim in his book – that professionalization, in the domain of literary study as a kind of deformation: 'The premise of my argument is that the most highly specialized, highly skilled forms of cognitive labor entail a correlative disability, or what has sometimes been called a "professional deformation".'[24] In her review of the book, Merve Emre identifies this argument as central: 'If there is a thesis that unites the essays in "Professing Criticism," it is that professional formation entails a corresponding "déformation professionnelle".'[25] Unidirectional mastery in a narrow domain, which is what scholarly professionalism has entailed through most of the twentieth century, is its own blinders, particularly oblivion to other ways of looking at things. Emre cites related terms that imply this professional deformation: John Dewey's 'occupational psychosis', Thorstein Veblen's 'trained incapacity', and Geoffrey K. Pullman's 'nerdview', going back to Nietzsche's scathing commentary about professionalism as crooked, oppressive, a debilitating aesthetic of claustrophobia and premature superannuation. As Guillory argues, 'Nietzsche's comment on the scholar's "overestimation [Überschätzung] of the nook in which he sits and spins" specifies the inflection of narcissism specific to "scholarship, as opposed to medicine or other professional fields".[26] John Dewey's criticism of the professionalization of disciplines, however, is more political, as for instance that of the blinkered perspective of economics, which he sees as particularly corrupted by industrial capitalism. The practice of poetry, on the other hand, has been defined by Kenneth Burke as the least 'psychotic' and therefore the least deforming: 'After all, the devices of poetry are close to the spontaneous genius of man.'[27] Guillory, however, reads Burke's position as a necessary error, as 'poetry is not being represented here as a privileged "occupation"; it is rather a figure for perspectivism itself'.[28]

The high price of the deep professionalization of literary study might have paved a context for the vigorous return of lay or amateur reader in the contemporary 'postcritical' debates. In his article 'Postcritique and the Problem of the Lay Reader', Tobias Skiveren has recently re-asserted the complex and implied importance of this figure. 'Throughout most of its modern institutional existence,' he argues, 'the field of literary studies has repeatedly framed the lay reader as its constitutive Other; the excluded subjectivity against which the proper literary critic defends himself.'[29] The phenomenon of postcritique has naturally involved a turning away from the professional, and a certain celebration of the amateur reader. Skivereen is sceptical about this celebration and feels that this merely indicates a historical overreach on part of the discipline: 'The return of the amateur reader, the "lover" of literature, is a curious unintended consequence of the profession's overestimation of its aims.'[30] The renewed interest in the amateur and a disavowal of disciplinary methods of reading is not likely, he feels to bring back the social prominence occupied by critics in the nineteenth century. What valence, then, might the figure of the amateur reader/critic have today?

Even within the history of Western modernity, the terms 'amateur' and 'professional' have shared a shifting and contradictory relationship. Marjorie Garber's provocative argument is that the two terms 'are always in each other's pockets. They produce each other and they define each other by mutual affinities and exclusions.'[31] They have, in many ways, been shaped by their reciprocal disavowal, and their mutual relationship, in the end, is not so much oppositional as dialectical: 'Not only are they mutually interconnected. Part of their power comes from the disavowal of the close affinity between them.'[32] Nowhere does the narrative of professionalization feel more embattled than in the field of study that takes culture as its object. 'For if culture is defined as the wholeness of a valued past,' writes Bruce Robbins, 'set against the fragmentation of the modern city and the division of labor, then a professional discipline that takes culture as its object must seem to have fallen from culture, to be untrue to culture, to be in a state of contradiction, from the very moment it becomes a discipline.'[33] The professionalization of the literary academic, therefore, has an element of contradiction within it, insofar as the amateur may claim to exist in a more seamless continuity with literature than the relatively detached scholar. The rise of the literary critic as a figure of expertise, Bruce Robbins tells us, 'Is thus necessarily the rise of the *anti-professional* specialist.'[34]

The respective prestige of the amateur and the professional, Garber has likewise argued, has been more historically variable in the humanistic fields of knowledge than elsewhere. By way of a recapitulation of the changing prestige of the amateur and the professional in the Anglo-American world of letters, she returns to the term 'virtuosi' (along with what she calls 'its more abjected companion, dilettante') as it was used in seventeenth-century England as a prestigious antecedent of the literary amateur. Throughout the eighteenth century, while the dilettante sat in a position of humility next to the 'better-informed' virtuoso, neither term had the trivial or derogatory cast that they would earn with the increasing professionalization of literary studies. It was through the nineteenth century that the virtuoso, the dilettante, and the belletrist gradually came to be devalued, to the point where an Oxford don could measure academic success with the claim that 'we have risen above the mere belletristic treatment of classical literature.'[35] And by the 1920s, John Middleton Murry was articulating what had become a decisive dismissal of the amateur: 'No amount of sedulous apery or word-mosaic will make a writer of the dilettante belletrist.'[36]

The professionalizing trajectory of the discourse of literary thought, however, is worth close examination in terms of the ideological cast that it revealed from the very beginning. Garber gives the striking example of Charles Eliot Norton, who 'in the antebellum period was an amateur intellectual in the best sense', but in 1874 came to be appointed professor of art history at Harvard. Quickly, Norton became a champion of scholarly professionalism, and 'began to add footnotes and technical notations to his formerly more sociable and personal translations of Dante'.[37] This professionalism came with a distinct gendered performance, where credible scholarly authority belonged to the masculine mind, and the amateur sensibility, now suddenly trivialized, was identified with the feminine. Even as he emphasized the importance of teaching and a broad liberal education at the undergraduate level, Norton was enthusiastic about the rise of graduate schools, which were beginning to push the academic pursuit of knowledge from the conversational and the personal towards the scientific. Once symbolic of the confluence of intellectual and economic privileges embodied by the aristocratic man of leisure, the idea of the amateur had now relinquished its prestige to the new masculine paradigm of professionalism.

Norton's ideological arc was in many ways symptomatic of the political climate surrounding the rise and consolidation of disciplinarity in the nineteenth century. The institutionalization of English as an academic discipline in England, Chris Baldick has demonstrated convincingly, was rooted in the aim of providing education to members of various subordinate social groups at home and overseas. The formative force was the figure of Matthew Arnold, who, both Baldick and Terry Eagleton have argued, looked to literature and its pedagogic application as a means of social cohesion in a world where both religion and the aristocracy were rapidly losing their authority and cohesive power.[38] Arnold, who significantly used the term 'culture' as a translation of the German '*Bildung*' (more commonly translated as education or training), was a staunch champion of the idea of formative training, of contact with good literary models in particular, in the hope that a new trained body of teachers could be brought "into intellectual sympathy with the educated of the upper classes".[39] Arnold's bold claim on behalf of the civilizing force of literary studies laid the ideological ground for the institutionalization of the discipline, but larger social and educational developments eventually made this institutionalization possible. Of these developments, Baldick lists three as most important: 'first, the specific needs of the British empire expressed in the regulations for admission to the Indian Civil Service; second, the various movements for adult education including Mechanics Institutes, Working Men's Colleges, and extension lecturing; third, within this general movement, the specific provisions made for women's education.'[40] If English was to be a 'civilizing subject', its civilizing impact was to play the most crucial role in the education of women and the working classes and in the business of empire, in the training of its civil servants as well as of colonized subjects. 'Arnold's conceptions of the humanizing and socially healing power of literary culture', writes Baldick, 'had in fact quickly taken root where Homer was unavailable: among women, artisans, Indians, and their respective teachers.'[41]

The professionalization of English studies had important ideological motivations and even more far-reaching ideological consequences. If the amateur signified an older world of aristocratic male privilege, then professionalization, while conferring on literary-critical discourse a clear disciplinary identity and distinct institutional status, was also a pedagogic gesture towards social cohesion in an increasingly unstable world, nowhere more so than in late-Victorian England. This aim took its clearest form in providing an accessible and ideologically appropriate subject to new social groups that needed to be trained and educated in a professional way. The study of English literature was felt to possess not only adequate intellectual value but also ideological capital that allowed it to be designed as a disciplinary condition of professionalization for subjects who were key to imperial administration. Gauri Viswanathan has done pioneering work to reveal the symbiotic relation between the institutionalization of English studies and the British imperial project in India. She has reminded us that 'English literature appeared as a subject in the curriculum of the colonies long before it was institutionalized in the home country'.[42] It was in fact as early as the 1820s, when the classics still dominated the curriculum in England, that English literature had already become a curricular subject in British India. If the institutionalization of English literature was, in turn, to become a condition for the *Bildung* of professional subjects, it had a twofold goal: to train and qualify British civil servants for service in India, and to educate a class of native Indians in English culture and values so that they became effectively English in their taste and sensibility while still Indian in flesh, a class of men who would be the intermediaries between the British rulers and the native masses.

More recent inquiries into colonial education have demonstrated the reality of this process to be far more complex than such a directly ideological project might be. Rosinka Chaudhuri has foregrounded the active will with which Indians in the early nineteenth century sought European education, while Sanjay Seth has troubled the complicated the linearity of 'intent' and even the trajectory of imperial ideology by foregrounding the radically disparate subjectivities Western education in the colony necessarily entailed. While the imperial goal remains a deeply contested issue, one thing remains clear – the study of literature was to occupy the central place in this education.

The accident of aesthetic education

The phrase 'aesthetic education' is as complex as it is rich, and as potentially debilitating as it is generative. Roger Kimball points out the 'peculiarly disengaged' nature of aesthetic pleasure as it is outlined in Immanuel Kant's influential treatise, the *Critique of Judgement* – the fact that it can experienced without sensory and the tangible.[43] Unlike the physical immediacy of sensory gratification such as thirst or hunger, aesthetic pleasure is not driven by a physical lack, and is hence an 'entirely disinterested satisfaction' that works as 'the free play of the imagination and understanding'.[44] Friedrich Schiller was fascinated by the Kantian understanding of aesthetics – and particularly by the moral dimension Kant saw in it. His extended essay, *On the Aesthetic Education of Man*, draws on this moral dimension of the aesthetic experience to develop an educational programme. It resolves the conflict between the 'sense drive', rooted in self-preservation and physical existence, and 'form drive', which seeks permanence and dignified abstraction, to the emergence of the 'play drive', which, by holding the two drives in harmony, frees humans from the exclusive domination of either. This harmony creates a unique freedom that different art forms seek to attain in their own way. Beauty comes to unite the rational and the natural, enabling an entry into the 'world of ideas' but without leaving behind 'the world of sense'.[45]

Colonial or postcolonial readers of metropolitan texts whose lives are historically distant and peripheral to the cultural contexts of such texts illustrate the absence of tangible, immediate reality in ways not imagined by Kant. Here too, is the need to enter a different cultural context and a radically different subjectivity – as Gayatri Chakravarty Spivak reminds us in 'How to Read a "Culturally Different" Book' – except in this case it is the peripheral subject who must enter a universe and worldview established as superior and historically more advanced by the ideology and educational apparatus of imperialism.[46] It is precisely the failures and challenges strewn in the path of this entry that I read as elements of postcolonial amateurism, driven by the anxiety that one must do so to become a reader and writer in the modern Western sense of the term. It is sobering here to recall the way in which Simon During reads Spivak's work, *Aesthetic Education in the Age of Globalization* as enabling an 'aesthetic transformation' that is situated rather than universal. During elaborates this by describing Spivak's position as an intriguing negotiation – between the 'progressive humanism' of Schiller's aesthetic theory and Louis Althusser's denunciation of such a humanism and the essentially aesthetic apprehension of art shaped by it, as evident in Althusser's 1966 essay, 'Cremonini, Painter of the Abstract'.[47] This indicates Spivak's desire to bring Schiller's centralization of imagination together with the Althusserian emphasis on epistemology. But according to During, the attempt to reconcile these opposed forces marks Spivak's programme of aesthetic education as 'tragic', riven by 'limits and impossible choices'.[48]

Is aesthetic education tragic when enacted in the (post)colony, particularly when it seeks to read metropolitan culture? The tension between the universal and the situated becomes a fracturing one with these struggling autodidacts as they aspire for genres of imagination globalized by European modernity; this is something I hope to show in the chapters that follow. The doubts and struggles are as real as they are, in the end, variously enabling, for a range of reader-writers that include V.S. Naipaul, Peter Abrahams, Nirad C. Chaudhuri, and Pankaj Mishra, as they grapple with the aesthetic and epistemological alienness of metropolitan texts that colonialism irrevocably taught them to desire. The unavoidable question for this book then becomes: what does modern Western knowledge mean in terms of literary aesthetic, beyond the larger fact that the aesthetic as a discrete category came into being with the European Enlightenment? Among other things, it appears to imply the Romantic notion of individual creativity, as it becomes evident in Naipaul's attempt to grapple with it from the jumble of a Hindu-Trinidadian culture and an imperially structured British curriculum. But it is intriguing that in the long run, such transnational passages become important modes of rejuvenation for canonical literature, as Ankhi Mukherjee has argued in her imagination of the Western classic in the postcolonial context: 'the canon of literature and theory renews and transforms, achieves novel combinations, and fights obsolescence by being constantly on the move.'[49]

Can a study of the non-metropolitan exploration of Western literary aesthetic derive inspiration from similar projects in the social sciences? My attempt to understand colonial education owes a great deal to the work of Sanjay Seth. In *Beyond Reason: Postcolonial Theory and the Social Sciences*, Seth explains his attempt to critique the colonial impact of modern Western knowledge while working from within its scope, using Paul Rabinow's revealing words: 'to anthropologize the West, to show how exotic its constitution of reality has been; emphasize those domains most taken for granted as universal; make them seem as historically peculiar as possible; show how their claims to truth are linked to social practices and have hence become effective forces in the social world'.[50] Literature, however, constitutes reality differently from the social sciences, even if their respective realities overlap considerably; the peculiar role played by personal, often idiosyncratic imagination in the reality constructed by literature makes it as rich with the promise of empathy as it makes it vulnerable to hegemonic ideologies such as that of colonialism in ineffable and invisible ways. The story of colonial reading of metropolitan texts is also a story of misreading, and I'm most interested in moments of misreading that are surprisingly and accidentally generative. However, if the influential account of misreading as the connective tissue of literary history is offered by Harold Bloom, acts of colonial misreading, reaching out to texts from cultures at a radical remove, could not possibly be more different. When Bloom argues that 'poetic history' is 'indistinguishable from poetic influence', I sense the breathing presence of T.S. Eliot's imagination of the symbiotic relation between tradition and individual talent – more pressingly so when Bloom argues that poetic influence makes poets not less but more original. But what is the tradition through which a young Dionne Brand reads *Lady Chatterley's Lover* alongside *The Black Napoleon*, Nirad C. Chaudhuri reads Edward Gibbons, Theodor Mommsen, and James Bryce, Toru Dutt or C.L.R. James reads Thackeray and George Eliot, Peter Abrahams reads Romantic and Harlem Renaissance poets, Pankaj Mishra reads Edmund Wilson? The material infrastructure of empire often explains the presence of these books in the reading paths of these colonial and postcolonial readers, but their encounter with them is still enabled by serendipity. And the intensity of these reading experiences is inseparable from the flawed nature of the readings, to be productively understood through the negotiation of the humanistic and the ideological – through the negotiation of Schiller and Althusser as that During sees essential to Spivak's programme of aesthetic education.

In *The Intellectual Life of the British Working Classes*, Jonathan Rose tries to touch the core of the impulse behind interpretation. In doing so, he invokes the sociologist Erving Goffman's celebration of the primitive question that comes to the human mind upon encountering an external universe, that which they 'continue to ask up to the moment of death: "What is going on here?"'.[51] This is the question, Rose argues, prompted 'people at the bottom of the economic pyramid' to read and make their own texts as widely varies as the Bible, *Jude the Obscure*, the *Girl's Own Paper*, Beethoven, the BBC, *Marines of Guadalcanal*, adult education courses, elementary school lessons, 'even the disciplinary thrashings administered by schoolmasters'.[52] To make sense of a situation, be it a book or sensory data, Goffman has argued, the human mind creates a frame, which does for it what the program does for a computer: 'it determines how we read a given text or situation'.[53]

My project has something in common with Rose's attempt to recover the reading and thinking lives of ordinary readers in Britain, particularly those outside the upper and middle classes who have traditionally articulated accounts of their engagement with books. Rose offers some striking stories of reading in unlikely places, and occasionally (though not always) of the social mobility that accompanied such reading habits. One such account is that of Will Crooks, Labour MP, who was wonderstruck by his reading of *The Iliad*, bought secondhand for 2d, while growing up in extreme poverty in East London:

> What a revelation it was to me! Pictures of romance and beauty I had never dreamed of suddenly opened up before my eyes. I was transported from the East End to an enchanted land. It was a rare luxury for a working lad like me just home from work to find myself suddenly among the heroes and nymphs of ancient Greece.[54]

Accounts of working-class autodidactism from metropolitan cultures remind us that the province is not just a function of empire but can also very well be within the national borders of the dominant countries. Tom Lutz has provided a compelling account of growing up as a provincial autodidact while at a blue-collar job in Dubuque, Iowa. 'The shadow of empire,' he writes, 'is cast very close to its center, cast there perhaps not dissimilarly to the way it shades its outposts.'[55] Referring to my earlier essay on the young Pankaj Mishra's autodidactism in 1980s Benares, Lutz narrates his youthful autodidactic energy in ebullient terms: 'like Pankaj Mishra, I'll say, I was an autodidact. I was a prickly, rebellious youth: reactive, Oedipal. I knew nothing and knew everything, especially knew that I didn't need the man to tell me what to read, didn't need college, I didn't need the establishment'.[56]

Lutz's account and Rose's ambitious survey bring up comparative questions about the differential impacts of class and colonial identity vis-à-vis their respective distance from literary archives canonized and cherished by metropolitan elites. Do figures like Will Crooks, in spite of his class positions that had kept them at a great remove from a classical education, enjoy a greater cultural connection with the world of European classics than the reader from the periphery of the British Empire irrespective of the latter's class position? Or do the colonial bourgeoisie and their postcolonial inheritors – particularly figures like C.L.R. James, Toru Dutt, and Nirad C. Chaudhuri – have a privileged access to the culturally alien world of European classics that had eluded Crooks in the poverty of the East End? There is, for instance, little doubt about the entrenched Victorianism and Puritanism of the early James or the elite, high-culture life led by the young Toru Dutt, and the affinity they variously create with the metropolitan canon, be it the classics or Victorian novels. I will have the occasion to return to these figures in details in the chapters that follow, but it may suffice to say here that Rose and I scale trajectories of reading that are sometimes very similar in the obstacles before them, and yet quite radically different in their cultural contexts.

But a greater difference separates our projects. As a social historian, Rose is interested in recovering collective patterns of action. The many striking individual stories he narrates must, in the end, build up to recognizable narratives about group behaviour – his final archive is not about exceptional individuals but forms, howsoever contrarian, of action exhibited in social formations. The valiant and important task he sets up at the very outset is 'to enter the minds of ordinary readers in history, to discover what they read and how they read it'.[57] In other words, he is interested in discovering the reading habits of the common, often impoverished or disenfranchised reader, as a social body, as indicated clearly in the title of his remarkable book. Projects of literary criticism may also etch sociological narratives, and I do seek to read a semblance of colonial and postcolonial pattern in mine, in the engirding systems of education as much as in the actual patterns of reading. But in the end, it is clear that this is a comparative work involving the remarkable but idiosyncratic reading habits of a group of extraordinary individuals whose experiences gain only some unity from the global nature of the British Empire. In the end, none of these figures can be reduced to the representation of any social or historical group; while they are that as well, the unique nature of their imagination and subsequent life trajectories as public writers and thinkers set them aside from the more invisible – and perhaps more inarticulate – readers in Rose's archive.

Visibility, individualism, self-expression – it is possible, however, to take these obvious markers of the literary memoir as granted, without noting their rootedness in bourgeois culture and their limited role in accounts of working-class selves. In her work on working-class autobiographies, Regenia Gagnier is keenly sensitive of this limitation; she is aware that such accounts often tend to be 'not revelations of self, but of class'.[58] And it is not by choice either; individualism is scarce when one's freedom and agency is cramped all around. Romantic conceptions of subjectivity based on self-absorption and self-contemplation 'is a misplaced model for writers whose impediments to literacy include lack of time, space, and adequate light'.[59] It was inevitable, therefore, that many of these autobiographers would present themselves and their family members not as exceptional or memorable individuals but as ordinary, even forgettable members of subordinated social classes. Does this distinction between a bourgeois literary individualism and working-class self-effacement get elided in this distinction I claim from Rose's project? Only a full consideration of the accounts I present can do justice to this complex and problematic question, but the short answer is yes. The formation of the modern Anglographic literary subject under colonial or postcolonial reality – whatever violence, resistance, or liberation defines that process – involves, for the most part, the emergence of a modern, individuated literary subjectivity, often acutely aware of their troubled location within traditional communities. This is particularly true of the English-language autobiographic accounts chronicling complex moments of literary autodidactism in the following chapters. The difference between Rose's archive and mine is therefore not merely between the methodological instincts of our respective disciplines; it goes deeper into the very imagination of subjectivity that shifts between our chosen archives.

Even while acknowledging this crucial difference, and the eloquent articulation of private subjectivity that marks my group of readers, it is perhaps more important to see this present work as undoing an opposition Rose sets up early in his project. This is the opposition of the ordinary reader with the professional intellectual. Compared to the challenges of recovering the pattern of 'ordinary' reading, Rose writes, 'it is relatively easy to recover the reading experiences of professional intellectuals: authors, literary critics, professors, and clergymen extensively documented their responses to books'. As opposed to them, he notes the unrecorded reading habits of an intriguing medley of peoples – 'freedmen after the American Civil War, or immigrants in Australia, or the British working classes'.[60] The fact that his archive in his book is really the third group might explain the clear opposition he creates between the 'ordinary' and the 'professional' reader, for indeed, as a social group they lack both the qualification and the will to become part of the professional groups as formulated early in his book.

Rose seeks the ordinary reader from disenfranchised social groups within Britain. But there is also a kind of a provincial reader and thinker created by the fracturing of metropolitan knowledge on the colonial periphery. Capable of articulating the narratives of their reading later in life through uniquely imaginative subjectivities, they are not the 'ordinary' readers that Rose identifies. But nor are they professionals in the metropolitan sense of the term – as writers, critics, and academics might be in the heart of the imperial metropolis, empowered by a greater harmony between method, pedagogy, experience, and archive. Dwelling within the conflicted realization of a strategic implementation of Western humanities on the margins of empire, this is a kind of reader who must fall through the cracks of the binary of ordinary and professional that Rose sets up. In my formulation, they are not quite ordinary but amateurs – valiant and bungling amateurs, at least in the early years of their *Bildung*, if not throughout their reading and writing careers. And it is these moments of unprofessionalism, of flawed amateurism, that is precisely interesting and even generative. My goal in this book is to show how the claim made by Stefan Collini about humanistic enquiry in general – wherein the 'existential state of intellectual dissatisfaction turns into something like a methodological precept' – takes on a heightened and historically situated dimension with the provincial readers from the margins of empire.

Rose is naturally less interested in individual figures than in larger social patterns; had his main goal been to retrieve individual (and therefore exceptional) champions of effective working-class reading capable of casting their experience into striking narratives, these figures might had some resemblance to the figure of the Black vernacular intellectual celebrated by Grant Farred. For Farred, however, this intellectual vernacularity exists only within a condition of blackness; in fact, blackness makes this necessary. 'In order for a black or marginalized intellectual (more so than for other figures) to be politically efficacious, the historical injunction is overdetermined: vernacularity is an absolute prerequisite.'[61] The configuration of the vernacular intellectual inevitably invokes Antonio Gramsci's idea of the organic intellectual, as one who represents a particular class – most often a 'working-class spokesperson who negotiates between his constituency of origin and the dominant classes'.[62] Farred includes one of the figures from my book in his group of vernacular intellectuals – C.L.R. James – the other three being Bob Marley, Muhammad Ali, and Stuart Hall, with James attaining vernacularity through his immersion into the popular sport of cricket, and the discourse he creates around it. Some of the factors that define the vernacularity of an intellectual for Farred, notably, colonialism, diaspora and immigration, also emerge as important in my work. But in the end, the category of the vernacular intellectual as understood by Farred is of limited relevance to me. Farred reads a certain grounded popular texture in the idiom of the vernacular intellectual that is hard to consistently identify in the figures I read from different parts of the British Empire, even though elements of such vernacularity can be seen as marking parts of the oeuvres of certain intellectuals of the Black Caribbean diaspora, and some of the writers associated with the *Drum* Magazine in mid-century South Africa. The bigger difference, however, might have to do with the question, and particularly, the character of marginality and resistance. 'In colonial and postcolonial societies,' Farred writes, 'vernacular speech belongs to the colonized or the ghettoized communities of the metropolis'.[63] Accordingly, it forms a clear contrast with formal speech: 'The vernacular is counterposed to (and is less valued than) the formal – or "proper" – speech of the colonizers or the metropolitanized discourse of the dominant society'.[64]

The amateur readers in my book have a far more unpredictable set of relationships with what Farred calls the 'metropolitanized discourse', just as it does with what he calls vernacular speech. Occasionally, the very project of colonial and postcolonial self-making is to own this metropolitanized discourse, which does not limit the participation of a resistant vernacular in the very trajectory of that ownership. A figure like Sindiwe Magona, Xhosa writer and social activist (writing in English) from the Cape province in South Africa, one who accounts for the self-learning of the female domestic, is a telling example of the latter, while the metropolitanized discourse feels more firmly entrenched in the language and idiom of Es'kia Mphahlele, described by Ngũgĩ wa Thiong'o as 'the herdboy from Maupaneng who became the scholar in Jo'burg', articulating a clearer trajectory of metropolitanization.[65] The metropolitan accent is heard even more clearly in the debates about culture staged later in South Africa by Lewis Nkosi and Njabulo Ndebele. The amateurism that I read often appears along the trajectory of this very metropolitanization, revealing cracks in this very aspiration and points of disjuncture between indigenous reality and metropolitan notions of modernity and cosmopolitanism. While these be telling cracks and moments of disjuncture, they are, in my understanding, deeply generative ones. I'm less interested, therefore, in a clear disavowal of metropolitanized discourse – that which defines Farred's vernacular intellectuals – than in the colonial and postcolonial subject's uneven relation with it, including many shades of assimilation, conflict, aspiration, and resentment.

These figures are of greatest interest to me when they appear as struggling, peripheral readers who come up with fascinating, unexpected readings, where the uneasy relation between metropolitan culture and colonial reality become enabling in ways not possible without this very disjuncture. Mistakes, anxieties, and misgivings, for many of these thinkers, pave the future path to becoming intellectuals within public, often transnational spaces. Is an intellectual with a public reach an amateur or a professional? Marjorie Garber responds to this question by saying there is, at the very least, an element of amateurism in the work of the popular intellectual which may very well be a post-professional performance, rather than an unprofessional one. Speaking about literature and the humanities more broadly on popular, more accessibly forums involves a certain unlearning of disciplinary discourse – perhaps (though not always) even the deployment of a grounded, popular idiom reminiscent of the vernacular intellectual as imagined by Farred. But even within Anglo-American metropolitan culture, Garber reminds us, 'intellectuals were, and still are, celebrated for their professional amateurism'.[66] In material terms, being an amateur has usually meant someone who works without an institutional affiliation, or at least without a regular one – which, Garber argues, accounts for a certain nostalgia for figures such as Kenneth Burke and Edmund Wilson, with the latter intriguingly becoming a key figure for one of the postcolonial amateur-public intellectuals in this book. While the desirability of amateurism continues to be a provocative issue in literary studies – more so given its not-too-distant memory of a troubled acquisition of status as a professional academic discipline – such examples, and many more of them, also continue to tell us that the amateur-professional dialectic will forever remain productively unresolved in the field.

A powerful case for the necessary and continued amateurism of the intellectual is made by Edward Said. For Said, amateurism implies disaffiliation with interests, lobbies, and institutions of power that seek to co-opt intellectuals to the hegemony of state and capital. Their amateurism is of a sharply polemical nature and is the precondition of the continuous vigilance for the preservation of their freedom and caution against bullying or absorption by the establishment. Said draws on Julian Benda's notion of the intellectual as a passionate, fearless rebels who fight oppression and authority and defend the weak, even though, written in 1927, also reveal the limitation of his time and keeps his list – which features Socrates, Jesus, Spinoza, Voltaire, and Nietzsche – confined to men valorized in European culture. That an intellectual is not defined or limited by a particular discipline, for Said, is best illustrated by Michel Foucault's construction of the 'universal intellectual' as opposed to the 'specific intellectual' who has increasingly come to replace the former figure. Said is passionate about the independent and adversarial status of the intellectual, and he feels the greatest threat to the integrity of the intellectual today comes not from the usual corridors of capitalist and state power and comfort, but from within, the attitude he calls 'professionalism', by which he means

> thinking of your work as an intellectual as something you do for a living, between the hours of nine and five with one eye on the clock, and another cocked at what is considered to be proper, professional behavior – not rocking the boat, not straying outside the accepted paradigms or limits, making yourself marketable and above all presentable, hence uncontroversial and unpolitical and 'objective'.[67]

Such approaches to the idea of the amateur go a long way to liberate the term from the indulgent dilettantism of feudal elites; it situates it within a field of resistance, disaffiliation, and non-conformance. Said himself is included, along with Charles Baudelaire, Fyodor Dostoevsky, Guy Debord, Hannah Arendt, and Jane Jacobs, in a list of exponents of free and unusual wisdom, in the intriguing and delightful book, *The Amateur: The Pleasures of Doing What You Love*, by Andy Merrifield.[68] Not unexpectedly, for Said, the great threats that diminish the power and integrity of the figure of the intellectual today are variously rooted in forms of professionalism, which articulates itself across various dimensions: the debilitating constrictions of academic and scholarly specialization, the fetishization of expertise and institutional certification that calls for correctness and cautious disciplinary territorialization, and perhaps most damningly, the hard-to-resist drift towards power and authority, to support and even be in direct employ by its institutions. The great threat of professionalism can only be resisted by what Said calls amateurism, which replaces profit and narrow specialization with the care and affection that must shape and drive the intellectual's vocation. 'The intellectual today ought to be an amateur', he writes, 'someone who considers that to be a thinking and concerned member of a society one is entitled to raise moral issues at the heart of even the most technical and professionalized activity as it involves one's country, its power, its mode of interacting with its citizens as well as with other societies.'[69] Beyond measured questions of profit and method, the intellectual must make her labour personal and daring. The question we are left with, as such, is rhetorical, with the answer already lodged in our intellectual and political conscience: 'How does the intellectual address authority: as a professional supplicant or as its unrewarded, amateurish conscience?'[70]

Every period in English studies reinvents this question for itself. In her January 2023 review essay on *Professing Criticism*, Merve Emre outlines Guillory's narrative of the academic professionalization of literary study in the twentieth century. But while professionalization 'secured intellectual autonomy for criticism's practitioners', enabling scholars to specialize in different periods, national traditions, themes, and even cultural artefacts, the cost of this autonomy has been influence, as the efforts of these scholarly specialization have not spread far beyond the classroom at all.[71] Scholarly rigour at the cost of public impact is a phenomenon easily recognized in the historical trajectory of literary criticism in the Anglosphere – and most of us in the academy would recognize it as a necessary, even productive sacrifice. But this professionalization brings a greater setback, which Emre correctly reads as a unifying thesis in Guillory's book – that of professional deformation, which finds a strange, if partial resonance with Said's suspicion of the professionalized intellectual and his subsequent championship of the amateur.

The crisis in literary studies is now acute enough – particularly in the Anglo-American academic world – for the old misgivings about the deep professionalization of literary study to resurface in new forms. Some of these anxieties, such as the loss of the popular appeal of traditional forms of literatures, are immediately recognizable, doubly aggravating in the age of instant digital culture and aesthetic gratification. Others, such as the debilitating employment crisis in academic humanities, seem to have taken an apocalyptic urgency not quite seen before despite several smaller warning signs through the last decades of the twentieth century. At such a moment, a celebration of the amateur reader might seem as galling to some as it might feel liberating to others. As Guillory points out, the rewards of non-institutional scholarship are dangerously low: 'To be a freelance scholar, no matter the quality of one's scholarship, is precisely to be excluded from the system of rewards.' But at the same time, it is difficult to see certain current conversations in the literary academy, notably those around the phenomenon of postcritique (with which I engage in detail in the next chapter) and the question of the lay reader, as disconnected to an attention to some of the virtues of amateur thought and reading. Guillory, too, has proposed a withering of sorts for cultural capital by seeking to free literary criticism as a specialized activity structured after capitalist division of labour. The result might be the liberation of the producers of imaginative and intellectual labours in the Marxist vision of the communist organization of society, where the work of writers, artists, critics, and thinkers will belong to everybody who will engage in such production among other activities of the day.

The most visible form of this drift is the increasing influence and popularity of varieties of cultural intervention by bloggers, social media participants, activists, and influencers, and experimental and interactive commentators such as writers of fanfiction, and the corresponding decline of the traditional guardians in the pages of newspapers, broadsheets, literary magazines, and awards. Increasingly, we dwell in a world where the traditional cultural capital that distinguished a leading newspaper review from one on Amazon or Goodreads (and interactive social media such as BookTok or Bookstagrammers for popular/mass-market books, on TikTok and Instagram, respectively) continues to dwindle, particularly with younger constituencies. I think anyone who recognizes the intellectual and imaginative uniqueness of literary discourse – and here the distinction between the 'creative' and the 'critical' is moot – finds this chaotic democratization of utterance and criticism less than satisfying. But at the same time, it is difficult not to see, as noted by many above, that much has been lost from the relentless professionalization of literary study in the academy, which, to a large extent, has modelled itself on knowledge-production in the hard sciences, a significantly misleading track for the institutionalization of literary study. It is from this troubled space that I join the voices of several scholars who have variously foregrounded the many, if uneven, virtues of amateur or lay reading.

I have personally sensed the enthusiasm around the idea of amateurism in the metropolitan academy, such as when in 2017 the journal *New Literary History* devoted a small cluster to amateur criticism which included an essay of mine that contained the germ of this project – 'The Critic as Amateur'.[72] Along with another contributor to that cluster, Aarthi Vadde, who has also written extensively about amateur criticism, particularly in contemporary and digital contexts, I edited a collection of essays, also called *The Critic as Amateur*, where many scholars, entrenched professionals all, offered a wide range of brilliant interventions on critical, scholarly, and readerly amateurism. For Derek Attridge, amateur pleasure in books is the essential precondition of professional reading, while Ragini Tharoor Srinivasan foregrounded the inspired amateurism of interdisciplinary cultural studies that defined her academic training. Tom Lutz offered a remarkable story of amateur literary *Bildung*, strikingly similar to some of the colonial and postcolonial amateurs I discuss in this book – but from within metropolitan culture, from the very provincial penumbra of the literary establishments of New York City. Melanie Micir gave us a spirited history of the role of the amateur sensibility in the history of the feminist press, while Kara Wittman, in the epilogue essay for the collection, read the undergraduate student as the amateur with the burden of saying something 'new, interesting, and original'. And these are just a few of the chapters.[73]

The present book is a deeper examination of a history of amateur reading and criticism that does not coincide with the discipline's academic history in any significant way – none of the thinkers examined here were professional academics – and yet, it is a history, that I feel, lies at an important angle to academic scholarship, and certainly to the larger idea and practice of literary criticism. Academic fields close to the themes in this book have derived genealogical energy from amateur debates. The most striking example is the exchange and argumentation with amateur historians writing for popular readership that shaped the work of historians such as Jadunath Sarkar and Govindrao Sakharam Sardesai as they sought to make history a proper academic subject in India.[74] Cultures of lay reading, often by marginalized or minoritized groups have also variously entered academic debates in both historical and literary studies, and in more recent years, have led to renewed attention to the non-specialist reader in the latter field. Apart from Rose's study of British working-class autodidactism, I'm thinking of Janice Radway's 1984 book, *Reading the Romance: Women, Patriarchy, and Popular Literature*, and more recently, Merve Emre's *Paraliterary: The Making of Bad Readers in Postwar America*, both of which, in their own ways, significantly depart from the canons of high literature in the choice of their archives as much from the social groups who read them for affective or functional reasons of their own.[75]

The present book is not about lay, poorly educated, or 'bad' readers as a sociological category, but rather some of the most inspiring practitioners of idiosyncratic non-specialist reading that is generative – perhaps particularly so – in its flaws and failures. Perhaps behind it is the belief that the most effective way to integrate the best practices of critical amateurism is to observe some of its most inspiring practitioners. And yet, my insistence on the uniqueness and particularity of literary discourse (and my scepticism about the growing digital influence of the citizen-reviewer) requires me to be attentive to readers whose amateurism is driven by striking imaginative and intellectual uniqueness of their own. Hence my focus on these figures, who, unlike Jonathan

Rose's ordinary readers, have all left vivid and striking accounts of their reading and thinking about literature, which have variously shaped their own aesthetic education at odd angles from systems of imperial education within which they found themselves situated. At the same time, this is also a plea to examine this question beyond the limits of the Anglo-American world, through the reality of English as a language of world literature. As a constellation of narratives about amateur reading that make up colonial and postcolonial programmes of aesthetic education, it is also an inquiry into the imperial history of literary humanities across the transcontinental expanse of the British Empire. To look towards the future of reading culture and humanistic study, a long glance at its past – particularly as it has embodied itself under flawed, oppressive, and exclusionary structures of education – is a simultaneously sobering and enlightening experience. It is a look that I hope, will reveal a different nuance to the textual relation between empire and colony, by revealing unexplored realms of what Dipesh Chakrabarty has called 'the anticolonial spirit of gratitude', to complicate larger patterns of cultural and material power with unique trajectories of individual imagination in ways only literature can. But I'm hopeful that the bungling acts of reading by these unforgettable peripheral readers, as celebratory as resistant, unpredictably affirmative and eclectically suspicious, will offer some roadmaps for the present where the reading of older texts, particularly from metropolitan cultures, is, to a great extent, determined by the vigilance and suspicion of #cancelculture. In my greatest moment of optimism, I imagine these remarkable outliers as offering revolutionary possibilities for the future.

Chapter 2

POOR READING, WEAK THEORY

> To this day, I pussyfoot along the stacks whenever I have to go to a
> library. I doubt I will ever be at ease in those institutions, just as I
> will never be at ease in restaurants, hotels, theatres, cinemas and all
> the other places which I never set foot in as a child.
>
> — Sindiwe Magona, *Forced to Grow*[1]

Is there such a thing as the posture of reading? Is it merely a cosmetic
act? Is it a deception when the posture is bereft of real textual
engagement? When you look like you're reading but in fact you're
not? I don't mean those moments of lapsed concentration may befall a
seasoned reader. I mean a situation where one cannot read but wishes to
look like one can – and 'appear' consequently immersed in a book that
comes only through literate understanding in the traditional sense of
the term. Is reading without such understanding an act of reading at all?

These strange thoughts come to my head as I read the opening pages
of *In Bed with the Word*, a deeply evocative, short book on the relation
between reading, spirituality, and the politics of culture by the Canadian
writer and scholar Daniel Coleman. Coleman opens the book with an
image from his past: a six-year-old boy skipping his second day in school
to spend his morning in bed with book. The child of White missionaries
in Addis Ababa, Ethiopia, the boy is Coleman's older brother, John, and
the setting of the scene was Bingham Academy, a boarding school for
missionaries' children in the city. The scene, which went on to become
part of family lore, is all the more remarkable because John doesn't
know how to read, which did nothing to prevent him skipping school
(where, among other things, he was supposed to learn to read), to stare
at length at the book with which he had decided to stay in bed.

'What are you doing in bed, Johny?' asks a woman's voice. 'You should
be in school with the other boys.'

'Oh,' says the tow-headed boy calmly. 'I just thought I'd spend the
day in bed with the Word.'[2]

This illiterate, childish relation with reading can be properly understood only with the full set of attendant facts around it. Perhaps the most important among them is that the book was a 'black, leather-bound King James Bible', which invariably also takes us back to the fact that the boys' parents are both missionaries trained in the evangelical Protestant tradition.[3] A stretch of quiet time with the Bible and their notebooks along with a hot drink every morning was an unfailing habit with his parents, as long as Coleman remembers, and it was clear where little Johny got the idea, and the desire for 'the posture, the position, the place of being a reader'.[4]

'The boy in bed with the word,' Coleman writes, 'presents in one picture pretty much everything I want to say in this book about spirituality and reading.'[5] Coleman goes on to elaborate a sensitive and relevant book on the relationship between reading and spirituality in the context of contemporary popular, academic, and literary culture. My particular interest in this image, however, is that it illustrates what I call an illiterate relation to a book – and perhaps even to the act of reading. The illiteracy renders reading impossible and yet cannot prevent this relation from coming into being. No one can miss the privileges that closely surround and structure this illiteracy – the White missionary parents, the safe and potentially nourishing space of the missionary school, and the evident impact of the parents' religious reading habits on the little boy. All of these nurturing influences shape a mimesis of the reading posture, but it is a posture that lacks the most crucial asset, that of literacy, only that which can enable the reality of reading.

The gesture of reading, but not a functional relation with books – or at least The Book, in this case, enabled here in the absence of literacy. Does this enabling happen in spite of this absence, or precisely because of it? That is the kind of inquiry into the child mind that is as important to ask as it is difficult to answer. To say that this is a relation with books, or even the gesture of reading, that has not received sufficient attention would be to state something counter-intuitive, possibly nonsensical or outlandish. That is because of the obvious reason that it is not act of reading in any conventional sense of the term, inasmuch as reading implies actual understanding of the material, no matter how partial, arbitrary, or subjective such an understanding may be. But the fact that books – or at least certain kinds of books – evoke relation to literacy beyond this conventional model is an important truth that accounts of reading need to acknowledge. If this be any act of reading, it is a reading driven by the poverty of literacy and experience even as that very poverty paradoxically deepens reverence for the book. The book here is a material object in its own right, not merely a repository of meaning inscribed by linguistic and semiotic signification, even if that signification has historically been a major precondition of its appeal. But a *major* precondition; not the *only* one. Even if this interpretative poverty is underwritten by familial and cultural privileges in this particular instance and is clearly a condition of childhood, this relation to reading – that of deeply affectionate illiteracy – is crucial for millions of people around the world, for whom, the power of a particular kind of text eludes literacy and understanding even as it emphasizes the very bookishness of that text.

Reading and spirituality have had a mutual relationship that is as historically deep as it is geographically and culturally expansive. That is an important part of Coleman's subject in his book. But while he focuses on real act of reading, and the consequent cultures of interpretation, hermeneutics, and self-awareness that have arisen from such acts, I'm most enthralled by what I would call an illiterate or imperfectly literate relation with reading. But perhaps I'm defining literacy too narrowly, in a constrictively instrumental sense of the term?

More expansive imaginations of literacy have been celebrated in recent times. 'Literacy,' writes Nathan Snazza, 'is primarily about affects and not conscious events of meaning making or representational constructions.'[6] Snazza is following up here on his reading of a significant scene in Toni Morrison's *Beloved*, where the illiterate slave Sethe is in the process of deriving meaning of the word 'characteristics' based on her eavesdropping of the schoolteacher's lessons and her own sensory encounter with objects. The development of Sethe's 'literacy', if it can be called that, does not involve reading, though it involves unintended, vicarious instruction about text and language; in *The Nation and Its Fragments*, Partha Chatterjee has documented similar ways in which certain Indian women eavesdropped their way into literacy in the nineteenth century by listening at the door while the male members of their family received private instruction.[7] What matters to me at the moment, however, is the affective aura around literacy that exists in spite of its actual absence, indeed, in some way, as inspired by its very absence. The absence of literacy creates an affective value around it – particularly around its material repository, books – that easily accessible, high-functional literacy cannot. Later in his book, Snazza writes about this affective aura shaped by the absence of a sustained legacy of literacy even as he embodies deep and sophisticated literacy himself: 'I am always affected by books even when I am not reading them. As someone who grew up in a working-class home, it's hard to separate the pleasures I experience with books from a decades-long attempt to rework my habitus, bodying myself into the forms of class privilege that enable flourishing in universities.'[8]

Why do I insist on pausing at the paradox of this awe or pleasure about books on part of those deprived of literacy – or even at the somewhat different pleasure of one simply deprived of its family legacy? Part of it, no doubt, is to remark on the repressive ideological content of this pleasure, in the manner in which Louis Althusser had revealed education to be.[9] The path to literacy, likewise, remains singular. 'There is,' Snazza argues, 'as any person who has moved through statist educational systems will know, a profound and disturbing pleasure that adheres in having read more, in having thought more about bigger ideas, bigger books, harder theories.'[10] Using Sara Ahmed's term, Snazza describes this kind of pleasure as 'white manning', because this path, after moving through the material and ideological structures of canon formation, offers the same pleasure as that which 'interfaces with the work of maintaining male supremacist, white supremacist, Eurocentrist capture of educational potential'.[11]

Forms of marginal consciousness have riven literary-critical study at least since the 1960s, when the radical recuperation of non-mainstream voices – in race, gender, class, sexuality, bodily ability and national-cultural origin, among other things – fundamentally altered the discipline's worldview as practised in the metropolitan west, from both a place of political activism and anti-foundational instincts in philosophy and linguistics. But as the historian Dipesh Chakrabarty reminded us in 2000, the inclusion of minority histories expands the archive and maybe even the canon, but this expansion can also happen without calling the discipline into a crisis – that is, without altering its fundamental epistemological mode. It is one thing to include indigenous tribal voices in nationalist, anti-colonial history, but another thing altogether to let tribal religious beliefs disrupt the rationalist mode that forms the core of history as a modern discipline.[12] Archival expansions, as such, do not naturally turn into epistemic alterations of the dominant paradigms of disciplines. Chakrabarty's description of history partially describes literary studies as well. Not being tied to institutions – judicial, bureaucratic, and others – the way history tends to be, literature has greater freedoms, but the caveat about the gulf between archival and epistemological expansion holds equally true in methods of literary criticism.[13]

Does this enable a possible return to the figure of the boy who wishes to spend the day in bed with the Word without possessing a literate relation to it? Is he, too, on the way to 'white manning' – overdetermined by his race and gender? Or can we take away something from his posture, this day of refusal to acknowledge the lack of literacy as a barrier to his relation with the book? Coleman does not return to John anymore, or tell us how his life turned out; this is, therefore, no speculation of future, but an attempt to read that moment in its own right. It is clear that religion holds a key to this inexplicable relation to books that lie beyond the conventional epistemology of humanist literacy. As Dipesh Chakrabarty, Ranajit Guha, and the subaltern historiographers have periodically reminded us, it is almost impossible to give a honest account of many marginalized social groups, and certainly impossible to articulate their stories, without attention to forms of religious consciousness.[14] While this has been a sobering epiphany for Marxist historiography, it also requires a reading of a literary act – that of reading itself – to take into account the impoverishment of all power, privilege, agency, indeed, the entire subordination of one's self that defines this particular relation to reading which eludes the literate, liberal, bourgeois relation to texts rendered in language.

Religious practice around the world has been characterized by a kind of faith that can be variously defined as pre-literate, non-literate, and post-literate. This reverence has thrived in equal measure in the presence or absence of literacy, often in perfect indifference to it. The Sikh devotion to the text of the Granth (literally meaning 'book') Sahib, and the custom of offering all human comfort to it, for instance, leaves a deeply figurative mark on the mind. What I want to take away from this is an alternative relationship to the culture of reading. When such 'reading', whether or not existent in the presence of literacy, is enabled by a submission of the need of intellectual control, or indeed of any kind of personal agency, it creates a peculiar loss of mastery that runs counter to all established conventions of reading. The loss of mastery, progress, or success as affirmative or celebratory conditions has been an important suggestion of critical theory in the recent years.[15] When it comes to reading, for Nathan Snazza, this condition is 'bewilderment', which is the 'particular affective state of disorientation' that opens up possibilities away from the inevitably humanist or human-centred direction education is traditionally expected to take. Seeking to expand literacy and its affect beyond human actors, Snazza recommends that 'instead of orienting all of the educational movement toward Man, what we need today is an education that does not know where it is headed' – an education with no mastery over its direction.[16]

A traditional humanist conception of education is synonymous with the development of intellectual and disciplinary mastery. But what, indeed, is the ethical and political significance of such mastery? In her book *Unthinking Mastery*, Julietta Singh has revealed the quiet complicities between colonial domination and other forms of mastery thought to be innocuous or even beneficial – including epistemological and intellectual ones. There is, as such, a moral connection between forms of mastery such as colonialism and enslavement on one hand, and on the other, with 'forms of mastery that we often believe today to be harmless, worthwhile, even virtuous'. To master an instrument, an archive, or a language is usually imagined as laudable, and 'yet as a pursuit', Singh argues, 'mastery invariably and relentlessly reaches toward the indiscriminate control over something – whether human or inhuman, animate or inanimate'.[17] Mastery involves an inevitable submission of something. Inasmuch as mastery requires 'a rupturing of the object being mastered' – since the object must be rendered weaker than the master – mastery becomes 'a splitting of the object that is mastered from itself, a way of estranging the mastered object from its previous state of being'.[18] Viewed this way, mastery ends up being a kind of exclusionary humanism, one driven by a decisive master–slave dialectic, where the emergence of a victorious human subject is contingent on the violence and domination it can inflict on subordinated modalities.

Singh opens up a sustainable strand of scepticism about epistemological mastery, paving the way for intellectual failure as redemptive, perhaps even indicative of a different ethics of knowledge. When such failure, indeed, the very absence of the attempt to succeed, confronts religious texts, it is impossible not to hear the echo of the encounter with otherness as imagined by Emmanuel Levinas, for whom, the ultimate, unknowable Other is God. When Derek Attridge translated the Levinasian modality of otherness into an act of reading, as for instance in his rich and complex reading of the novels of J.M. Coetzee, he interpreted the experimental nature of the text, and of its consequent 'difficulty' as an ethical claim to otherness.[19] Turning away from the question of the alienness or difficulty of texts, I would like to examine possibilities latent within the reader's silence before the text, or the refusal to interpret, sometimes even to read, and all the hesitance, resistance, refusal, and failure that remain aligned to what Singh sees as the negation of mastery.

What does it actually mean to read against the epistemological goal of mastery – particularly in the face of power and domination that lays down specific structures of education and literacy? In an intriguing book, *World Literature for the Wretched of the Earth*, J. Daniel Elam has offered some illustration of this disavowal of mastery. He looks at British India where Western authors, texts, and curricula inscribed models of authority and professional development, just the way reading and critique was, for many anticolonial thinkers, also a path to resistance and emancipation. However, Elam's provocative focus is on readers who read as a means of disavowing authority and expertise, and escape power and domination through such disavowal. His examples are the leader of the California-based anti-colonial Ghadr Party Lala Har Dayal, the political leader and social reformer B.R. Ambedkar, the celebrated champion of non-violent resistance, M.K. Gandhi, and Bhagat Singh, the revolutionary nationalist executed by the British. 'As an anticolonial practice,' Elam writes, describing the various reading cultures foregrounded by these figures, 'reading could mark modes of refusal, nonproductivity, inconsequence, inexpertise, and nonauthority'. His radically utopian argument is that "in direct contrast to the values of British liberalism, these recalcitrant ideals were perfect for envisioning a radical egalitarianism rooted in communal reading and collective textual criticism".[20]

Viewed this way, the values of 'unrecognizability, indecipherability, unintelligibility, untraceability, and untranslatability' become ways of escaping and resisting colonial authority, including the Macaulayian prescription of the brown mimic man. Emerging as a critique of colonial selfhood, such practices of readerly failures, according to Elam, pave the emergence of an 'anonymous, interpenetrating, multitudinous collectivity'.[21] One thinks of the collective, rather than individual identification in British working-class autobiographies noted by Regenia Gagnier, who offered the important caveat that 'Cartesian subjectivity was not assumed by most working-class writers and as a consequence autobiography often meant something different from emplotted self-sufficiency'.[22] But these self-frustrating modes of reading enacted as part of anti-colonial resistance do not just dissipate the emplotment of individualism; they also signal conceptions of worlds that are variously impossible or utopian. 'Bhagat Singh's "universal brotherhood" demanded "chaos" and assured death,' writes Elam, as evident in his reading habits and goals in prison in the face of a death sentence. Likewise, 'Ambedkar's "fellowship" was produced by a commitment to shared suffering, which necessarily stalls abandoning the world as it is. Gandhi's philosophies were rooted in perpetual failure and loss. The citizens of Har Dayal's "World-State" were the descendants of the present, but they inherited an impossible past.'[23] For Elam, these impossibilities variously evoke the universal impossibility of larger collectivities such as that of comradeship as imagined by Frantz Fanon and world literature as imagined by Eric Auerbach. Does that mean that failure-shaped reading practices can only lead to anarchy, nihilism, and impossible utopias? Can acts of reading framed by failure – or conditioned by the impossibility of epistemological mastery – be generative in any sense of the term?

The limits of interpretation

Reading is central to this book. Most of the writing I read here is inseparable from the reading experience of the writers; often, the chapters foreground direct accounts of such reading, and the obstacles, missteps, and bewilderments on its way. I would like to spend some time in this chapter looking at what reading has meant to literary study in its most specialized and professionalized domain in the modern and contemporary world – the academy. In the most obvious ways, the academic study of literature, as conducted in the metropolitan Anglosphere, is unrelated to the kinds of reading experience that make my central archive in this book, which happens on the provincial peripheries of the Anglophony. I have two primary reasons for returning to academic study here. First, I find the most compelling debates in literary criticism today happening around the ways and cultures of reading. Secondly, and perhaps more crucially, it seems to me that academic debates around reading may have something to glean from the kind of struggling, marginal, and amateur practices of reading that I focus on this book. I think some of the energy of meandering and offbeat approaches to reading is already evident from the discussions around surface reading, lay reading, and postcritical reading. My return to these academic questions of reading that drift away from the traditional centrality of depth and mastery is however, not so much to cast light on these colonial and postcolonial amateurs, though I hope some of that happens too. The greater goal is rather the other way around – to see if these variously marginal, meandering, and flawed cultures of reading from the provinces might be helpful to any of the professional debates I examine in this chapter.

Reading has comprised the traditional core of the labour of literary study. It has been a particular kind of reading, playing hide and seek with visible and hidden meanings, literal and figure-cast, consolidated and scattered in places least expected – in a certain kind of imagination at least as much as in socially accepted reality. The ancestry of literary hermeneutics in the interpretation of scriptures from various religions around the world is well-recognizable to us – the quest for the meaning implied by absent God or gods and their various prophets and incarnations, often hidden in parables, metaphors, or simply in the eternal invisibility of the Giver of these words. This has initiated a culture of interpretation that is, over time, smoothly migrated to the study of languages and linguistic representation where the literal and the visible have ceased to be the sole goal of the quest for meaning.

These are all histories deeply familiar to serious readers and scholars of literature, so there is no need to elaborate on the variously alternating importance of reading or the centrality of its pursuit in literary academics. Its more recent shifts, however, might be more interesting. Over the last couple of decades, the metropolitan sphere of the literary academy has taken a probing, deeply reflexive look at the practice of reading as the defining pursuit of literary study. The question of mastery, both interpretative and archival, has been both touchstone and lightning rod in this drawn-out exercise. 'Reading "more" is always a good thing, but not the solution'. Franco Moretti wrote in the widely discussed 2000 issue of *New Left Review*: 'world literature is not an object, it's a *problem*, and a problem that asks for a new critical method: and no one has ever found a method by just reading more texts'.[24] Moretti, a painstaking reader of Lukacs and himself one of the key figures of Marxist literary theory, embodied, I felt, the structuralist impulse at the heart of Marxism – the approach to the archive through large patterns and structures. Moretti, technology, Stanford, Silicon Valley – that is how a mental image of the then-emergent field of digital humanities, soon to sprout in the Stanford Literary Lab, has been etched in my head. I should also say that that image had very little to do with that sudden feeling of certitude that had Lukacs lived in the present, he might have been a digital humanist. That image of Moretti – somehow separable from my image of the writer of books such as *The Way of the World* – was keen to get the big picture, very much in the structuralist-Marxist tradition in which I read a theorist of the novel as Lukacs. The immense reading, cataloguing, and classifying power of the computer, an important element of the early days of the Stanford Lit Lab and Digital Humanities on the whole, was a natural ally to the project of distant reading. If close reading, as Moretti said in the *NLR* article, indicates the primacy of a small number of texts seen as deserving of sustained and intimate attention, distant reading, especially in its digital version, enables attention to thousands more and consequently, a far larger sociology of literature than might have been possible without this massive technology of assessing thousands of texts within a remarkably brief period of time.

As expected, for the longest time, academic criticism has been looking for mastery, be it epistemological or archival, as well as for elements of conflict and collaboration between the two. It is only in recent years that things have started to shift. The traditional quest of knowledge in English literary study, as evident in the first half of the twentieth century, took place through the practice of close reading, which, Joseph North has argued, defined the act of criticism. Through methods of practical criticism and close reading, 'the archetypal critic was a generalist, sometimes even a "public intellectual", and thus was susceptible to caricature not only as an amateur or a dilettante, but also a mere journalist, popularizer, or educator'.[25] The amateur leaps out as a figure who both struggles and plays with their ownership or mastery over method or archive. But it is just as important to note that North reads 'the field's central axis of dispute was between literary "scholars" and literary "critics"'. The key distinction, as such, was between those who treated the study of literature as a means by which to analyse culture, and those who treated the study of literature as an opportunity to intervene in culture'.[26] What is of even greater consequence is that North sees the scholars eventually winning over the critics in a decisive way to shape the discipline of literary studies since the 1970s, following which the latter's goal primarily became that of historical-contextual analysis, rather than the cultivation of aesthetic sensibilities, which had been the aim of the critics in the past. As he sums it up:

> There has been what I will call a 'scholarly turn,' by which 'scholarly' approaches, which have tended to treat literary texts chiefly as opportunities for cultural and historical analysis, have replaced "'critical' approaches, which, in their day, had tended to treat literary texts as means of cultivating readers' aesthetic sensibilities, "aesthetic" here of course being understood in a range of rather different senses.[27]

The Arnoldian-Leavisite project of literary study as 'criticism of life' consequently becomes an object of residual nostalgia. For North, the key moment of this historicizing impulse is the appearance of Frederic Jameson's *The Political Unconscious*, with its celebrated slogan 'Always historicize', which, North argues, 'is the horizon beyond which the discipline of literary study have so far been unable to see'.[28] The far-reaching impact of that slogan has subsequently inspired literary studies to become essentially interchangeable with social theory, which, North argues, has laid an absolute claim to the progressive, left-leaning conscience of the discipline. Criticism as a means of aesthetic education goes missing from both the research and the teaching aspect of literary study, now dominated by reading as a means of cultural diagnosis. Here North seems to ignore the fact that this cultural diagnosis can also be an act of genuine aesthetic education, such as studies of the relation between realism and historical modernity have revealed, just to take a random example. One is not necessarily exclusive of the other.

Even so, I agree with North about the larger scholarly turn of the discipline. But some fundamental methodological questions remain: Do we use texts to reveal historical-contextual knowledge? Or do we use historical-contextual knowledge to better understand texts? In many ways, this binary is more epistemological than ontological. In actual practice, this binary does not quite exist in the fullness with which North seeks to demonstrate it. Be that as it may, I feel North is right when he identifies historical scholarship as the currently accepted index of the progressivist, even left-leaning impulse of the discipline. If criticism hinges on a historical-contextual reading, it must be committed to social justice, particularly structures of race, gender, sexual orientation, the ownership of property, and other modalities of power that mark individuals and societies, and which have often been lost in singular and monolithic perceptions of the aesthetic. There is a deep trust in the progressivist impulse of historical consciousness here that is, ironically unrecognizable in the most reflexive and conscientious historiographers of today. I'm thinking here not only of the subaltern historiographers' identification of the limits of history as a discipline of bourgeois rationality that falters around myth and religion – crucially wedded to the global inevitability of European imperialism in Dipesh Chakrabarty's 2000 book, *Provincializing Europe* – but also of more recent declarations of scepticism about the canonized impulses of history as a discipline, such as those in Priya Satia's 2020 work, *Time's Monster*. Focusing primarily on British history, Satia has persuasively shown the discipline to be one of the greatest ideological and policy-making forces of imperialism. As we look into the actual workings of the discipline, historical consciousness by itself becomes hard to accept as the evidence of the progressive and just social vision of an interpretative approach.[29]

Perhaps North gave the historical-contextual approach greater currency than it actually possessed in the second decade of the twenty-first century. For Sharon Marcus and Stephen Best, writing in 2010, the historical model of criticism committed to excavating meaning from the depth of the text already has 'a nostalgic, even utopian ring to it'.[30] Curating a special issue of *Representations* on the theme of 'surface reading', Marcus and Best, too, see Jameson's book as initiating the decisive turn towards symptomatic reading, driven by the assumption that the true nature of a literary text, particularly its complicity with structures of power and hegemony, can scarcely be understood from attention to its surface but must be excavated from the layers of hidden meaning underneath. The two prime determinants of hidden hegemonic meanings are capital and the unconscious, with Freudian (also particularly, Lacanian) and Marxist reading of cultural phenomena, which Jameson's influential book brought together in its title as in its argument. If 'the nineteenth-century roots of symptomatic reading lie with Marx's interest in ideology and the commodity and Freud's in the unconscious and dreams', they wrote, 'Jameson's *Political Unconscious* pioneered symptomatic reading in modern criticism.' The act of recovery of meaning from invisible depths conferred an image of labour to criticism that was deeply heroic, and therefore worth serious professional weight. The powerful influence of Jameson's 'version of symptomatic reading', they point out, was to be felt in the centrality of two crucial critical projects from the following decade: Eve Kosofsky Sedgwick's *Epistemology of the Closet* (1991) and Toni Morrison's *Playing in the Dark: Whiteness and the Literary Imagination* (1992), texts which 'showed that one could read a text's silences, gaps, style, tone, and imagery as symptoms of the queerness or race absent only apparently from its pages'.[31]

The harnessing of deep interpretation to the cause of progressivist politics would pave the way of an argument such as that North would make in 2017 – about the historical-contextual paradigm of criticism as laying full claim to the left-leaning conscience of the discipline of academic literary study. In the process, progressivist politics became fully professionalized: 'For in the Anglo-American world, the literary disciplines are now quite evidently disciplines of professional scholarship, of "technological expertise," much along the lines of the social sciences, and quite as a result of the turn from criticism to cultural analysis'.[32] The ascription to a fully professionalized scholarly agency to interpretation attuned to political inequities has important implications for my formulation of failed reading, and I will return to that question soon.

What has variously been called lay, amateur, or common reading has had a rich, complex, and often contradictory relationship with reading practices internal to the disciplinary history of literary studies. John Guillory reminds us that unlike legal, technical, bureaucratic, and scientific writing, literary texts are open to reading by non-scholarly readers, which has historically created a certain resistance to the formation of literary studies as an academic field even as scholars transformed their mode of reading to a disciplinary practice. But even as lay reading remains largely unrecognized within literary scholarship (except within the subfield of the history of the book), Guillory constructs it as essential to the discipline – partly as the historical antagonist of professional reading, and secondly, as 'a back-formation of professional reading, analogous to the concept of "orality" as the antecedent to literacy'.[33] There are, hence, oppositional elements within the relationship between lay and professional reading, which have added layers of complexity and possibilities of confusion about this relationship. But none of these elements can be disavowed.

The phenomenon of lay reading, moreover, has been intimately connected to the project of criticism as the historic function of the critic has been to guide and instruct lay readers in their reading and appreciation of literature, particularly as the reading of vernacular literature (as opposed to the classics) became widespread popular practice. 'The critic', Guillory argues, 'sought to instruct the reading public as one of them.'[34] The subsequent polarization of lay or common reading with professionalized scholarly reading as such comes across as an unfortunate event and was perhaps avoidable in the history of the discipline. Even though conflicts between critique and interpretation on one hand, and the simpler responses of taste and preference on the other have sometimes widened the gap between lay and professional readers, I feel that Guillory overstates the distance, as the instincts of lay reading indeed remain embedded within the established practices of professional reading, as he himself goes on to acknowledge through the mechanisms of sentence meaning and aesthetic pleasure, through which lay reading becomes 'in fact the inescapable condition of professional reading'.[35]

The empathy with modes of lay reading has never really vanished from the scholarly discipline of literary study. It has remained submerged, and in recent years it has made a vigorous comeback through the postcritique debate, which, among other things, has looked at interpretative suspicion with a fair degree of suspicion of its own. If meaning hides from the surface, suspicion must become both affect and method for interpretation. In her widely discussed book, *The Limits of Critique*, Rita Felski invokes Paul Ricœur's formulation of the hermeneutics of suspicion and the detective work it does on texts. While for Ricœur this hermeneutic mode traced Freud, Marx, and Nietzsche as its immediate antecedents, Felski, who is keenly sensitive to the affective meaning of suspicion, points to its possible connection to more contemporary influences, such as 'Cold War politics, late capitalism, or postmodern paranoia'.[36] Felski's project, in this book – one she continues in her 2020 work, *Hooked* – is something of an affective counterpart to surface reading, to renew affirmation and celebration as counter to the hegemony of suspicion over interpretative methods.[37] That affirmation, she knows, can be just as easily a part of the interpretative act: 'the art historian, the psychoanalyst, and the detective all pounce on the insignificant trace as the gateway to a hidden reality'; the critic of today, as such, joins 'a transhistorical community of interpreters, decoders, and sign readers'. At the very 'moments of wonder, reverence, exaltation, hope, epiphany, or joy' that visit the critic, the hermeneutics of suspicion is replaced by what she calls a hermeneutics of 'restoration'. It is, for Felski, the 'difference between unveiling and unmasking'.

What is particularly important is that Felski too reads scepticism as something coming from 'below', from the poor and the dispossessed, who naturally incline towards a suspicion of the powerful. To that end, they don't need to be literate in the interpretative methods foregrounded by Marx, Freud, or Nietzsche; the disenfranchised refract a natural suspicion of words that belong to power. 'Servants have often been skeptical of the promises of their masters,' writes Felski; 'factory workers learned to treat the words of their bosses with a pinch of salt; African American slaves developed an oblique practice of signifying to convey their disdain for those who enslaved them'. Suspicion and resistance to power is therefore an organic element of critique, which does not so much discipline or censor as resist. 'Critique', Felski points out, 'is iconoclastic in spirit; it rails against authority; it seeks to lay bare the injustices of the law'.[38]

Felski draws attention to critique's rootedness in resistances against new forms of regulation that emerge in the fifteenth and sixteenth centuries, as well as to the religious and spiritual struggles of the Middle Ages. But as North argues, the interpretative model of critique is now primarily historical-contextual. The various moments of attention to textual surfaces or the attempt to depart from suspicion as the emotion accompanying critique has not done much to change the importance of the historical approach. It is only natural that the historical approach has been able to retain its prime claim to progressivist politics in literary studies.

In other words, interpretative and contextual knowledge is key in order for critique to retain its resistant character and progressive social vision. We've heard partial dissent coming from a champion of surface reading. By way of studying rumour, Stephen Best reads first-person testimony by Caribbean slaves who believed that the British monarch had freed them, 'viewing their words neither as evidence irredeemably corrupted by the sovereign power that extracted them, nor as verbatim speech through which we can recover subjects lost to history'.[39] They make a decisive call to neither affirmation nor suspicion. Their truth lies hidden in plain sight, on the very surface; they are "exactly what they appear to be: "impossible speech" that oscillates between loyalty and insurgency, speech and paraphrase, fact and prophecy, confession and coercion, and in that sense reflects back to us the deeply felt uncertainty of the enslaved'. The equivocal nature of rumour resonates with the unfreedom of the speakers. They lack information and conviction. But when read with a humanistic attention to linguistic texture, their affective lack of certitude becomes a valuable index of their very own lack of freedom.

The status of depth, knowledge, and expertise in the relevance of effectiveness of reading has become shakier in recent academic scholarship, even as the erosion of these traditional elements of reading has been questioned repeatedly. Reading without goals of depth or mastery has, in other words, appeared more relevant, but this unexpected relevance has also invited caveats from rethinkers of critique. Tobias Skivereen's 2021 article 'Postcritique and the Problem of the Lay Reader' sees the figure of the lay reader as a largely unhelpful distraction from the most significant questions of the postcritical debate, even as the identity of the lay reader moves from the intuitive and essentially emotional responder to literary texts to the politically naïve individual easily deceived by invisible structures of power that shape and enable literary texts (recalling the importance of North's historical-contextual reader). Instead of celebrating the lay reader, he advocates something he thinks can be called 'potentianalysis', where rather than repeating analyses of literary texts to reveal the failures of neoliberal capitalism, the reader might read possibilities of generative actions, such as the realization of "societies of welfare, care and trust".[40]

Alternatively, Skivereen wonders about the likelihood of 'a postcritical decolonialism that focuses not on undoing Eurocentrism but on coming up with new ways of fostering environments of hospitality'.[41]

I was a little surprised to realize that Skivereen sees such models of 'potentianalysis' still merely as unrealized potential in discussions of reading today, as I thought I'd put forward the model of something very much like postcritical decolonialism in 2017 in the pages of the same journal where he articulates his argument. 'The Critic as Amateur', which had the seeds of this current book, outlined new and unexpected environments that transformed Western texts rather than simply undoing them. Perhaps it is not what Skivereen was looking for, as indicated in the very title of the article, my reader was an amateur, albeit an inspired one, who stumbled upon the texts concerned by accident that were, however, not fully separable from the colonial history of their own identity as well as of the environment where such 'accidents' took place.

Skivereen's argument does not take into account the kind of lay reader that may actually be helpful to postcritical approaches to reading. There is, in his approach, an urgency for a certain ethical position that gets priority over the actual practice of reading. Merve Emre has identified this inclination for ethical positioning in her 2017 book *Paraliterary*, where, as she puts it, even the more daring interventions about cultures of reading can 'seem more eager to legitimize a particular ethical subject position than to parse specific practices of reading'.[42] By ethical subject position, Emre implies 'a particular kind of human being in the world', but this figure of the reader is presented "without first elaborating how a historically and institutionally contingent, explicitly mediated, and public technique of reading results in the creation of that particular kind of human being'. This attachment to the position indicates an unwillingness to abandon their proclivities as critics formulated by certain ideological forces in scholarly education.

All readers, it goes without saying, are situated in their own historical circumstances. So are the readers that I seek to read in this book, even though concerted efforts to go beyond these very circumstances often define their very relationships with reading. It is difficult to include such readers in the academic debates about reading, and yet, I feel that these debates have something to gain from these struggling but imaginative readers – among other things, as viable and enriching models of lay reading. What happens when the reader is someone with an indifferent, incomplete, stumbling sort of knowledge, when their very arrival at the text is an accident? Here is the story of an imagination quickened by a strange concoction of chance, misdirection, ignorance, and a subconscious sense of identity, all coming together in a moment where none of the aims or resources of literary reading is even a remote possibility. Shortly after introducing us to the boy who wishes to spend the day in bed with the word in Addis Ababa, Daniel Coleman takes us to another side of the world, to 'the fishing village in Guayguayare, Trinidad, where an eight-year-old girl also took to her bed with a book'.[43] Books were not on the little girl's mind; she was raiding her grandmother's wardrobe: 'What made me fall into this book was probably some raid on my grandmother's cakes or sweet breads. I was probably trying to steal her Klim milk powder or the sugar she buried there also, as if it were not the sole ambition of children to seek out secrets.'[44] Here too, the Bible was a staple read, and there were sweet treats for the children hidden away, which lured the narrator and drew her in, purely by accident:

> My grandmother read the bible from that drawer, putting her finger under each word, then tiring, her eyes or her grasp giving out, she placed it in the recess at the head of her bed before falling asleep, some psalm dying on her lips … But when she was asleep we forgot her power. Then the wardrobe drawer was a lure of tablecloth-covered cakes soaked in rum to keep them moist and crumbling shortbreads in tins from away, powdered milk and Ponds pink face powder, dates, chocolates melting to cherry centres in the heat, Andrew liver salts which frothed in the mouth, avocados left in brown paper to ripen. What led me to this book, then, were my senses, my sweet tooth, my hunger, my curiosity, the intrigue, the possibility of outsmarting my grandmother.[45]

Slavery can be the strangest of memories in the Caribbean islands, both elusive and oppressive at the same time, the destroyer of communal memory and ancestral culture but the historical enabler of ideological chains. V. S. Naipaul, with his Hindu-Indian ancestry, recalled a time in his school when word 'slavery' brought up an inexplicable pain. There was some talk of the subject in school one day, and he remembered 'trying to give meaning to the word: looking up to the hills to the north of the city and thinking that those hills would have once been looked upon by people who were not free'. But it was a difficult exercise: 'The idea was too painful to hold on to.'[46] Jamaica Kincaid hit out at the only language slavery and colonialism left her with, the only one with which to critique their pillages now: 'For isn't it odd that the only language I have in which to speak of this crime is the language of the criminal who committed this crime?'[47]

For an eight-year-old Dionne Brand in Guayguayare, the accidental discovery of *The Black Napoleon*, a book on the 1791 Haitian Revolution in her grandmother's cupboard was a sudden encounter with a history of which she had no prior knowledge, having received a very different education through her school curriculum – or with the idea of a pain with which she had little personal familiarity herself, and yet, which seemed to ineffably belong to her. The book is accompanied by another one which brought out the inadequacies of her child mind and reason in the most obvious way. 'The geometry book', she only remembered, 'as pages of drawings, signs and symbols with thick dense writing which I could not follow, though I remember elaborate structures, a kind of inexplicable intelligence which I knew I would never conquer but felt I ought to.'[48] That book was forbidding and difficult, but the other book was actually forbidden, which eventually made it irresistible.

> I cannot recall the day I decided to read the book, but it must have been the day after my uncle said not to touch it. Then it became as irresistible as the other contents of the drawer. I opened the book, at first leaving the drawer open with the book lying inside, and began to read … It was the book that took me away from the world, from the small intrigues of sugar and milk to the pleasure and desolation of words on a page. For days I lived with these people I found there, hoping and urging and frightened and elated. The book was about the uprising led by Toussaint L'Ouverture against the French on St. Domingue … I had never met Toussaint L'Ouverture until I saw him at the bottom of the wardrobe drawer with the cakes and sugar. Perhaps I also met there things I had never felt before. I did not know about slavery; I had never felt pain over it. In fact I had never felt pain except the kind of pain that children feel, immediate and transient; I had never seen – well, what can one see in eight years or so of living?[49]

The eight-year-old is not only debilitated by her lack of knowledge and experience of life, but is additionally limited by the falsities of a colonial curriculum. There was a pain in the account that drew her like a magnet and yet about which she knew nothing, not only because it had been kept from her, but also because at the age of eight, she had not gathered much of life yet. The reading itself could not have been anything but a flawed awakening from a greater system of flaw and injustice, and it is the poor and accidental nature of such moments of reading that make up the most crucial points of the self-making of deeply imaginative individuals who emerge from conditions of such poverty and injustice. 'Finding *The Black Napoleon* in the drawer that smelled of cane sugar and rum,' Coleman goes on to write, 'she says, "made her the girl who grew up to participate in the Grenadan revolution, to win the Canadian Governor General's award for poetry, and to write books that, in their own turn, burn the skin and wake readers to the world they had not known they inhabited".'[50]

A poor reader, lacking knowledge of context or history – even when that history belongs to her, but without her knowing – gravitates back to herself, to the world around her. For Dionne Brand, the Haitian Revolution would remain inseparable from the smell of cane sugar and rum in her grandmother's cupboard in Guayguayare. For another poor reader in a crucial moment of his growth, Pankaj Mishra, the politics of the petty bourgeoisie in nineteenth-century France would hark back to casteism and corruption of late-twentieth-century rural Uttar Pradesh, to the point where a reading of Flaubert by Edmund Wilson would throw the most unexpected light on lives around him in his own provincial location. Historical-contextual knowledge, in both instance, veers between the erratic and the missing, pushing these readings as far from professional standards as possible. The poor cultural literacy in the lives of these imaginative individuals living precarious lives on the provincial margins, and the accidental, misdirected readings that emerge from their chance encounter with unexpected texts, yield truths about human life, identity, and history that professional scholarship, endowed with the right kind of contextual-historical knowledge, would almost certainly would have missed. Accidental affective connections with the text, indeed, a strange hermeneutics of affirmation, enable these readers to touch the surface of these texts and then veer in unexpected directions – to an unexplored depth within oneself in one instance, and to other people and communities on the other. The lack of the professional apparatuses of the literary historian enables both a strange universalism and the revelation of a dormant personal identity.

Poor reading, in the sense it is of interest as a method of interpretation, is a sharply circumscribed term. It is a unique mingling of the disabling lack of resources, intellectual, historical, and material, the vagaries of life, and the keenness of imagination in figures subjugated by the reality of racial, gendered, or colonial domination. Such reading is offered in the spirit of affirmation, but affirmation of a strange sort that is usually unimaginable in the original cultural context of the text. And its final commitment is neither to the surface nor to depth. If anything, there is a strange laterality to it, one with many holes. To set it up in a simple comparison to the academic study of literature, be it formalist criticism, historical scholarship, or anything else, would be silly; their context, energy, and goals are radically different from any mode of academic reading. My introduction of these various instances of poor, flawed, anarchic, and even nihilistic reading next to a discussion of academic debates about criticism, I hope, has not created the impression of the attempt to compare these disparate entities. My question is different: we have heard long enough that the amateur should professionalize, but does the professional also have something to learn from the amateur, perhaps claim some fragments of their self they might have had once, and some, never? Is there something in these various instances of poor reading which systems of professional literary interpretation learn something? Would that be an act of learning or unlearning?

Defining figures of contemporary criticism have already begun to make gestures in this direction. In *The Limits of Critique*, Felski called for a 'less strong theory', one that could leave 'room the aleatory and the unexpected, the chancy and the contingent'. It would have to be a theory of reading that would not "trace textual meaning back to an opaque and all-determining power', while assuming the critic to be a figure immune from its control. I read this as an imagination of the critic as a vulnerable figure, more dependent on chance and contingency than professional scholarship has imagined her to be. The depth model of criticism that Best and Marcus discuss, as well as the historical-contextual model that North sees as dominant, has all been variously seen as enacting forms of critical heroism, serious labour worthy of institution recognition and remuneration. I sense Felski asking for a diffusion of this agency, of the experience of the fallibility and susceptibility of the critic. 'Such a framework', she writes, 'would need to clarify how agency is distributed among a larger cohort of social actors; to refuse dichotomies of inside versus outside, transgression versus containment; and to more fully acknowledge the complication and entanglement of text and critic.' The slow erosion of heroic critical individualism to the emergence of 'a larger cohort of social actors' evokes J. Daniel Elam's imagination of 'anonymous, interpenetrating, multitudinous collectivity' foregrounded in his celebration of anticolonial thinkers in place of an expected colonial selfhood, noted above. Elsewhere, I have read in a different model of polymath amateurism a resistance to the formation of a professionalized colonial subject in British India.[51] And as Mishra demonstrates in his glorious misreading of the Edmund Wilson's historic rootedness, one of the key elements that gets misplaced in such instances of poor reading is the valorized focus on context. 'Rethinking of critique', no wonder Felski writes, 'also means rethinking our familiar ideas of context.'[52]

One of the more earthbound forms of that question might look like this: what happens to reading when the goal is not original interpretation, the quest for truth, or even the enhancement of knowledge? Anticolonial utopia is scarcely the only venue that excludes these traditional humanist practices and gestures. Very different, workaday mass spaces that reveal widely popular but blatantly reductive deployment of reading – and that too of literary texts – have been identified in post-war United States by Merve Emre. In *Paraliterary*, Emre examines the social phenomenon of the relationship of literary texts with 'lived experiences of public communication', where such communication includes such widely disparate but instrumental discourses of 'diplomatic and ambassadorial missions, private and public cultural exchange programs, multinational corporations, international magazines, or global activist groups.'[53] If the traditional humanist goals of interpretation and aesthetic education, as practised in elite educational institutions, made up instances of good reading, the functional deployment of reading as acts of public communication constituted defined the practice of the 'bad readers' against whom good literary reading had to stake its distinctive identity. The former, pervasive as widespread social phenomena was just about everywhere: 'lecture transcripts, elocution primers, conduct books, publicity stills, advertisements, consumer guides, financial instruments, magazines, journals, intelligence reports, bureaucratic files.'[54]

The modes of reading recorded by Emre are just as intriguing in their distance from the ambition of literary humanism, even when their archive is literature, whether high or middlebrow – Henry James or Erica Jong. 'Imitative reading' is deployed to set up books, or public lectures around them, as forms of learnable discourse, even when the discourse is far from textual or literary, such as the imitation of modes of conduct in Henry James novels by young women around the nation. 'Reading as feeling' was far more pragmatic than it sounded on surface, consuming American texts to generate a certain international idea of America, usually a 'love that was thus capable of governing not only an individual's emotional responses but also an increasingly unruly geopolitical order at midcentury.'[55] Reading and writing brands in literature energized patterns of American consumerism like the identification of 'traveler's checks, travel guides, and customs declarations' as well as 'experiences like tourism' as globally readable discourses, at least for those who could afford them.[56] 'Sight reading' illustrates modes away from verbal discourse to the importance of images and photographs in the consumption of texts, particularly as magazines rose in their popularity through the century.[57] Finally, 'bureaucratic reading', examining particular forms of institutional, official, and diplomatic discourses, asked the question: 'What might it mean to write and read like a bureaucrat?'[58]

Paraliterary seeks to unveil what 'other people learn to do things with literary texts'.[59] The echo of J.L. Austin's speech act theory in the linguistic texture of this argument is suggestive, but no less suggestive is the 'othering' of people who deploy literary texts for non-literary purposes, as set out in institutional venues of advanced education and high culture, such as literary periodicals. It reveals the wide mid-century popularity of a certain canon of texts as somewhat strange and unexpected, as that popularity translates en masse into modes of imagination and epistemological practice far away from those considered literary or is otherwise consistent with aesthetic or humanist education. But reality stages its own mode of persuasion, as 'the dizzying rise of institutions of international mass communications and the sheer volume of texts they produced and circulated made it impossible to ignore the heteronomous attitudes toward literature embraced by readers conscripted by the state and acting in the service of the nation'. While on one hand Emre's inquiry brings us close to the once revolutionary and democratizing subfield of cultural studies, on the other, it indicates a disambiguation, indeed, a disappearance of the traditional agency of literary hermeneutics.

The latter is of particular interest to me here. In recent years, the academic study of literature has experienced a conscious withholding, indeed, a deliberate diminution of intellectual agency on part of the scholarly interpreter. This has been driven by a range of impulses – the need to reduce interpretative 'suspicion' and raise the quotient of wonder, slow down the relentless quest for underlying patterns and structures – all various attempts to prevent the reduction of messy, undisciplined archives to powerful, omniscient theory that is given to us by the European Enlightenment as well as its radically contrarian interlocutors. In foregrounding what he calls a deliberate weakening of critical theory, Paul St. Amour writes, 'the various loads borne by weakness can productively decenter what they encounter'. Affective and epistemological embodiments of weakness, which have emerged from 'fields that address difference, stigma, and inequity', such as queer studies, lead to a generative estrangement of both theory and archive. 'These emergent, alternative methods', St. Amour points out, 'explore, among other things, what would happen if strength were no longer the presumptive master-criterion for art, thought, research, argument, and teaching.'[60]

How can methodologies be imagined as weaker, more diffused or scattered? Among other things, this entails a rethinking of the traditional relation between theory and archive, and the inevitable hierarchy of power between them through which the former ends up controlling the latter, and even dictating its shape and limits. As methods of reading, St. Amour is right in invoking Jeffrey Williams' description of these approaches as 'the new modesty in literary criticism' in cataloguing 'post-critique, surface reading, distant reading, thin description, the sociological turn, and new formalism' as recent instances of weak theory in reading methodologies. These are the approaches that seek to replace the depth-model hermeneutics of 'symptomatic reading' which seek to reveal hidden hegemonies of capital, the unconscious, or other structures of powers within texts. Such acts of relinquishment, or at least the diminution of agency on part of theoretical methodologies, one hopes, will lead to a celebration of the chaotic amorphousness of archives that have been subjected to the epistemological violence of reductive and suspicious interrogation for too long. As St. Amour says in relation to modernist studies, among other outcomes, such a weakening allows the archives to breathe and expand farther rather than be reined by the overpowering and therefore limiting control of strong theoretical methodologies.

I do see my celebration of poor reading as part of this conversation around weak theory. But more importantly, I also like to think of such readings as practices that have historically existed, both regularly and erratically, among real practitioners marginal to the various establishments of literacy, education, and interpretation. In other words, I do not see them as primarily internal misgivings of the discipline, but rather as material practices that have always existed in the world. It is time for the two to meet, coming as they do from opposite directions – reading as historic acts of scraping and scavenging, and the self-detection of malaise by academic practice. I won't deny that there is a ring of utopia in the dream of this mutual conversation, because it remains as difficult to theorize a system of poor reading as it is difficult to link it to a real institutional practice. One can link it to the reality of the colonized and the provincial, but only if one also acknowledges the specialness of individuals who have established memorable instances of its practice. This difficulty, I would say, is its uniqueness. But at the same time, poor reading is carried out every day in different parts of the world, in many forms, in varying degrees of accuracy, relevance, and effectiveness, at varying gradients of amateurism, sometimes on their way to professionalism, sometimes away from it, sometimes at odd angles to it. Can this inform or enrich our teaching practice rather than merely be seen as obstacles to be removed? In the epilogue to our edited collection, *The Critic as Amateur*, Kara Wittman raised this very question. 'Do we hope', asks Wittman, 'students will hold on to the aspects of their amateurism that allows them to wonder and explore without feeling constrained by professional expectation, to remain, as Roland Barthes put it, in the epistemological "as if" of the "Amateur," the subjective and intimate pinnacle of [their] particularity?'[61] Even students privileged to be initiated to literary study in the precincts of professional institutions have something to learn from the contingent richness of poor reading. The depletion of interpretation often comes with the unasked grace of bewildered joy. The study of literature, in the end, would be wealthier if we can acknowledge poor reading, not merely as a lack or failing on its way to correcting itself, but as an essential part of aesthetic education.

Chapter 3

AUTODIDACTIC NATION

'You must go to college, my son, and come and look after me and your brother and your sister. They must also go to school.' So said my mother when I went to high school. This kind of pep talk has launched thousands of Africans into the uncharted seas of insecure education in an insecure life (57).

— Es'kia Mphahlele, *The African Image* (1962)

Why is it that education often becomes the most acutely sought after thing in communities that are most sharply deprived of it? Where does this seeking come from? With many of the communities I discuss in this book, this lack is not a simple structural absence but the strategic instrumentation of an exclusionary or repressive system. The hunger for education that sometimes appears in the subjects of such systems does not merely reflect the desire for upward socio-economic mobility, but something far deeper – a compelling call to make oneself in the image of the full humanity denied to them by that very machinery. How does one access the humanities from within a system that refuses to acknowledge the humanity of those it wishes to incorporate? It is both a mystery and wonder of human resilience and imagination that some of the most heroic attempts of self-making through a scattered, scavenged, and relentlessly autodidactic practices of reading has been carried out by Black and Coloured thinkers, writers, and activists in twentieth-century South Africa.[1]

In a revealingly titled essay in his collection *The African Image*, 'These Cheeky Kaffirs, Those Impertinent Natives', Es'kia Mphahlele narrates the harrowing story of educational and career (im)possibilities before the Black African in apartheid-era South Africa. 'Detribalized', the Black African has 'no allegiance to tribal authority, except in a detached academic way.'[2] Moreover, if they 'tried to go back to their tribe, they would find no land to occupy'. But the path to White modernity, and the jobs and careers it brought up, were also closed to them for the most part. Educated Africans, he points out, are clearly not wanted in the city, where illiterates or semi-literates are preferred, who accept menial jobs and errands with a sense of gratitude. The teaching profession was the most accessible, and therefore it became the most common among Black African people with post-secondary education. During the times Mphahlele describes, the teacher's course took two years if 'one had done a three-year course in high school'. It was far more expensive to study medicine – even though nursing, particularly for Black women, closely followed teaching as a popular choice of profession.

It feels like an ironic inevitability that education would become a defining concern for Black South Africans in twentieth-century South Africa long before apartheid was formally instituted in 1948. The profession of teaching was one which drew many educated Black Africans as the only career choice, making them more deeply entrenched than ever in the inequitable and impossible conditions under which some semblance of education was to be achieved, with little scope of a fulfilling career to follow. The result could only be the making of human beings who are strangely cut off from everything – from their traditional communities as well as from the violence of modernity. 'It is a lonely man,' wrote Mphahlele, 'who is not taken seriously by his own people, yet cannot keep aloof from them and their daily miseries.'[3]

The White man, too, resented the educated African deeply. Writing a couple of years after Mphahlele, Bloke Modisane, Mphahlele's fellow writer at *Drum* magazine, known for its representation of Black township life under apartheid, explained that White resentment of the educated African was not so much due to his alleged cheekiness, but because the latter frustrated the sanctified stereotype that the Native must be humiliated into submission. At the same time, the educated African, particularly if speaking English, is resented by fellow Black people, as English is one of the symbols of White supremacy: 'he is resentfully called a Situation, something not belonging to either, but tactfully situated between white oppression and black rebellion'.[4] He is regarded as a curio by the English, who listen to his accent and pronunciation with critical attention and then pronounce, 'with almost divine tolerance and Christian charity', that the African speaks beautiful English. The colonial tongues, English and Afrikaans, have deeply loaded histories and very different associations of power, oppression, and aspiration – and to the Afrikaner, the English-speaking Black African is a violation and an offense. 'The Afrikaners,' writes Modisane, 'are almost psychotic in their reaction to the English-speaking African, whom they accuse of talking back with insolence and aping the white man.'[5]

What are the conditions within which Black and Coloured South Africans educated themselves in the twentieth century, till the dissolution of apartheid in 1994? Mphahlele points to the similarity between patterns of co-existence between Black and White populations in different countries in sub-Saharan Africa. Unlike Uganda or West Africa, where the Black population posed no threat to the small group of White expatriates and hence Black education was encouraged, in South Africa, like Kenya, the Black person 'is being resisted by the minority group which has entrenched itself economically and politically and which cannot bear the thought of competing against an overwhelming number of black people'.[6] A particularly fierce opposition, it is historically clear, came from the Boer/Afrikaner population, who resented the liberal education policy of the mission schools that apartheid would eventually put out of practice. Descended primarily from Dutch settlers in the Cape in the seventeenth century, the Afrikaners were shadowed by the economic and political modernity of the English since the nineteenth century and finally defeated decisively by them in the Second Anglo-Boer War that concluded in 1902, leading to the end of the Boer Republics and the establishment of the Union of South Africa as a Dominion of the British Empire. This created an unprecedented two-tiered imperialism, with the English firmly entrenched as the aspirational culture of modernity and the Afrikaner designated as a relatively backward and unsophisticated farming people subordinated to the advanced industrial capitalism of the English. Under this subordination, the threat of the Black African was arguably felt the most fiercely by the Afrikaner population. It is partly this threat, and their perception of being an embattled group, that consolidated Afrikaner nationalism to shape the institution of Apartheid in 1948, following the general election victory of the Afrikaners that would also lead to the formation of the National Party in 1951.

In their introduction to the *Cambridge History of South African Literature*, David Attwell and Derek Attridge discuss the imposition of a common history on radically heterogeneous South Africa, a history which has itself been violently absorbed into the modern world system. 'Colonialism and then apartheid', they write, 'do not define all of South Africa's history, certainly not its cultural origins, but it is axiomatic that European expansion from the seventeenth to the nineteenth centuries set in train processes that would lead to the development of the nation-state.'[7] These were also the processes that would lead to contention over education, and the hierarchy between languages – including that between the languages of the White colonizers, English, and Afrikaans, marking the former as a language of aspiration and the latter as that of oppression. The Soweto uprising of 16 June 1976, which involved over 20,000 school students from across the nation and led to the death of over 700 in the face of police brutality – was essentially a protest by Black students against the imposition of Afrikaans as a language of school instruction as spelt out in the *Afrikaans Medium Decree* of 1974. But the defining education legislation of apartheid-era South Africa was The Bantu Education Act of 1953, which formally enacted racial segregation in the South African education system, directing Black children and youth in a different set of ill-funded schools and depleted, simplified curricula that would essentially exclude them from any intellectual or white-collar careers. Only the church continued to offer a limited space, from where the Federal Theological Seminary and liberation theology would later provide an intellectual foundation for the radical anti-apartheid movement of Black Consciousness.

Writing before the Act was passed, Es'kia Mphahlele says, 'Thus we hear whites in South Africa talk of "Bantu culture" and apartheid which is meant to give us an opportunity to "develop along our own lines"', which 'will save us the frustration that results from trying to compete with the whites in spheres of life already preserved for them as a birthright!'[8] What kind of educational opportunities did the Act provide to them when it was finally instituted? Njabulo Ndebele, the Black writer born in the fateful year of 1948 and affected more directly by Bantu Education, points out that the Act was simply a consolidation of what was already a socio-political reality, the lack of a proper education of the African people of South Africa, barring the mission schools, which educated a small minority of the African leadership, including, for instance, Mphahlele at St Peter's, Nelson Mandela at Healdtown, and Albert Luthuli at Adam's College. 'Although the African was to get an education', Ndebele wrote, 'it was only so that he could be a better servant who could understand simple instruction and read simple messages.'[9] Providing nothing more than basic literacy through poorly funded, impoverished schools, Bantu Education essentially cut off the mass of Black Africans from the written word and in turn deprived the African elite of any 'educational base within the larger African community'.[10] Such is the loneliness and alienation of the Black intellectual, as articulated by Es'kia Mphahlele above.

Education, aspiration, and literary subjectivity

The precarious and complex relation between education, labour, and personal growth becomes a defining concern in much of South African literature through the twentieth century, even if we limit ourselves to

English-language writing. It takes on a particularly urgent and sensory form in narratives of growth and development, be it the *Bildungsroman*, memoir, or the hybrid mix of autobiography and criticism left by many writers, some of the most poignant, painful, and memorable of which have come from Black and Coloured writers. Zoë Wicomb's linked story collection, *You Can't Get Lost in Cape Town*, strings together a Künstlerroman which, published in 1987, chronicles the growth, education, and literary development of a mixed-race woman from Namaqualand very much like its creator, also born in the critical year of 1948.[11] While the anxieties of a relatively prosperous mixed-race family (that of a village school-principal) around the education and career of a girl who can pass as White seem one of privilege say, next to those of the young Black boys in Njabulo Ndebele's collection, *Fools*, Wicomb's Frieda Shenton's anxieties – and those of her father – strikingly parallel the educational anxieties of 'Coloured' South Africa.[12]

The very opening story of the collection, 'Bowl Like Hole', presents a village community flush with the excitement and importance of the arrival of the Englishman, Mr. Weedon, who arrived in a big fine car, 'enquiring about sheep or goat or servants'.[13] In the admiration for Mr. Weedon, presented most pronouncedly in the Shenton family, we see the clear hierarchy constructed by the 'Coloured' population – between the English, who represented civilization and sophistication, and the Boers, who represented uncouth savagery, and not far behind, the jagged cruelty of apartheid. Mr. Weedon is admired more because he 'spoke not one word of Afrikaans'. Nor could be, as 'for people born in England the g's and t's of the language were impossible, barbaric'.[14] Mr. Weedon, with his admirable English speech that they do their best to emulate, leaves them with a pronunciation of the word 'bowl' that confuses them. 'Bowl like hole, not bowl like howl', wonders Frieda's father. 'Do you think that's right?' Even though Frieda's mother is equally confused, she knows who must be right: 'Of course, he's English, he ought to know'.[15]

Frieda's family seeks upward mobility desperately and this dream turns successful in Frieda, who receives a college education, is seen writing essays about Thomas Hardy's novels, and becomes, much like Wicomb herself, a successful writer who emigrates to the West, to return again, and to write what strangely feels like the very collection we're reading, giving it a clear metafictional flavour. But the recorded experiences of Sindiwe Magona, a Xhosa writer from the village of Gungululu in rural Eastern Cape, are far harsher. As a domestic servant who completed much of her education by correspondence in the most intense years of apartheid and Bantu Education, hers is a story of autodidactism that is as harrowing as it is inspiring. The stories of the collection *Living, Loving and Lying Awake at Night* chronicle the painful lyricism of the life of a Black female domestic serving White families, and the conflict of rage, aspiration, and indignation narrated with a visceral intimacy. The story, 'Joyce', for instance, is made up entirely of a conversation between two female domestics articulating this rage, and the desperate hope of transcending this life of dehumanizing labour.

'My mother got me this job,' says the opening speaker, 'but believe me, I'm not going to be a maid for long.'[16] The other speaker tells her that she was a student doing matric but her classes were disrupted by the riots. 'So Mother said: "Ntombi, go to work until this thing is over and then you'll go back to school."' The response contains an appalling statistic: 'Do you know how many African women doctors there are? In this whole country? Five, FIVE – that's all!' But the speaker is optimistic that 'there will be six – that, I promise you.' The conversation continues in the staccato music of protest. There is agreement with the White mistress' idea that 'the domestic worker should improve herself'. But as one might expect in a country striated by sharp education apartheid, 'I don't agree with what that improvement means … Thank you very much, but I don't want to learn to iron starched shirts better. I don't want to learn the ways of laying the most attractive table.'[17] But segregated education and labour policy makes race an inevitable reality in menial domestic work, and when will that change? 'And the color of the maid should not automatically be black.'

It is a world where fair and deserved rights appear as mercies granted out of gratuitous generosity. White women, who refuse to pay rightful wages to their domestic workers, appear generous when they buy books for the children of the same workers – who naturally can't afford to buy them themselves given her abysmally low wages. The result, among other things, is disastrous for female solidarity. 'How can I,' asks one speaker, 'be a sister to my father, the white woman?' The White woman does not hesitate to ask the Black woman to share her knowledge with her White child: 'Read Penelope a story from her Xhosa book.'[18] – but there is no acknowledgement of the lack of the Black woman's education, or that of her children: 'But that does not make them think of me as a student whose learning has been disturbed and who is pining for school.' There is no possibility for the poor Black domestic worker, no option, no education to aspire to, no air to breathe in this segregated nation, just the desperate hope: 'I am not going to see my twentieth birthday in this job. There is only one way for me to go from here: and that is: OUT! … OUT! … OUT!'.[19]

When education is cut off, the air to breathe is gone – that is the cry of suffocation we hear in Joyce's voice, in Magona's story. The claustrophobic predicament of Black youth, male and female, looms large in Njabulo Ndebele's significant collection, *Fools and Other Stories*, where teachers and students are key dramatic characters, particularly in the title story, where the teacher tells the student he meets on the railway platform: 'You see, there is no education for us in this country.' And then he accounts for its history, clearly referring to the Bantu Education Act: 'The damage was done way back in 1953. Now it is 1966. Yet, we keep complaining as if the injustice began yesterday.'[20] Educated Africans, that is, those who had received some semblance of education before the Act made it illegal, now found their hands tied. 'I cannot determine the kind of education my daughter shall have,' wrote Bloke Modisane, 'and it is a criminal offence for me to give my daughter lessons at home; if it is proved that there was a blackboard, chalk, paper and pencil, then I'm guilty of conducting a private school, thus contravening the Bantu Education Act.'[21]

This life of education deprivation and constriction is everywhere in Black South African writing. Miriam Tlali, whose education at the University of Witwatersrand was interrupted when it was closed to Black people, eventually went to secretarial school because of lack of funds, and trained as a bookkeeper. The life of an office-clerk, and quotidian racism to which it was subject, made her semi-autobiographical novel, *Muriel at Metropolitan*, a novel that struggled to find a publisher and was banned immediately upon its publication in 1975. While Wicomb's Frieda Shenton gets access to a university education of indifferent quality, it is just as easy to see connections between the female domestic workers in Sindiwe Magona's stories and Muriel in Tlali's novel, who can at best afford an education that keeps her a clerk in a furniture and electronics store, a long way from the doctor that is the aspiration of Magona's domestic worker. Education and its disruptions haunt Tlali's fiction in direct and indirect ways, also finding expression in her novel *Amandla*, based on the 1976 Soweto uprising, and also banned soon after publication.

Literature, self-learning, and the telling of freedom

The damage was done, says the teacher in Ndebele's *Fools*, way back in 1953. But Ndebele himself, writing in the 1980s, provides a more capacious view of this damage, which extended much farther back in history: 'The coming of Bantu Education in the early fifties served to consolidate what was already a socio-political reality: the lack of an adequate education for the mass of the African population'.[22] What did the prehistory of this consolidation look like, and what did it do to the education of the Black intellectual under apartheid – particularly education in Western literature and humanities? What fragments of education were drawn from uncertain and often accidental experience of reading, of meeting unlikely texts in unlikely places? Hedley Twidle, in his study of narrative non-fiction in South Africa, has arrived at similar conclusions about autodidactic self-making derived from 'mostly useless' literary inheritances chanced upon by accident, say in Njabulo Ndebele's accidental discovery, in his father's garage, of a whole box of banned memoirs and personal histories by a range of writers such as Es'kia Mphahlele, Bloke Modisane, Todd Matshikizia, Mary Benson, Peter Abrahams, and other lesser known books and copies of magazines. Chronicling several similar accidental encounters with books that left lasting impact in the lives of Peter Abrahams, Thabo Mbeki, Jacob Dlamini, as well as more canonical figures such as Nelson Mandela and M.K. Gandhi, and White writers such as J.M. Coetzee and Nadine Gordimer, Twidle describes them as 'reminders of how the most important intellectual work in or about the country has often taken place outside formal institutions: in marginal, covert, or exile spaces', constituting an ongoing tradition of 'autodidactic, unaffiliated intellectual labor'.[23]

How did such an education, snatched in the face of heavy odds, hard to access even before 1953, shape a literary subjectivity for the Black writer? These are questions that interest me keenly, and I've found some of the most moving moments of its realization in Peter Abrahams' 1954 memoir, *Tell Freedom*. It is an account of poverty, pain, and violence, structured by the strict lines of apartheid, which gives young Peter, born of a Black father and a Coloured mother, an early lesson on the cost of hitting back a local White boy while he grows up, after his Ethiopian-origin father's early death, in the impoverished household of his uncle and aunt. His uncle Sam is forced to beat him brutally under the supervision of his White neighbour – his baas – after Peter dares to return a blow to the White man's son who abused and brutalized Peter and his cousin Andries earlier in the day. It is a harrowing life in Johannesburg's Vrededorp, constricted by his Black identity and the limited freedom of movement afforded by the required passes. Haunted by his dream of ancestry in the kings of Abyssinia, he does stints of work selling firewood and at the smithy, cleaning cars during his lunch hour, and shortly after his tenth birthday, runs into 'the short-sighted Jewish girl' in the office of Mr. Wylie whose car he cleans. She asks him how old he is, and on knowing that he is 'going on for eleven', asks why he doesn't go to school. He can say nothing beyond 'I don't know, miss,' which is also his answer to her question if he wants to go. 'I don't know, miss,' is also his answer to her question as to whether he would like to learn to read. And then she turns the pages of the book before her and starts to read and something happens to him: 'The story of Othello jumped at me and invaded my heart and mind as the young woman read. I was transported to the land where the brave Moor lived and loved and destroyed his love.'[24]

The 'short-sighted Jewish girl', Sarah, is a teacher who, when she wishes to take Peter in her class, is told 'that education is compulsory for whites and no one cares about whether this boy goes to school or not'.[25] And yet it so happens that in a class that is three times as big as it should be, with some students nearly adults who are hard to control, without enough benches to seat them all, 'a boy at work hears a story and the story makes him come here', and he says, 'Please, I want to learn.' Sarah's superior, the school-principal who is also the 'Mad Boer Poet', goes on to admit that Peter should be admitted to the school, driven hard, caned if he fails. The classroom that follows is both absurd and moving. Peter has no slate to write on, so Thomas, another student, offers to share his slate, which 'is cracked across the middle', and he can sit next to him too, as there is room there. Jones, who sits there, is not coming back since 'his father's gone to jail, so he must go to work to help his mother'.[26] Peter's father is not alive, and the teacher knows that as a consequence, 'things are not too easy'. As they learn the alphabet and the numbers, a question strikes Peter: 'Are all the books in the world made from the alphabet.' To hear that they are creates great wonder in him.

Letters, rather than numbers, appear to be Peter's calling, and soon, he has trouble with arithmetic. The principal calls him and has a stern chat that is meant to be both a reprimand and a motivation, reminding him that arithmetic stands between him and everything he wishes to do, 'like a lion barring your road'.[27] He has similar problems with scientific principles such as gravity and the roundness of the earth. But during his three years of regular attendance at the school, he really takes to literature. Lamb's *Tales from Shakespeare* continued to be a favourite since the first magical revelation with his teacher Sarah, and along with Palgrave's *Golden Treasury* and the Everyman's edition of John Keats, he writes, 'were my proudest and dearest possessions, my greatest wealth'.[28] Tales from Shakespeare and *The Golden Treasury*, modern classics by that time, have enjoyed immense canonical and popular appeal across the British Empire. Shakespeare, particularly distilled as a repertoire of thrilling tales in the Lamb collection, offers mesmeric entertainment to any literary autodidact, and it is momentous how the story of the moor Othello and his romantic self-destruction reached out to the ten-year-old Abrahams, already imprisoned by his embattled Black identity.

But readers of English literature in the colony live in a reality radically different from the world of literature in which they may dwell through their imagination. They must reckon with their strangely conflicted, incompatible duality. Such too, was the experience of Peter Abrahams. 'With Shakespeare and poetry, a new world was born. New dreams, new desires, a new self-consciousness, were born. I desired to know myself in terms of the new standards set by these books. I lived in two worlds, the world of Vrededorp and the world of these books.'[29] But the world of material reality was too keenly present, and overpowering in its presence. Late in the nights, walking alone through the White neighbourhoods of Johannesburg, he could not help but marvel at the strong-brick-made houses that kept its residents warm, dry, and sheltered against the intensity of wind and rain. Looking into their windows, he saw 'the magic of electricity' and could not help think that 'a boy could read Lamb's Tales without strain in such light'.[30] The book-hungry child could often see 'whole walls of books' in these houses and marvel 'what a sight!' – but at every sharp turn, be it the public parks or the lavatories reminded him with loud signs that this world was 'RESERVED FOR EUROPEANS ONLY'.

But the two worlds, that of reading and that of his own reality, would soon come together unexpectedly. One day he saw a well-dressed young Black man in an eating house reading a paper called *Bantu World*, one Peter had never heard of, and whose look took him by surprise. 'Yes, the pictures on the front page were of black people! All the papers I had sold had only pictures of white folk.'[31] As he tried to read the paper, the young Black man asked if he could read. When he said he could, the man asked him to read a bit to him, and after Peter did so successfully, the man wondered what Peter was doing there working at the market. 'I want money to learn some more,' said Peter. 'What do you want to learn?' asked the man. 'To write stories,' said Peter. While he was unable to help with that, the man said that he might be able to offer him a job, and directed him to the Bantu Men's Social Centre. Tentatively arriving there in the best clothes he could find, Peter saw a Black world he did not know was possible. He heard the voice of Paul Robeson – 'the voice of a black man!' – and naturally drawn to the bookshelves, he browsed through the catalogue slips: 'novels, history, sociology, travel, Africana, political science, American negro literature'. He stopped there, astounded that there could be something called 'negro literature'. Taking out a fat black book titled *The Souls of Black Folk* by W.E. B. Du Bois, he turned the pages, and realized that the book spoke of people who were 'black, and dispossessed, and denied'.[32] Skimming through the pages, these lines hit him: 'For this much all men know: despite compromise, war, struggle, the Negro is not free.'[33] The Negro is not free – the line kept echoing in his head as he thought of the 'reserved for Europeans only' signs all over the Johannesburg, the White sections, the park benches, the tearooms, all the places he wasn't allowed; he remembered his Aunt Mattie going to jail, he remembered the spittle thrown on his face, all the while that line echoing in his head – 'the Negro is not free'.

He wondered why he had not thought of it himself. Reading it, he felt he had known it all along. But till he read these words, he felt that he didn't have the language to express the knowledge. 'Du Bois's words had the impact of a revelation.'[34] It was all the more powerful because it crystallized the sum total of his own life experience so far – the pain, the humiliation, the endless exclusion, the lack of voice and existence, suddenly given language, with the clarity of an incisive poem: 'The problem of the Twentieth Century is the problem of the colour-line – the relation of the darker to the lighter races of men in Asia and Africa, in America and the islands of the sea.'[35] As he read, Abrahams recognized the people in the book. But for the lack of laughter in that solemn book – 'here, in our land, in the midst of our miseries, we had moments of laughter, moments of playing' – Du Bois gave the young boy all the keys to understand the very world he inhabited.

He picked up other books: *Up from Slavery*, *Along this Way*, by Weldon Johnson, a slim volume called *The Black Christ*, a fat volume called *The New Negro*. Turning the pages of *The New Negro*, Abrahams realized incredulously that 'These poems and stories were written by Negroes!'. He had an instantaneous reaction: 'Something burst deep inside me. The world could never again belong to white people only! Never again!'[36] He went on to read the words of Countee Cullen, Langston Hughes, Stirling Brown, Claude McKay, Georgia Douglas Johnson, and Jean Toomer, who spoke:

> Caroling softly souls of slavery,
> What they were, and what they are to me,
> Caroling softly souls of slavery[37]

Peter spent as much time as possible amidst the bookshelves of the Bantu Men's Social Centre. He read each and every one of the books on the shelves marked American Negro Literature. 'I became,' he writes, 'a nationalist, a colour nationalist, through the writings of men and women who lived in a world away from me. To them I owe a great debt for crystallizing my vague yearnings to write and for showing me the long dream was attainable.'[38]

Racial and literary subjectivity sprout simultaneously in the young Abrahams, one making the other possible. From his first recognition of Othello the moor in the voice of his teacher, at a time when he knew no letter, through his love for Shakespeare and English poetry, the words of Du Bois and the verse of Jean Toomer, all acquired on his own through dedicated hours at these bookshelves, gave him a sense of his self, a deeply racialized and a literary-imaginative existence at the same time. His experience at the Bantu Men's Social Centre inspired him to sign up for a correspondence course in 'General Education' at ten shillings a month, as well as to acquire ten bound volumes of a series called Practical Knowledge for All. It was an atmosphere where others were also setting out on correspondence courses as well as independent programmes of study, so there was community support around their attempts to make their way through the uncharted terrain of knowledge for which the mainstream institutions of White South Africa would offer them no support.

The distant lands from which these knowledges and literatures came called out to these young men, where they could live in freedom not available to them in their own country. Most of them wanted to go to America, which held the promise of hope, opportunity, and freedom. But Peter was divided between America and England. While America had limitless opportunities and the appeal of Harlem, England had Charles Lamb, John Keats, Shelley, and the poetry that had first set the young boy's mind to music. He could not decide easily. The voice of the American Negro, his freedom to voice his unfreedom, made him feel that America offered more to the Black man. But England, unable to offer the comfort of the company of his own kind, 'could counter that call because men now dead had once crossed its heaths and walked its lanes, quietly, unhurriedly, and had sung with such beauty that their songs had pierced the heart of a black boy, a world away, and in another time.'[39]

He decided that he would like to go to England first, if he ever got the opportunity – maybe to America later, but first to England. But he couldn't stop thinking of Harlem, 'a Negro city!' – where Countee

Cullen and Langston Hughes walked the streets together, joined by Paul Robeson, Du Bois, and Stirling Brown in his boyish imagination. It is his imagination of these faraway lands that kept him going while he put the little money he had in his books and correspondence courses. It felt natural, perhaps melancholically so, when he wanted to go to college to train to be a teacher and realized he would get the opportunity to do so in the Diocesan Training College in Pietersburg, he was overjoyed. But his people were uncertain. For the provincial, self-taught youth, sharply marginalized by his racial identity, any institutional education implied a leaving, a far journey, a great distance from his family and community. His people were uncertain. 'All these books and all this learning of yours,' said his sister Maggie, 'sometimes worries me. What'll you do with it? And will you be happy?'[40] But his mother felt differently. As he walked away from Vrededorp, his mother said in a heavy voice: 'It is a bad place. I'm glad you are going out of it.'[41]

In college he studied while working, sweeping and dusting the office, doing occasional typing, and working hard on the monthly college magazine. Mathematics still gave him trouble but he did well in all the other subjects. He also played sports and learned to 'turn the earth and make things grow from it'.[42] Most importantly, there he met a friendly group of teachers and priests who were to become 'the first white men whose colour I forgot'.[43] They taught and played with the students. The Afrikaner, Mr. Jansen, 'a big, gentle-natured man with a tentative manner', helped him overcome the 'reserve all non-whites have towards Boers'. It was a significant moment, as Afrikaner people and the Afrikaans language represented for many Black and Coloured people the worst of the racial oppression in South Africa and the actual institution of apartheid. But personal connection, mentorship, and most importantly, literature created a bridge there too. 'Through him I discovered the rich body of Afrikaner literature and the beauty of the language itself'.[44] But it was the tall and thin Father Adams who was the 'literary expert', and Peter was thrilled to have written an essay one day that pleased him. Father Adams was a champion of simple and moving writing, and whenever Peter used 'big words or made clumsy and almost meaningless sentences', he directed him to the Bible and its moving, simple expressions. That, he said, was how 'English should be written'. Peter read the Bible and saw what he meant.

Peter's progress towards his own literary idiom almost feels inevitable at this point. Initiated by the oral rendering of Shakespeare's tales in the voice of his teacher, moving through the magic of English Romantic poetry, struck to an awakening by African American writing, introduced to Afrikaner language and literature, and finally, the simple cadence of the Bible, it was time for him to start writing. He sent a few poems to *Bantu World*. They were published and earned for him a letter from the Zulu poet, H.I.E. Dhlomo, and a few months later, a payment of five shillings and another letter from the new editor, Fezile B. Teka, who wrote: 'They will all praise. Few will think that a poet must eat. This is an investment so that you will speak for us one day.'[45] Teka continued to encourage his writing for as long as he was the editor of *Bantu World*. He spoke to him about the dangers and hardships of Black and Coloured writers in South Africa, and the possibilities they might have had if they were in another land, but celebrated the fact that against all these odds, Peter's poems had reached him. 'We hope, my friend,' he said, 'we all hope. We know the road is hard, but still we hope. Perhaps it is unfair, but we hope.'[46]

Though he was studying at a Teacher training college, Peter didn't have the clear goal of becoming a teacher. But the reality of the state of education for the non-European population stared at his face. It was a reality through which he had made his own way this far, and while the data was overwhelmingly depressing, it wasn't just data for him – it was visceral, personally felt reality. He records that an abysmally small 6.5 percent of the non-European population was in school, with only 2.4 percent going beyond primary education. While the government spent 10,000,000 pounds on the education of the children of 2,000,000 Europeans, only 1,000,000 pounds were set aside for around 8,000,000 non-Europeans. It was clear that 'the real burden of non-European education was carried by the missionaries', particularly the Anglican missionaries, but for whom less than .5 percent of the non-European population would have received any post-primary education.[47] The data clearly establishes what Njabulo Ndebele would say decades later – that the Bantu Education Act was merely the institutionalization of a stark education apartheid that had defined South Africa for many decades before it.

His literary education continued in the meantime and he became familiar with the work of Auden, Day Lewis, Isherwood, and Spender. He also found a new mentor, a teacher of English, Mrs Williams, who 'took over where Father Adams had left off, and she helped on my journey into the golden realms of language and literature.'[48] Eventually, in 1938, he came to be 'discovered' by the European press and came to be known as the 'Coloured Boy Poet', but one day, that identity turned against him. Applying to the job of a clerk-and-messenger job shortly after the feature article identified him by that title, he heard the White man tell him: 'I know your face. You're the Coloured Poet.' And then, 'Well, we don't want you.'[49]

Learning comes full circle at the end of *Tell Freedom*, when Abrahams enters 'the desolate world of the Cape Flats' and tries to set up on the impossible mission of educating the children of the poorest of the poor in South Africa. His plan is to stay there a while and help with the school. He has no money and can't get any, but he hopes to go to Cape Town nearby where he hopes to 'get books and slates and the other things a school needs'.[50] The poverty there is nothing like what even he has experienced in his life. 'Man is so strong,' an old man there tells him, 'he can live where nothing else can live.'[51] Even here, the education is managed by the missionaries, and the next day, 'the skinny, dried-up, ragged mass of children fought and scuffled their way into the little church'.[52] From the office of the *Guardian*, 'South Africa's only "popular" Socialist paper', he procured school supplies, and 'the children formed relay teams and carried the books, pencils, slates, chalks, and paper into the church'.[53]

The children were eager in their learning, and within a month, they had started a night school for grown-ups. Peter became so immersed in the work of teaching that he forgot his plans to leave the country. But before long, he became so ill himself that he could not carry on any longer. The community wept their farewell to him, and the book ends with these poignant lines: 'Early next morning I walked across the sandy earth to the station for the last time. And the children watched me go. I would have to make up for leaving them.'[54]

That would be Peter leaving South Africa in 1939, as a twenty-year-old, to work as a sailor and then to settle in London for a while. The children he left behind in that church school were versions of what he had been in Vrededorp, from where he sought to make himself against all odds. His story remains one of the grittiest narratives of self-learning, indeed, self-making in a hostile climate where neither education nor intellectual life was made for the non-European people of South Africa. Even before the formal institution of apartheid in 1948, and the great educational apartheid of the Bantu Education Act of 1953, these were the conditions in which a Black South African which had to work through their aspiration for education. With Peter Abrahams, this autodidactism led to the formation of a unique literary subjectivity that would have its impact in due course. Stumbling upon literature almost by accident, he gravitated towards it with a strange inevitability, and it was literature that would develop a subjectivity that was as sharply racialized as deeply as it was human.

Domestic worker, matriculant, writer

Does the autodidact have a keener commitment to learning than the learner well-supported by institutions? As the decades move on and apartheid becomes more and more entrenched in every sphere of life, we see an intriguing and unmistakable pattern among Black South African thinkers, writers, and activists. The preoccupation with learning grows deeper and more intense the more elusive and unattainable real education becomes, culminating in the segregating vision of the Bantu Education Act. The philosophy of this education is articulated with a brutal honesty by Sindiwe Magona, who was born in 1943 and who experienced the cruel divisiveness of apartheid education while in school herself:

> In severing the education of the African child from that of the white child, the powers that be had announced, in Parliament, that the aim was to ensure that the black child would be protected from frustration; she would not be put through an education that would make her believe she was being prepared to graze the greener pastures. The education that would be given to the African child, the Honourable Dr. Verwoerd had enlightened us, would fit her for her station in life, service to her master, the white man, woman, child, and in permissible ways, the white economy. Service, not participation, never mind access, would be the operative, the key word.[55]

There is something magical and powerful about the two volumes of memoir published by Magona – a debilitating diffidence about learning matched by an honest and passionate eagerness to teach and champion the cause of education whenever she can. This powerful tension shapes her learning through correspondence while working as a domestic servant, her career as a teacher in poor African schools, and finally, her postgraduate study in social work from Columbia University, sponsored by the Institute of International Education.

The titles of these memoirs are deeply revealing. The first volume, *To My Children's Children*, is written as a letter from a Xhosa grandmother to her grandchildren: 'When I'm old, wrinkled, and grey, what shall I tell you, my great-granddaughter? ... How will you know who you are if I do not or cannot tell you the story of your past?'.[56] The title of the second volume, *Forced to Grow*, contains the bitter tension of a *Bildung* that must have seemed perverse to the eyes of individual and society, subject and history. What kind of growth was promised to the African woman in this traumatized society, where the conflicts between books, marriage, children, and the nation seemed irresolvable?

Growing up in a Xhosa family that never bought 'any reading material, even the daily newspaper', for Sindiwe Magona, books in English, the language in which she would write herself, 'was greatly aided by a white family I never knew' – through the books they discarded, brought over to Magona's by Mrs Waya, a neighbour who worked as a domestic in the family. 'There must, therefore, be children my age in that family', she conjectures, as the discarded readings contained many comic books with characters that would become 'childhood friends I have passed on to my own children'.[57] Chapter books, those for grown-ups as well for children, were read with 'limited comprehension'; these included *Pride and Prejudice, Cry the Beloved Country, Great Expectations, Lorna Doone, The Mad Hatter,* and *Treasure Island,* which were 'some of the spoils Mrs Waya threw our way'.[58] But discarded books did not come whole. Sometimes the young Sindiwe would reach the end of a deeply engrossing book to find that the last few pages were missing. But it did not thwart the reading entirely, as she confesses: 'I learnt to make up my own endings'.[59]

Even small triumphs of learning feel sweeter when achieved against heavy odds; they feel unreal and unexpected. Magona does not recall 'greater joy than that experienced when learning my very first English word'.[60] The moment remains 'as vivid in my mind today, nearly four decades later, as if it were yesterday'.[61] The knowledge came from her older brother, Jongi who had been going to school. It was the word 'Vaseline', which had been taught to her as it was pronounced in Xhosa, 'Varcelinah'. It was a triumphant moment when she learnt the original English word and its spelling. Jongi, later to go to Oxford as a Rhodes Scholar and settle in England, was in fact to be a role model and an inspiration. She read all his books. It was a crucial familial model in a community where most parents had no education themselves but were desperate to give their children the opportunity they never had.

Since the law stipulated that African children start school only after their seventh birthday, Magona was seven years and five months old when she joined school, when most White and Coloured children, under no such stipulation, were already in their third year. The school where she went was poor and overcrowded, and it was hard for her family to afford the books, uniform, and other school supplies. In spite of all adversities, she grew fond of school. But poverty stood in the way sometimes, such as during the time she was forced to play truant, having failed to persuade her mother to give her the equivalent of five cents that she needed to buy a ruler, a pencil, and a rubber. It was impossible to show up in school as 'the teacher had warned us she would deal with any child who dared show her or his dirty face in her class the next day without these things'.[62]

Much as the parents wanted the children to get school-education, the learning they brought home sometimes created disagreements, most intensely when it led to the 'straddling of two worlds, the world of school and "civilization" and the world of ancestor worship, witchdoctors, and traditional rites'.[63] So if they wanted to open their windows at night, having learned the benefit of ventilation and fresh air, their mother would have none of it as she feared witches would peer into the house while they slept unaware of their eyes.

But even this education they brought home was soon to be brutally truncated. Magona was ten when the Bantu Education Act was formally passed, and within a few years, when she was in high school, the debilitating effects of this racialized dilution of education were being keenly felt. Magona, from 'the old stream' that had a few years of learning preceding the act, could not help but feel 'not a little superior' as they were 'faring much, much better than the products of this exclusively African system'.[64] After completing three years of high school, she was in a position to begin training as a primary school teacher, in a course that 'still existed; for Africans only'.[65] But exactly at that crucial moment, distraction appeared in the form of irresistible sexual attraction, when she met a man on a bus ride to Cape Town. It was the time to turn one's back to all good advice! On the threshold of real work in the form of a teaching career, a genuine well-wisher advised her to complete high school, but she was in no frame of mind to listen: "'Sindiwe, don't leave school. Finish high school. Do your matric." This suggestion, bordering on lunacy in my opinion, came from Mrs. Mbombo,' a nursing sister several years older who was married with one child, and who would later complete her medical education to become one of probably less than ten African female doctors in the country at that time, fulfilling the impossible ambition of a female domestic servant in one of the stories in Magona's collection, *Living, Loving and Lying Awake at Night*.

Life intervened quite literally. Magona started teaching in April 1962, but had to leave the job six months later when she became pregnant. The next four years stormed by as it witnessed her 'get married, have two more children, work as a domestic servant, and lose a husband'.[66] She was four months pregnant with a baby when her husband abandoned her, claiming to go to see his parents but never coming back to her. It began a nightmarish cycle of condemnation, rejection, and desertion by the major institutions of society. The Church told her that she was reaping the results of her sins, while society around her found her worthless as she was without a husband, and 'the department of Bantu Education, standing on high (if mythical) moral ground, rejected me as unworthy of serving its young wards whom it was energetically stunting all the time'.[67] Not formally separated from her husband, she was a married woman in the eyes of law, and therefore not considered the primary breadwinner of the family, which prioritized men and even unmarried women before women in her situation, abandoned in reality but not on paper. She took the only option left before her, becoming a domestic worker. She worked as a domestic for four years, for different households, the experience of which has clearly shaped the visceral texture of the stories of *Living, Loving and Lying Awake at Night*. It felt like a miracle, therefore, when she received a job with the Langa School Board, after the sudden pregnancy and unexpected resignation of two unmarried teachers had created vacancies. It created a whole new chapter of trials and tribulations for her, most pressingly that of obtaining care for her small children while she went to work, but at least she was employed, and that too, in the profession for which she felt destined, that of teaching in a school.

Too young, imperfectly trained, and weighed down by uneven and unexpected demands of life and profession, Magona became a teacher who seemed more driven by her ignorance than her knowledge, by her imperfections more than the complete education and qualification that felt destined to remain out of her reach. She taught languages over which she has insufficient command herself – English, Xhosa, and Afrikaans – of which she felt qualified to teach only English; a ragtag bundle of subjects thrust on her, through which she could only grope her way through, trying to make pedagogic sense: while history was manageable, geography far less so, and little of the Scriptures and Needlework that she was supposed to teach along with them. She worried that she ended up transmitting her own diffidence, insecurity, and incomprehension to her students while trying to teach them. There was little choice but to start to take lessons herself even as she fulfilled, in whatever way she could, the duty of the teacher – in Needlework as well as in Religious Instruction, from the same person, Mrs Rozani, the wife of a Dutch Reformed Church Minister. But nothing would put her misgivings to sleep: 'My inadequate education was forcing me to pass on a legacy of inadequacy to the next generation, my pupils.'[68]

When your life is severely limited in scope and promise, the range of disciplines can only feel like an irony. Such is the range of a subject like geography to learners whose mobility feels perpetually challenged. Magona remembers her own feeling at the age of ten – that it was an irrelevant discipline to her. "'What use is this knowledge to me?" I asked myself … "What does it matter that the monsoons bring rain to India and the rice crop can then be planted? Don't I know where to get my rice? From the Indian shop at the corner of Fifth Avenue and Main Road."'[69] Convinced that she would never see faraway lands in her life, or even other parts of South Africa, she had cast geography to the bin of irrelevance.

The pursuit of knowledge would continue to look absurd in someone in her place, a mother of children, for whom carrying her babies was considered normal but not alien objects such as books. While for society, married, divorced, widowed, and single mothers were all grouped together, the strongest censure, she found, came from other women, who would ask her: 'Why are you carrying books? Don't you have children?'[70] Quickly become persistent agents of patriarchy, women imposed cruelty on one who dared to be different, to look for something beyond old age and death. 'As I carried books with the surreptitiousness of a kleptomaniac,' she writes, 'derision followed me from real, no-nonsense mothers who, highly satisfied with being mothers, found my behavior weird if not wanton.'[71]

An indomitable will brought her to world of books, for the longest time she felt no confidence in that world. For this world seemed to know who owned its spirit through inheritance, and who did not. Even though she started going to public libraries, she never became fully comfortable there. It was a habit, she felt, that was best cultivated early in life, something her life had not allowed her to imagine. 'To this day,' she confessed, 'I pussyfoot along the stacks whenever I have to go to a library. I doubt I will ever be at ease in those institutions, just as I will never be at ease in restaurants, hotels, theatres, cinemas and all the other places which I never set foot in as a child.'[72] For people excluded from the natural environs of learning and culture, education happened in isolation, through staccato, self-directed attempts with no critical glance lingering over them. Listening to radio programmes was one such habit, through which she picked up better English and Afrikaans, and accepted her flaws with much embarrassment and humiliation.

As a teacher, she also came to accept the pervasiveness of lack; it was a culture of lack and inadequacy that defined the schools set aside for African children following the great education apartheid. The lack came from the homes of the children as much as from the system, and they met and collided in the classroom, creating an anarchy of illiteracy, where every act of learning was a deep and bitter struggle. 'Lack of books', Magona writes, 'was endemic in African schools.'[73] Those who had the textbooks did not have exercise books, and vice versa, while many had neither; hardly any students had both. There was no greater moment for the teacher to realize the sad inadequacy of her teacher-training. In a world where less than 1 percent of African homes did not earn depressed wages, she was not trained to teach children from poor homes; trained to teach children with a mother and a father, she found herself teaching a majority of children of single mothers, of which many were tending to White children for their livelihood, forced to neglect their own children on the way. It was a system where even the best-intentioned of teachers could only give their minimum: 'Minimum is all I could give, that thinly stretched I was.'[74] On their part, the children were a heartrending contradiction – of childlike innocence and worldly experience at the same time: 'They had seen too much, too soon. It was there in their shifty eyes and their lies … these children, were, above all, just children: even on such barren soil they would grow.'[75]

Thinly spread as she was, she did pour all of herself into teaching. And its rewards took material shape as well. With her first pay cheque, she opened a bank account, a first not only for her but her entire family, because 'mother and father had never been inside a bank before'.[76] But it was all an uphill trek as nothing came easy, much less improved job prospects, as she trudged along with all her burdens, studying, single parenthood, work demands, even the innocent ambition of wanting to complete high school. But while enhanced educational qualification held out the official promise of a better job, the advertisements did not include 'the one criterion that was crucial in getting a job' – 'a white skin'.[77]

For such a bruised, diffident learner and teacher, the arrival at self-expression through writing – the very reason we have these realities alive in this tangible form – was a miracle that refused to make sense. For the teacher used to the discipline of structure, the generic freedom of spontaneous writing was a shock and a gift: 'I learnt that an essay did not have to be any specific length. An essay, *mirabele dicta*, could be just the beginning or the ending of a story or a piece of composition. How exciting, practical and creative.'[78] But it would take much longer, and much greater exposure to the world, including her trip to the United States in 1978 to think of herself as a writer, a term which came with its own scathing self-doubt. The hanging of the guerrilla fighter Solomon Mahlangu let out a pall of sadness and anger that turned into a frenzy of writing. Once she started writing, she was struck by how tremendously fulfilling she found it. 'I needed no car, bus or train to get to it. It could be done without interruptions from others.'[79] But when someone told her the publisher Ravan Press would be interested in the kind of writing she was doing, including the 'township pen sketches' for which she had already been paid by a magazine, the fear of the unknown overcame her. 'I did not know I could write. I did not know anyone like me who did.'[80] Even the Xhosa writers she knew were much older, all men, and no one lived around her. 'Writing was no less of a myth to me than Icarus and his attempt to reach the sun.'[81] Hers was no unique case; she knew it in her heart. It was the daily battle to survive drained energies in townships where many stories will forever remain buried. It was her magical will, commitment to the real, and a love for the word, malnourished as it was, that gave us the honest accounts of the story of this unlikely reader, teacher, and writer.

Herdboy, teacher, scholar

It is almost a given that autodidacts feel more strongly about education than most people whose education has moved through the sequenced and supportive institutional order consider appropriate in its time and place. It is certainly the case with autodidacts who had to fight a hostile environment that did everything to stand in the way of their education. As Magona's story reveals, many Black South African youth were drawn to teaching. There was also a practical reason behind this – of all the educated professions, training to be a teacher cost the least, as Es'kia Mphahlele has pointed out. Even so, that couldn't have been the overarching reason for someone like Peter Abrahams, who must have seen a young version of himself mirrored in the impoverished children he taught in the church in the dreary Cape Flats. It was inevitable that such self-taught people would be dismayed further by the formalization of the education apartheid in the Bantu Education Act. Like Peter Abrahams, Es'kia Mphelale, also born in 1919, was educated before the institution of the Act, but much like Abrahams, his education, which concluded with a Ph.D. in Creative Writing at the University of Denver, was a valiant attempt at self-making that eventually drove his involvement in the opposition to the divisive legislation – which led to his removal as a teacher in South Africa.

Ngũgĩ wa Thiong'o, in his foreword to Mphahlele's classic autobiography, *Down Second Avenue*, identifies Mphahlele's crucial role in education, particularly that in identifying future writers. As he travelled through schools holding seminars and talking to students, many saw his project as eccentric and hopeless, a 'latter-day Don Quixote who mistook shadows for writers'.[82] Ngũgĩ sees Mphahlele as capably bridging the creative, the critical, and the pedagogic. Such a bridge had much to do with his own unlikely *Bildung*, an unexpected growth, 'the herdboy from Maupaneng who became the scholar in Jo'burg would link the rural and the urban'.[83] The product is *Down Second Avenue*, an exquisite hybrid of history and poetry, an autobiography that reads like fiction and has the vitriolic power of a political pamphlet. That was in fact the kind of writer he was to become, including later works such as *The Wanderers* and *Africa Is My Music*, where, as Ngũgĩ writes, 'he blurred the boundaries between writer, scholar, and educator, between writer and journalist, between genres – prose, poem, and drama – and between literary and social critic'.[84] His activism had deep roots in his commitment to education, and his faith in the role the arts played in society.

It was not an activist commitment that came from the stability of structured institutional learning, which was not available to him. It came from the anarchy of accidental education, brought into existence not by an inherited infrastructure but by the force of will, which ended up giving him a fierce commitment to it, and to those excluded from its institutions. 'Mphahlele', writes Ngũgĩ, 'started as a herdboy listening and reciting stories'.[85] He went on to become a teacher, but his teaching career was cut short by his activism against the Bantu Education Act. 'For being an educator, a writer, and a defender of the artistic space', writes Ngũgĩ, 'he was as it were thrown out of the city into a wilderness that he would turn into a platform for his educational mission and literary prophecies'.[86]

Though Mphahlele was born in Pretoria, he was brought up in Maupaneng village, in GaMphahlele, from the age of five by his paternal grandparents. When at the age of twelve he came to live in Marabastad, Second Avenue in Pretoria, the physical reality of segregated urban life struck him hard:

Now why would people go and build houses all in a straight line? Why would people go to a bucket in a small building to relieve themselves? Why would people want to be cut off from one another by putting up fences? It wasn't so at Maupaneng. Houses didn't stand in any order and we visited one another and could sit around the communal fire and tell one another stories until the cock crowed. Not in Second Avenue. And yet, although people didn't seem to be interested in one another, they spoke with a subtle unity of voice. They still behaved as a community.[87]

Life in school was a medley of humiliating contradictions. The principal and everybody else considered him 'backward', and he seemed to substantiate the designation: 'I was in a class of about eighty. In the half-yearly test I took 77th position in our class.'[88] His poor performance was put down to the low quality of country schools, which he had attended till then. As he 'scraped through to Standard four', he met a terrifying class teacher, nicknamed Kuzwi, who caned children for almost any reason. Hit by him many times, the boy cried but kept his tears to himself. It was a puzzle how hidden under this poor academic performance and constant physical punishment he learned to read much faster than his peers. While watching the silent films of the day, his friends looked to him to read the dialogues and titles on the screen aloud so that they could follow the story. That was the boy's moment of importance – that he could read so well, and so fast. Bewildered, his friends asked him how he read so fast. He couldn't explain it, but he knew his own inner compulsion to read. 'The truth of it was that,' he wrote, 'I used to pick up any piece of printed paper to read, whatever it was. It became a mania with me. I couldn't let printed matter pass.'[89] Even though he was poor in English, the medium of instruction, he 'read, and read, till it hurt', because he 'got a good deal of pleasure out of it', and he felt pride because he 'was overcoming my backwardness'.[90]

Backward he was, in the measure of curricular progress. He passed Standard Five at the age of fifteen. Like Abrahams in *Tell Freedom*, he too, hated arithmetic. But reading was both passion and a promise of progress, particularly reading in English, of which his mother was immensely proud. She could not afford to buy him books outside the two reading books in school, one in vernacular and the other in English. The White family for which she worked gave her their old newspapers and periodicals, never bothering to ask why she wanted them. It is intriguing how he craved for their conscious benevolence, that they realize that they were supporting an unfortunate creature who was craving their level of literacy. He wanted them to acknowledge with admiration that he could read English. In reality, they never cared and remained unaware of his desperate attempts to read, and to scavenge for reading material. 'I continued to rummage,' he writes, 'for discarded, coverless, rat-eaten, moth-eaten, sun-creased books for my reading.'[91] That was how he came across an old translation of *Don Quixote*. He read it over three times, and in the process, its pages fell out.

Things started to look up in Standard Six. In spite of 'harrowing conditions at home', he felt his career at school was taking a clear shape. Slowly, he moved ahead of his classmates in every subject but arithmetic. English poetry left a strange impact on him, particularly under the incantatory instructions of European instructions. Two of his favourites were Tennyson's 'Half a League, half a league' and Byron's 'The Destruction of Sennacherib's Host'. The instructors insisted on physical action during the recitation, and the students came up with all kinds of bodily contortions to impress them. 'We shouted and barked at the audience. We leapt forward to show how "the Assyrian came down like a wolf on the fold", and stamped on the floor, and I think we drowned our voices.'[92] They understood nothing of the significance of their own actions, and when they asked the teacher to explain some of the lines, all he said was 'It's poetry, boys and girls, it's poetry, can't you see?' They left it at that, 'feeling awed'.[93]

Education was a mix of confusion and commandment. The educators of these unfortunate children never failed to make them feel excluded from its magnificent edifice and grateful when crumbs were thrown at them. Education was progress but also alienation, as it had no connection with any of their life experience. But their own life was what they had to leave behind, as without that they would be no 'progress' – as that promised by education. When Mphahlele passed Standard Six in the first class, the question arose about his future direction. Two of his uncles had gone to higher institutions, one for a teacher's course, and the other to St. Peter's Secondary School. The latter was suggested for the boy, if his mother, who made three pounds a month in domestic service, could afford the fifteen pounds a year for the school fees.

She decided to send him to St Peter's saying exactly those words had launched countless Black Africans in the chaotic world of post-primary education with tragically limited career options: 'You'll come back and be able to look after yourself and the two you're leaving behind.'[94] This was a family where a son had been made to feel sorry for his education, as after three years training as a motor mechanic he could only work as a bus inspector as neither the government nor the European trade unions allowed Africans to work as skilled workers. In spite of her son's experience, Mphahlele's grandmother insisted, 'You must starve yourself, stinge yourself rice and stew if you want your children to go to college, and some people don't know it.'[95]

High school was bewildering: 'I hadn't the slightest idea what high school education was for, so for a long time I was bewildered.'[96] But through the bewilderment, a certain subjectivity had started to shape up, through the study of literature and languages. While mathematics, physics, and chemistry were new and alienating and he retained his old loathing for arithmetic, he 'was easily the best in English and Latin', and therefore managed to keep up a respectable place through the promotion tests. A strange new awareness also started to grow in him, 'an awareness of the white man's ways and aims'.[97] While the students felt deeply connected to the White teachers in the school, they realized that the White world outside was different and dangerous. 'Slowly I realized how I hated the white man outside the walls of St. Peter's'.[98]

The time was ripe for a momentous, yet almost accidental friendship – that with Peter Abrahams, one of his 'two Coloured friends'.[99] For Abrahams, as we know from *Tell Freedom*, the architect of an independent literary education on his own, a literary subjectivity was by then deeply racialized, and the language of imagination inseparable from the utopia of liberation. Mphahlele remembered him talking about Marcus Garvey as if all the boys knew him already. 'And dreamily he said, what a wonderful thing it would be if all the negroes in the world came back to Africa'.[100] Abrahams was already writing poetry in his notebooks, and Mphahlele admired them, seeing in them something like the texts they were studying in school at that time. But he also remembered 'how morose the verse was: straining to justify and glorify the dark complexion with the I'm-black-and-proud-of-theme'.[101]

As with all learners who find themselves at an odd angle with their institutions, Mphahlele found his treasure in the school library, and it's intriguing how he expresses it. 'For the first time in my life since I met Cervantes, a vigorous figure in tattered garments, during my primary school years, I shook hands with notable men'.[102] They included Robert Lynd, Alpha of the Plough, Addison, Steele, Goldsmith, Shakespeare, Dickens, 'Q', R.L. Stevenson. Robert Herrick's 'To Daffodils' became a favourite poem to read and learn by heart. As recitation and dramatics drew him, he outgrew the 'crude elocution' displayed on the concert stage in Marabastad, yelling Tennyson's 'Half a League, half a league'.

But whatever his attempts, education remained a self-willed process, as it brought few rewards or opportunities to the Black African afterwards, and few career options that made use of his learning. A rude jolt came during the 1937 final examination, when he saw an older boy, Thomas use the last name Bennet in the registration instead of his African one. He said that an African last name would disbar him from entry into the Coloured and Indian Normal College for teacher training, and he didn't want to go to an African school as the salaries were abysmally low there. It was the truth. A Coloured or an Indian teacher could get a good teaching job even without a university degree, and would also be paid four times as much as an African teacher with the same qualification. The career of teaching, one of the few options open to the educated African, was riddled with tragic iniquities.

Mphahlele didn't feel let down by what Thomas did. But, he writes, 'I didn't wish I could do the same thing.'[103] The attempt felt too huge.

In 1938, he too, decided to go to Adams College in Natal to get his Teacher's Certificate the next year. But before that, he looked for a job in Pretoria, and started working as a messenger in the Department of Native Affairs, for £5 a month. While his job was to carry files between offices, make tea, and run errands for the typists, he read books in the small room where he made tea and waited for someone to buzz him for an errand. In this way, he read R. L. Stevenson's *Black Arrow*, Dickens' *A Tale of Two Cities* and a book by Scott, also reading at home whenever he found the time. A tall, thickset lady who supervised his tea-making and was always knitting, reminded him of Madame Defarge, the austere and ominous knitting woman from *A Tale of Two Cities*.

Always independent in shaping his learning and self-making, it was inevitable that resistance would rise in him if any authority tried to constrict the path of his learning. The errand boy reading nineteenth-century classics in between making tea for his employers etches not just a picture of recreation but of the formation of a literary subjectivity. It is the kind of free, eccentric, and strong-willed self-making that would refuse to accept impediments thrown in his way, particularly those on account of his racial identity. That is exactly what the plan for Bantu Education was going to do – keep such literary subjectivities, along with any advanced intellectual identity out of the reach of Black South Africans. After teaching English and Afrikaans in high school through the 1940s, during he also got his B.A. as an external student at the University of South Africa, studying English, Afrikaans, Psychology, and Native Administration, in 1950 he had to deal with the great historical irony of the report of the Commission on Bantu Education, which was to decide the framing of the Act three years later. As it happened, he was also elected secretary of the provincial body of teachers in the winter of 1950. His racial identity, particularly his resistance to White oppression, would now get rooted not only in the project of education, as it already had been, but particularly in the struggle for full and unrestrained education for the Black and Coloured population, not the reduced and constrained version that was to be legislated in the impending Act.

Mphahlele's protest against the education apartheid started even before the appearance of the report, which, as others have observed, intensified, and institutionalized what had essentially been existent practice. He read a paper at a conference of Transvaal African teachers ('in South Africa', he wrote, 'one isn't simply a *teacher*: he is an *African* teacher or an *European* teacher or an *Indian* or *Coloured* teacher'), where he criticized the existing 'Code of Syllabuses in Native Primary Schools'. He dismissed the 'code as being for a race of slaves; for pupils who were not expected to change as well be changed by the environment, but to fit themselves into it; for unsettled communities doomed for ever to shift from one place to another, without the necessity to become either a stable peasantry or urban communities'.[104] The textbooks ordered for use by the Education Department for use in African schools came under heavy attack in this paper: history texts that glorified White colonization and rule, frontier wars, the defeat of African tribes; Afrikaans grammar books full of examples such as '*the Kaffir has stolen a knife; that is a lazy Kaffir*'; Afrikaans literature teeming with offensive words for non-White characters, depicted as 'savages or blundering idiots to be despised and laughed at', characters who inevitably get frustrated with city life and return 'home' – to the Reserves.

Younger than him by a few years, Bloke Modisane, later Mphahlele's colleague at *Drum*, the magazine about African life, articulated similar exclusions in the school curriculum. The son of a murdered Black man, whose mother had to turn a shebeen-queen to make a living, he felt stimulated by his history lessons and yet could not miss the glaring distortions and omissions: the glorious histories of classical Greece, Rome and the Renaissance, and the magnificence of Europe, without any mention of the slave labour that upheld them. When it came to South African history, the Black students learned about 'the wars of the Boers against "the savage and barbaric Black hordes" for the dark interior of Africa'; the great chiefs whose stories they had heard from their parents were described as 'blood-thirsty animal brutes'.[105] When a group of students confronted the teacher, the teacher told them that textbook history, which was what they needed to pass exams, was subject to the exigencies of time. Modisane understood that 'truth may have a double morality standard; the White man petitioned history to argue his cause and state his case, to represent the truth as he saw it'.[106] Learning to describe his own ancestors in the White man's inhumane terms, Modisane learned to hope for good marks in the exams.

It becomes easy to understand, therefore, why Mphahlele's relation with Afrikaans came to change, and it was a painful change with respect to a language he had been studying and teaching for several years at that point. Here I cannot help but think of Peter Abrahams' relation with Afrikaans in college, where he studied between dusting and sweeping, of his Afrikaner teacher, the gentle-natured Mr. Jansen, who not only helped the non-White students overcome their natural hesitation with Afrikaners, but moreover, instilled in Peter a love for the Afrikaans literature and language. It is one of the great cultural tragedies of twentieth-century South Africa that Afrikaans, the creolized language of southern Africa, once written in the Arabic script and spoken by Coloured and non-White immigrants, eventually came to be identified as the language of oppression. Perhaps it was inevitable that it would, given the initiative of the Afrikaner-led National Party in the institutionalization of apartheid. Zoë Wicomb's short story, discussed above, makes this hierarchy between English and Afrikaans clear in the minds of the villagers in Namaqualand, especially to those aspiring upward mobility. 'I taught Afrikaans as a mere duty,' wrote Mphahlele, 'and it was a most painful thing for me to feel that, together with my pupils, I was caught up in a situation where a language had been thrust upon us which was the instrument of our oppression and the source of our humiliation.'[107]

But even the Code of Syllabuses in Native Primary Schools, Mphahlele points out, was considered as outmoded by Dr W. Eiselen, who headed the Commission on Bantu Education, arguing that 'it turned out frustrated Black Europeans, cut off from their "Bantu Culture", and therefore made the "educated native" a stranger to his people'.[108] The son of a Lutheran Missionary, Dr Eiselen had for many years worked as an Inspector, and subsequently the Chief Inspector of African schools, where he instituted this code. His suggestion of a complete new basis for African education earned him the position of Secretary for Native Affairs under the Nationalist government. His argument about the educated native being a stranger to his people, however, makes for poignant irony. Writing in an essay collected in his later volume, *The African Image*, discussed above, Mphahlele would speak of the loneliness of the educated African, one who is not taken seriously by his own people but one who is unable to cut himself off from their misery. This loneliness is a condition acknowledged by adversaries in the education debate, and this loneliness, I would like to emphasize, is the inescapable condition of the Black or Coloured African who sought to educate themselves beyond the limitations of learning opportunities readily available for them. On one hand there was the inevitable alienation from a community who, without the fierce will of the autodidact, possessed no such education, and on the other, the absence of the possibility to turn this learning, fiercely, privately, and idiosyncratically acquired, into a career of any scope beyond the very constrained and impoverished version of teaching available to African and Coloured people.

Was there a viable trajectory of the formation of an educated, particularly literary subjectivity for a Black or a Coloured individual under the heavy educational apartheid of twentieth-century South Africa? The arc etched in Abrahams' *Tell Freedom* – from Lamb's retelling of Shakespeare to Romantic poetry to the prose and verse of the Harlem Renaissance – comes across as both intriguing and strangely convincing. 'The white man has detribalized me,' wrote Mphahlele in *The African Image*, 'He had better go the whole hog.'[109] The detribalized African cannot also be deprived from the full scope of Western education in the humanities and the sciences. And if the Black subject should have their own path to self-making, that blazed by Abrahams becomes an exemplary one – one which eventually led him to the Harlem Renaissance, and its free articulation of unfreedom. It is no surprise therefore that these literary autodidacts, themselves committed to teaching and education in different ways, including accidental and peripheral ones, were among the most vocal critics of Bantu Education that would cut off subsequent generations of non-White South Africans from the kind of subjectivity, movingly aesthetic and sharply political, that they had earned on their own, driven by fierce private will and aided by accidents, serendipity, and scraps of generosity occasionally cast their way.

The movement against the education policies, however, led to Mphahlele's dismissal from his teaching position, though no reasons were given. He, along with his fellow protestors, was not to teach 'anywhere in the Union.'[110] But most teachers dared not risk their jobs by openly sympathizing with the protestors. Conditions of employment for African teachers were such that neither could a dismissed teacher question their dismissal legally, nor was the Education department required to offer any reason behind their decision. However, a number of pupils decided on their own to stay out of school in protest against the dismissals of Mphahlele and his colleagues, but this resulted in the latter being arrested 'on charge of inciting the boycott and consequently public violence.'[111] Future applications for teaching positions were rejected on grounds that he had been 'dismissed for subversive activities.'[112] Protest against diminished education for Africans threatened to displace him from the teaching profession altogether. He had to work for Arthur

Blaxall, the welfare worker, as a shorthand-typist, but he could not suppress his longing to be back in the classroom. 'The yearning', he wrote, 'was choking me and I felt my nerves were giving in.'[113] Hoping against hope, in January 1954, he applied for a post at a Basutoland Protectorate high school and was employed as an English and geography teacher.

This was also the time when he started to read for a BA Honours degree in English. It was not a professional aspiration, but one done for passion: 'I did the degree for the sheer love of studying English.'[114] Literature gave him company in his loneliness: 'I loved particularly the papers on practical criticism, poetics and Shakespeare and Victorian literature. Gerald Manley Hopkins kept me company in my lonely moments.'[115] But the pay was poor, 'life was stagnant; people apathetic', and his urbanized nature felt unhappy and isolated in country life. That August, instead of returning to the Protectorate, he accepted an invitation from his alma mater, St. Peter's, to teach Afrikaans and mathematics. Since he could no longer be recognized as a teacher by the government, he was to be paid the paltry sum of £18 a month. But by the end of the year, he was not allowed to remain any longer and he accepted a job with *Drum* magazine in Johannesburg as a journalist and literary editor. His reservations about what he felt to be the sensationalist yellow journalism produced by *Drum* were mitigated by the responsible political reporting by Anthony Sampson and Henry Nxumalo, and eventually he became a writer and editor for the magazine. *Drum*'s role in capturing an African modernity has attracted some controversy, but as Ntongela Masilela has argued, it was in fact the writings of Peter Abrahams that was 'central in persuading *Drum* magazine to switch from celebrating "tradition" in its earliest copies to emphasising "modernity", thereby capturing the zeitgeist of the 1950s', called the *Drum* Decade.[116]

Mphahlele's trajectory – that of the self-learner and teacher into a public intellectual, eventually affiliating with *Drum* – reveals the bridge between the scholarly, the creative, and the pedagogic that Ngũgĩ identified in Mphahlele. 'In the year I joined ANC', Mphahlele writes, 'the Bantu Education Act arrived in the African primary school.'[117] He reported it for *Drum*. The ANC, which had not given sufficient recognition to educational and cultural matters as part of its activities, failed to mobilize resistance against the Act, about which the leadership was 'terribly divided and confused'.[118] The churches, which had borne the largest burden of non-European education, were also divided on the issue. They were being asked to hand over their precincts to the government who refused to subsidize them for 'teaching the Black man that he can be equal to a white man'.[119] While some churches acquiesced and even justified Bantu education, there were churches like the Johannesburg Diocese who did 'the painful and therefore courageous thing: it closed down its buildings and refused to have them used for an inferior system of education'.[120]

An almost ceaseless struggle with educational apartheid shapes a subjectivity where the imagination of literary identity is inseparable from race. This was the epiphany for Peter Abrahams when he felt the Harlem Renaissance poets were speaking in his voice. This would shape Es'kia Mphahlele's thesis research for his MA degree at the University of South Africa. His subject was '*The Non-European Character in South African English Fiction*'.[121] Intriguingly, this arose from his reading of Afrikaans literature and its stock non-White character, which led him to explore the latter's depiction in English-language literature. It is something that had troubled him in his critique of the code of curriculum for African schools – in the perpetual depiction of the non-White character as lazy, dishonest, or deceptive, and this thesis signifies a coming together of his educational crusade and a keenly developing literary identity – both ironically driven by a climate hostile to a full and free literary education, including his sharply conflicted relation with Afrikaans language and literature. The latter drove him to English, and he surveyed English literature from Africa and from outside, ranging from British and American authors such as Conrad, Forster, Kipling, Faulkner, Steinbeck, Harriet Beecher Stowe, writers from outside the Anglo-American world such as Mulk Raj Anand, and a range of Harlem Renaissance writers such as Carl van Vechten, Countee Cullen, Langston Hughes, and others. Then he looked at the way in which the non-White character gets limited in its depiction – 'either as a barbarian on the battlefield or as a noble savage' – in literature about South Africa from Thomas Pringle to H. Rider Haggard. This was followed by a study of four major South African novelists: Olive Schreiner, Sarah Gertrude Millin, William Plomer, and Alan Paton, followed by a group of writers for whom non-White characters are less important. While reading Peter Abrahams, whom he knew briefly in school, he began to understand the writer's need to justify himself, which he turned into a dominant symbol through his characters: the 'tragic longing for socially forbidden things'.[122]

Living, learning, and writing in the darkest and most brutal years of apartheid, Es'kia Mphahlele shaped a literary-critical sensibility that is daring and original, one that admired a literary aesthetic that was not just a reduction of crude political messaging, something which, perhaps inevitably, took over South African literary life in the decades to follow. In the aftermath of Chinua Achebe's vital critique of *Heart of Darkness* and subsequent generations of African resentment of the White creation of Black characters, it is hard to appreciate Mphahlele's admiration of now-canonical writers like E.M. Forster, Joseph Conrad, and William Faulkner, and his acceptance of them as 'standards for faithful portrayal of non-White character, untrammelled by some such political message or preachments as bedevil South African fiction'.[123] But the emotion behind this admiration leads him to make a bold critique of contemporary South African writers, one admirable for someone in the midst of a debilitating struggle with racial oppression in all spheres of life: 'The main weakness in South African writers is that they are hyper-conscious of the race problem in their country'.[124] He goes on to say that he admires William Plomer's and Laurens van der Post's 'poetic sense of irony' over 'Paton's sermons'.[125]

Mphahlele is able to see the stereotypical representation of non-White characters and the crude racial politics that comes up in its opposition as two, unfortunately cast sides of the same coin. The latter, he realizes, is not the solution to the former – not in terms of racial justice and not in terms of literary aesthetics. In the literary subjectivity that emerges at the end of *Down Second Avenue*, that which also shapes the literary criticism of *The African Image*, racial justice and literary aesthetics are inseparable and yet they cannot be brought to a mutually reductive relationship. He looks far and wide for a meaningful path that already anticipates a post-apartheid nation: 'There can hardly be a healthy common culture in conditions,' he quotes from his thesis, 'that isolate whole communities and make social and economic intercourse difficult or impossible. And the problem of a national culture is per se the problem of a national literature. It must remain sectional and sterile as long as such conditions prevail'.[126]

The reality of culture: the late apartheid years

Arriving through a long and rocky trajectory of inequity, deprivation, and inspired aesthetic, Mphahlele's understanding of culture fascinatingly echoes with the critique that would be famously launched on South African protest literature nearly three decades later – that by Njabulo Ndebele in his groundbreaking essay collection, *The Rediscovery of the Ordinary*. That book, particularly the title essay, is a sobering evaluation of the literary fetishization of the spectacle in the understanding of race and racial oppression, to the obvious loss of understanding of the insidious, quotidian way race has continued to shape life in twentieth-century South Africa, which has eluded the loud practitioners of protest writing. The source of Ndebele's understanding of the ordinary, is intriguingly rooted in a capacious understanding of culture which on one hand, evokes Mphahlele's delineation of 'national culture' in his thesis, and on the other, the Marxist understanding of the ordinariness of culture that has been memorably articulated by Raymond Williams.

Contrasting a more limited and instrumental understanding of culture as merely tied to books and art as championed in a famous ANC seminar by Albie Sachs, Graham Pechey has tried to establish the far more expansive understanding of culture that Ndebele represents: 'Ndebele's view of "culture" is far broader and (in the best sense of a now often rightly discarded term) more "materialist" than Sachs's: "culture" for him means, quite simply, the ineluctably symbolic dimension of the "infrastructure"; its purview as a category runs all the way from the composition of stories to the messages given off by the built environment.'[127] In the light of Pechey's criticism of Sachs, it is impossible not to remember Mphahlele's criticism of the party in the immediate aftermath of the arrival of the Bantu Education Act in the African primary school – about the leadership of the party being 'never really interested in educational and cultural matters as an important flank to its activities', with all its time taken up 'in organizational work around purely political ideology'.[128] It would appear that the ANC's understanding of culture had not progressed beyond the narrow and predictable aesthetic venues, if we are to attach by representative value to Sachs' albeit well-meaning seminar in 1989, where he calls for a ban on the expression 'culture is a weapon of struggle' and for an end to the art of 'fists and spears'. Even though Sachs' appeal has been read as an effective critique of the spectacular stage of protest literature – as I have done myself in an earlier book – it remains important to acknowledge, as Pechey says, the contrast between Sachs' (and possibly the ANC's) limited understanding of culture and Ndebele's far more capacious conception of it.[129] It is from this conception that the latter's argument about the rediscovery of the ordinary comes into being.

Njabulo attributes the narrow, reductive understanding of both culture and racial oppression to, among other things, what he calls 'the intellectually stunting effects of apartheid and Bantu education'.[130] Much of protest literature, he points out, can be traced to the eruptive events of 1976, in which the Soweto uprising played a central role. Like Mphahlele, he understands the inseparability of education and racial liberation – and the place literature and culture must occupy across this inseparability, omnipresent but not easily reducible to messaging or formulae. This is in fact the most striking feature of the racialized literary subjectivity that is celebrated by the accounts of self-making under the hostile educational landscape of twentieth-century South Africa – the complex and symbiotic relation between race, education, and culture. While Ndebele reads a large group of writers – including, perhaps the simplistic chroniclers of protest literature – as being poorly served by a harsh and inadequate education, it is fascinating how the most imaginative self-learners turned these very limitations as the essential precondition of an alert, humane, and capacious subjectivity.

Writing in the 1980s Ndebele points out that the issue is no longer about opposing Bantu education – as indeed it had been in the years chronicled by *Down Second Avenue* – but it was about the creation of a new kind of education. In the past, the slogan was that of 'liberation first, education later'[131]; but soon enough, this position had to be rejected, and it was replaced by one that recognized the very integral place to education to the process of struggle: 'people's education for people's power'.[132]

Ndebele's arguments about the culture of reading and the choice of reading brings to life the inseparability of education, politics, and literature. What can reading mean? What has it been historically used for? These questions lie at the heart of this chapter, and the book on the whole. How reductive has the use of reading been under Bantu Education? 'Where before,' writes Ndebele:

> [R]eading was a mere function of social advancement; where it has been chiefly an indicator of acculturation; where it has been a functional activity to enable workers to read instructions and become better servants; where to read fiction has been to read industrially produced romance and superstition, then the most creative, liberating, and positive values of reading have to be restored.[133]

These are values that have been embodied by all the readers discussed in this chapter, notwithstanding the often-accidental, arbitrary, and unlikely circumstances of their reading under an educational landscape that did everything to contract the possibilities of deep reading for the non-White population. But it was the very hostile nature of that landscape that brought out the most generative dimensions of reading. Ndebele, who has made the strongest argument in twentieth-century South Africa for a nuanced reading of politics as well as culture, remains an important corrective for an anti-racist movement that has often centralized the crudely ideological over issues in education and culture, as is unfortunately often inevitable for political movements. 'Politically', he wrote, 'reading will be seen and regarded as an important extension of the democratic process itself'.[134]

Reading, theatre, and other modes of artistic entertainment, Ndebele goes on to say, should constitute the practice of 'committed leisure', which must be considered as an extension of the democratic process, as art and leisure make up 'the only social context in which people are uninhibitedly themselves'.[135] It is impossible to have a democratic society where a wide range of cultural practices are not progressively institutionalized. But aware as he is of the experiential and affective power of performative forms such as drama, he remains keenly focused on the power of writing, which he calls 'essentially a subversive act'.[136] The written word can affect the reader in a deeply personal way and can potentially change the course of their life forever. This has historically created the awe around the written word, often making access to it a socially exclusive affair. That is why, Ndebele argues, the written word acquired centrality in a range of world religions, leading to the formation of 'texts containing ultimate and unquestionable wisdom',[137] as well as various kinds of official documents containing uncontested truth and authority.

Deprived of the empowering force of a literary education, indeed, any attempt at a true, humanized education, the Black African seeker of the word inevitably read without discipline, in a kind of a chaos, but one of magnetic passion. In *Home and Exile*, one of the most riveting collections of literary essays to come out of twentieth-century South Africa, Lewis Nkosi offers an account of such reading – 'reading always badly without discipline', driven purely by a quest for beauty of language, dwelling in disbelief that not everyone found books, words, and language as magical as he did – the kind of relation with literature, particularly Western literature, that was impossible to imagine in a Black African person in this educational landscape. 'I walked about the streets of the bustling noisy city with new English words clicking like coins in the pockets of my mind', he wrote, 'I tried them out on each passing scene, relishing their power to describe and apprehend experience; I used words to delineate faces I saw in the streets and through them I evoked the luminous figures from the closed world of the imagination.'[138]

The same experience of living in radically contradictory worlds – just as those experienced by Peter Abrahams reading European poetry in a racially segregated South Africa – came to haunt Nkosi. 'In those days I had two sets of reality'; he wrote, 'one was the ugly world in which I lived my trapped life and the other, more powerful one, was the world of the books I read.'[139] It was a deeply ironic double life, where he derived his sense of honour from the romantic novels of Dumas, Kingsley, and Marryat, and his sense of romantic love from the chivalrous traditions of medieval Europe. It was not as if the irony of this dual life was hidden from him. He knew Western literature had become an escape for him, a defence against a life of 'grime and deprivation' (8). 'Those days all I needed', he wrote, 'to go galloping down the highway in search of a "white" dragon was a high horse and a shining armour.'[140]

Home and Exile, however, is a book of unique perspicacity. Nkosi is quick to realize how far apart, and how incompatible this Western literature-derived romantic vision is with the gritty and painful reality of contemporary South Africa, especially its urban streets. More importantly, it felt irrelevant before the profession of journalism, particularly that of *Drum* magazine that he would soon join, to cover the violent realities of Black life – a profession that 'does its best to rub the nose of those who follow it in the mud of ugly reality'.[141] It was a world of drunken shebeens, flying bullets, raiding police, much of which *Drum* has been accused of exploiting to the effect of sensationalist journalism. For Nkosi, however, literary duality, indeed, the impossible mutual relationship of the worlds of imagination and reality, craft and street, continued to be harrowing but strangely generative. Indeed, as Ntongela Masilela has argued, *Drum*'s use of emergent popular forms was in keeping 'with the desire for modernity by the newly formed working class'.[142]

Going back to his own indictment, in the very opening *Home and Exile*, of Alan Paton's *Cry the Beloved Country* and the hero it offers in the Reverend Stephen Kumalo, Nkosi deplores the inability of Black South Africa to create literary heroes of its own. They were still in the wait for the great South African novel. In the meantime, Elizabethan England did not feel as distant as it initially seemed: 'Ultimately, it was the cacophonous, swaggering world of Elizabethan England which gave us the closest parallel to our own mode of existence; the cloak and dagger stories of Shakespeare; the marvellously gay and dangerous time of change in Great Britain, came closest to reflecting our own condition.'[143] If an African musician were to return home late at night, he goes on to write cheekily, he might be stopped by thugs to whom he would have the occasion to say, 'Unhand me, rogues', and indeed they would unhand him. It was incredible how the psychedelic poetry of Shakespeare resonated with the street life of urban South Africa, with the thugs who 'delighted in the violent colour, the rolling rhetoric of Shakespearean theatre' (13). Unbelievable as it sounded, 'their favourite form of persecuting middle-class Africans was forcing them to stand at street corners, reciting some passage from Shakespeare, for which they would be showered with sincere applause'.[144] This bizarre play of poetry and violence as a pulse of urban South African life was also the worldview of *Drum* magazine, where much of this writing was first published.

The most unexpected sparks of self-driven engagement with Western literature emerge from Nkosi's accounts, where the two absurdly distant worlds come to reflect each other in shockingly unexpected ways. He vividly captures a moment in the *Drum* magazine office, with the writer Can Themba 'leaning against the jamb of the door, a glass of brandy in one hand and a volume of Oscar Wilde on the other', quoting lines from the Rubaiyat of Omar Khayyam from memory.[145] From early issues representing Africans as tribal and rural, *Drum* quickly became urban and commercial, crafting its growth into the venue of new African voice and language in ways that run parallel to the figures I read here – three of whom, Modisane, Mphahlele, and Nkosi – served as its editor between the mid-1950s and the early 60s. An exceptional, turbulent, imaginative gang of young writers, the *Drum* magazine group revealed unexpected connections between the distant world of literary imagination and the gritty reality of contemporary South Africa, and as Dorothy Driver has pointed out, through the 1950s, the magazine revealed as much about the development of a Black South African reading public as about Black South African writing. Accordingly, it mirrored the diminished education and literacy of this reading public by reducing literary content and transforming itself to a racy, pictorial mass-market magazine, later attracting criticism, such as by Njabulo Ndebele, for giving in to spectacle and sensationalism. But this striking jumble of experimental, radical, popular, and lowbrow culture was precisely what the magazine was, distilling, much like its autodidactic writers, a dissonant medley of influences, as Driver points out: Hollywood B-movies, British and American detective fiction, the Harlem and Sophiatown Renaissance. It led to a style where resistant bravado mingled with 'linguistic and generic experimentation', often venturing into images of urban horror through its depiction of both domestic and township violence.[146] Consequently, the magazine cast a significant formative influence, credited with 'producing an African English in the making, inflected variously by a creative colloquialism and a *tsotsitaal*, along with a vocabulary of erudition and literary allusion, as well as inventive neologisms and vigorous syntactical structures that commentators have associated with jazz'.[147]

For Nkosi, however, this encounter of book and reality was not limited to the streets of South Africa, and neither was it limited to literature in English. His first journey to Paris and France, he goes on to write, began with the works of Dumas, Flaubert, Balzac, and Hugo. The attraction, initially, was as physical and material as it was literary, as the very appearance of the books embodied an affluence far from the boy's reality: 'I grasped at the Collins classics primarily because for any slum boy the neat leather-bound books looked invaluably posh and expensive.'[148] The rewards inside came with their own thorns, as 'the vocabulary gave me as much pleasure as it gave me trouble'. But in the end, the pull of romance was irresistible, and in the final instance, a learning experience as that which could not be enacted in any classroom: 'such is the power of adventure and romance on a boy's imagination that I struggled through the novels with an array of dictionaries until I had garnered a formidable word-list that astonished my essay master'.[149] One consequence of this immersion is a familiar one for the colonial subject who encounters the reality of the metropolis through literature long before they have a chance to visit, because the mobility required for such a visit does not come easily to them. The image of Paris that came to belong to him was 'stubbornly eighteenth and nineteenth century', with its romance, intrigue, revolution, a city of horses and cobblestoned streets. Dumas and Hugo had, for him, 'ruined forever the actual city'.[150] Even in a Paris hotel room in 1965, he would feel the tumultuous presence of characters from nineteenth-century novels. He stared at the large stone on the finger of a French lady pouring tea, for he'd learned from the nineteenth-century French novelist that there would be 'a thimbleful of poison' 'stored up inside the gleaming stone, the contents of which might be emptied into somebody's cup at the flicker of modest eyelashes'.[151]

Perhaps the greatest force generated by the self-motivated, amateur reader from the Global South, particularly one who has to transcend, or deviate past available educational opportunities to engage with Western literature is that of the explosive relation between the world of imagination and that of reality – one distanced in time and space, and the other physically, immediately, inescapably present. We see this in Nirad C. Chaudhuri's relation with the streets of Paris and the performance of Shakespeare's plays in Stratford-on-Avon after decades of textual engagement with both; in Nkosi's imagination of Elizabethan reality and Shakespearian speech in South African cities at night and the dream if nineteenth-century Paris in the city in the middle of the twentieth century; in Pankaj Mishra's experience of the Flaubertian petit-bourgeoisie in the violent, caste-ridden politics of late-twentieth-century Uttar Pradesh. For the postcolonial amateur reader, encounter with European texts often happens in a radically disembodied manner, far from their time and place, often, as through most of twentieth-century South Africa, in difficult and hostile conditions. There are always two worlds, absurd in their relation with each other. Their mutual conflicts and alienation are as important as the strange and unexpected ways they come together, be in Shakespeare in Johannesburg or Flaubert in Uttar Pradesh. The absurdity of this relationship speak of the exception will of these eccentric readers as much as it reveals the humanizing power of literature that cuts across erected structures of racial and colonial power.

Chapter 4

BOOKS, ROOTS, PASTS

> My grandfather said he knew what people we came from. I reeled
> off all the names I knew. Yoruba? Ibo? Ashanti? Mandingo? He said
> no to all of them, saying that he would know if he heard it. I was
> thirteen. I was anxious for him to remember.[1]
> — Dionne Brand, *A Map to the Door of No Return*

Of all places colonized, exploited, and dominated by European powers
across the world, the Caribbean islands have been haunted by the most
poignant and impossible questions about identity, origin, and tradition.
Here, the answers are the most likely to be fragmented, disembodied,
elusive, evocative of strange dreams and nightmares, the past as an
eternal will-o'-the-wisp. Old and new world colonialisms, before and
after the European Enlightenment, have coalesced in these central
American islands like nowhere else, joining the shackles of slavery and
indentured labour, bringing the tragedy of the Middle Passage with the
eroded agency of migration between the voluntary, the involuntary, and
the inexplicable. It resembles South Africa in its racial diversity, with
peoples from different parts of Africa, Asia, Europe, and of traceable
and un-traceable racial intermixing, but unlike the host of indigenous
languages in the African nation, the languages of the various European
colonizers and their creolized variants remain scattered across these
islands, overpowering the faded memories of the Asian and African
languages from which the enslaved, transported, and colonized peoples
have been severed over centuries.

There is something in the scattered island realities of nations that
posits identities on the brink of a kind of precarity. Such precarity
has historically bred hybridity as an inescapable condition of its
being. Writing about Francophonie and creolization in locations such
as Mauritius and Martinique, Anjali Prabhu drew attention to the
languages associated with hybridity, terms such as 'diaspora, métissage,
creolization, transculturation', all of which finds deep resonance in the
Caribbean context. What is the role of agency and knowledge when

one's identity is marked as hybrid? Hybridity, Prabhu pointed out, has been represented by Bhabha, Hall, and Lionnet as the resistance and triumph of the subaltern over the hegemonic, but has also been criticized as an elite concept by critics such as Benita Parry, who argue that the concept applies far more to 'metropolitan elite emigrés and far less to migrant diasporas and even less to those who have "stayed behind" in the (ex)colony'.[2] Where, then, can we locate hybridities? It is the third position outlined by Prabhu that resonates most with the tormented legacies of the Caribbean: 'Hybridity, when carefully considered in its material reality, will reveal itself to actually be a history of slavery, colonialism, and rape, inherited in terms of race.' As a painful history of 'interracial identity', Prabhu reminded us, 'it joins up with issues of choosing one's affiliations or having one's affiliations thrust upon one'.

The reality of having one's affiliations thrust upon one, in the context of the Black Diaspora, is often the plundering of all affiliation, or at least the knowledge of it. The lack of an archive and historical memory leads to the most fundamental quest, of the most painful kind. Dionne Brand calls the threshold of this loss 'the Door of No Return'. 'The door', she writes, 'casts a haunting spell on personal and collective consciousness in the Diaspora. Black experience in any modern city or town in the Americas is haunting. One enters a room and history follows; one enters a room and history precedes. History is already seated in the chair in the empty room when one arrives.'[3] No matter how real, the map of the Black Diaspora always feels spectral. 'As if walking down a street someone touches you on the shoulder but when you look around there is no one, yet the air is oddly warm with some live presence.' Bodies without embodiment, characters without names, movements without maps – the Black diaspora is always a history in search of itself.

Walking around Soufrière village in St. Vincent, on the Caribbean island of St. Lucia, Brand meets three children, 'slender and inquisitive', in the manner of local children – two girls and a boy. As they walk, talk, and let her watch their games, one of them looks at Brand and asks, 'Miss, you from Town?' Brand is dumbfounded by the question, as she does not really know where she is from, not from anywhere she can explain to them. Town is the farthest the children can imagine – they've only heard about it – and yet she cannot say she's from Town, as she is from beyond it. 'I feel like a child called on in the game of school but who doesn't know the answer to a simple question.'[4]

Dwelling in nothingness, the child Dionne had a defining door to the world: the BBC: 'The news of the BBC is a door to "over there," it is the door to being in the big world.'[5] When history is spectral and identity an abyss, the imprint of imperialism is more pervasive and inescapable than ever. Not only is it the source of news, history, and culture – to islands that lack all – the empire is the source of education and the force behind the shaping of a full and functional personhood: 'The time between the BBC at eight and the BBC at four was filled with brown school uniforms and lessons in the proper use of English; the proper use of knives and forks, the proper use of pens and inkwells, and the proper use of leather straps, the proper use of speech; the proper use of everything.'[6] Once the diaspora is past the Door of No Return, imperial culture treats it like a blank slate and shapes it after its own image, with its elaborate paraphernalia of education, culture, and perhaps most irrevocably, the church.

Christianity heavily weighed down on the Black diaspora of the Caribbean with moral and spiritual legitimacy. Past the threshold of the Door of No return, this sense of the moral and the spiritual would now become anchor. 'The entire globe', wrote George Lamming in The *Sovereignty of the Imagination*, 'was the spiritual property of the Christian God.'[7] But here was the trick – the religious authority was represented by its secular trustee, conferring an ethical and spiritual authority to the latter that now lay beyond question or critique. And within the Caribbean British Empire, rival powers, such as French and German, 'were interlopers who represented a heretical challenge to what had been divinely ordained as the limits of human reality: the Christian God, as creator of the universe, and the British Empire, as His temporal trustee'.[8]

Lamming's understanding of the pervasive and inescapable power of religion and education in the British Caribbean resonates as deeply with the French Marxist critic of ideology, Louis Althusser, as it does with the Kenyan writer and activist Ngũgĩ wa Thiong'o's delineation of the complicity of the bullet and the chalkboard, in winning wars on the battlefield and in the classroom. For Althusser, family, church, and school are all venues of soft and hard enforcement of the dominant ideology of the capitalist state that confers the deception of independent subjectivity to its citizens. For Lamming, both church and state in the British Caribbean were, willingly or unwillingly, 'agents of an intellectual and moral deception', reflecting the values of the imperial rulers. It was therefore inevitable that the religious functionary would, for him, become firmly imprinted as the force of preservation of the status quo, which, 'in Barbados … meant racism, economic exploitation, and a profound contempt for all that was black'.[9] But such was the forceful entanglement of material and ideological power embodied by the church that this did nothing to weaken its hold on the imagination of the colonized. Lamming cites an example from Sierra Leone, where a sixteen-year-old student had been asked: 'What do you think the letters BBC stand for?' Her reply had been, 'Before the birth of Christ?'[10]

The severance from the past represented by the Door of No Return creates the blank slate where European modernity can etch its unquestioned supremacy. Historicism, Dipesh Chakrabarty has argued, enabled European domination of the world in the nineteenth century. Historicism, or the philosophy that sees in history a linear progression from savagery to civilization, constructs colonialism as the necessary condition through which the world can progress as 'savage' cultures follow the trail blazed by 'civilized' ones. And that is the only way the former, asleep outside history, can enter its domain and its canon of events. That is why an island-nation such as Antigua, as Jamaica Kincaid points out, remains 'a small place' of still breathtaking beauty where nothing happens, whose aesthetic appeal derives as much from its exclusion from historical temporality as from its atmospheric features:

> They have nothing to compare this incredible constant with, no big historical moment to compare the way they are now to the way they used to be. No Industrial Revolution, no revolution of any kind, no Age of Anything, no world wars, no decades of turbulence balanced by decades of calm ....The unreal way in which it is beautiful now that they are a free people is the unreal way in which it was beautiful when they were slaves.[11]

Smallness of these island nations is not just a physical fact. The smallness is as temporal as it is spatial, and smallness is also quality of the minor, the nation excluded from the narrative of history and modernity. The inevitable consequence of such exclusions is a deafening silence, a crippling muteness, and the complete inability to reflect on their own circumstance. It is traceable as much to their exclusion from the dominant discourse as from the lack of memory Dionne Brand mourns in *A Map to the Door of No Return*. Kincaid reveals the inevitable consequences: 'The people in a small place cannot give an exact account, a complete account of themselves. The people in a small place cannot give an exact amount, a complete account of events (small though they may be).'[12]

That is perhaps why holes, silences, and lacunae, painful as they are, have a curiously enabling quality in Caribbean languages of imagination.

'Antillean art', Derek Walcott said in his 1992 Nobel lecture, 'is [the] restoration of our shattered histories, our shards of vocabulary, our archipelago becoming a synonym for the pieces broken off from the original continent.'[13] There is no exact account, no account that can be complete, as any account must bear the damaging burden of empire, slavery, genocide, and indenture that shaped the diasporic peoples who make up these islands. The consequent hybridity is the most painful and violently inhabited form of cosmopolitanism that there can be. The forced removal and consequent scattered resettlement of the diasporic people of the Caribbean were the reasons why George Lamming called 'The West Indian … perhaps the most cosmopolitan man in the world'.[14]

Falling into language, narrative, and history

If history is elusive, language fragmentary, and imagination full of abysses, what does one read, and what does one learn? Does one just surrender one's agency to the BBC, be it 'born before Christ' or the British Broadcasting Corporation, and the 'proper' use of pens, inkwells, speech, as directed by the Christian Church and the British Empire? Or are there other ways of arriving at knowledge, knowledge not limited by what Lamming called the intellectual and moral deception enacted by the state and the church? If there be such arrivals, they must happen through accident, mistake, and disobedience.

For Dionne Brand, it is arrival at desire, through desire. The very first book she recalls reading was a book about the Haitian Revolution of 1791. The act of recalling says at least as much about the texture and trajectory of her memory as about the subject of the book. She remembered it belonged to her uncle, a teacher, and it had no cover, and she remembers the thick and absorbent quality of the pages. For as long as she could remember, the book lay at the bottom of her grandmother's wardrobe, in the company of a geometry text and a Bible. It was the same place where her grandmother kept rice and sugar, syrup shine breads, black cakes for Christmas. As far as Brand can recall, it was an attempt to raid her grandmother's larder that made her fall into the book. 'What led me to this book, then', she writes, 'were my senses, my sweet tooth, my hunger, my curiosity, the intrigue, the possibility of outsmarting my grandmother.'[15] Hunger, curiosity, sweet tooth – what a serendipitous set of impulses with which to be drawn, at the end, to a book! But such unlikely forces were the only possible portals of discovery in a world dominated by colonial, racially myopic education.

She remembered the title running atop each page: *The Black Napoleon*, and she remembered names – a Toussaint, Henri Christophe, Dessalines, though she could not remember the name of the book's author. Did such a book actually exist? She never came across it since, but it must: 'I prefer to think of it still at the bottom of the wardrobe drawer, waiting for me to fall into its face.'[16] But she did read the book, and that too, as a forbidden act – deciding to read it after her uncle told her not to touch it, which immediately made it as irresistible as illicit candy. Opening the book, she started reading it with the drawer open. But soon, she took it to her spot behind the house, and then to her hidden nook under the bed. She began to realize that her uncle must have also fallen into its face, and that he didn't want any more of its pages torn out. The reading filled the young Brand with 'sadness and courage' and it 'burned her skin'. It became 'the book that took me away from the world, from the small intrigues of sugar and milk to the pleasure and desolation of words on a page'.[17] Reading was a sensory experience quite in the literal sense, and then quickly one that transcended the senses and revealed the austerity of its pleasure. 'For days', she wrote, 'I lived with these people I found there, hoping and urging and frightened and elated.'[18] In the book she met a history she had never encountered in her colonial curriculum. It was about the uprising led by Toussaint L'Ouverture against the French on St. Domingo. It was nowhere in the school history books that were given to the young Brand, which opened with Christopher Columbus 'discovering' Santo Domingo in 1492, as part of the 'new world' he brought into existence with his 'discovery'. The young Brand had nothing else but the first sighting of land by Columbus as her own beginning. 'His eyes, his sight, his view, his vindication, his proof, his discovered terrain. These were to be mine. All the moil and hurt proceeding from his view were to be good, evolutionary, a right and just casualty of modernity.'[19] Much was missing from that story. So the little girl had never met Toussaint L'Ouverture until she 'saw him at the bottom of the wardrobe drawer with the cakes and sugar'.[20]

Accident, desire, childhood mischief, and curiosity brought the young Brand on the discovery of a history and an account of her own self that had been made invisible by the colonial education she had received in her school. It was not just the discovery of a vital segment of history, but the realization of experiences and sensations that lay far beyond her child sensibility. It wasn't just the knowledge of slavery, so far withheld from her, but the kind of pain carried by its reality and its legacy – not having experienced anything but the most transient and immediate of pains in the eight years of life till that point. The book with the torn cover, stumbled upon at the tip of her sweet tooth, miraculously gave her an identity and a history: 'I did not yet know how the world took people like me. I did not know history. The book was a mirror and an ocean.'[21]

That is what books do – they lift one beyond the sensory range of the empirical and make a larger swathe of history part of one's experience. And that experience expands one's sensory being if it speaks to one's personal identity, one's body and the bodies of one's ancestors. The schoolbooks in Brand's life had no interest in her body or her experience, or that of her ancestors. But the sensory quest of sugar and cakes brought her to a book which ended up linking her physical being with a trajectory of history that far exceeded her moment and returned to her identity – but one which had found no place in her school curriculum. The result was passion – passion for the Haitians fighting the French. 'I recognized them. I was them. I remember my small chest – my grandmother called it a bird's chest – wracked with apprehension over the outcome.'[22] The Black Napoleon, and the history it held, was now irreversible part of her identity and her body, along with the taste of milk and black fruitcake and wafers. Childhood was never the same again.

Books discovered through accident, in secrecy, in violation. Brand talks about such books that were experienced with the body at least as much as with the mind, books that physically changed the growing child that she was. The other book that left a defining mark on her was one that was very much part of the English literary canon, by an author placed in the Great Tradition by T.S. Eliot and F.R. Leavis. But just stepping into her teens, Brand knew nothing of the contested cultural capital of D.H. Lawrence's *Lady Chatterley's Lover*, and how would any of it matter? 'This book,' she remembers, 'began as a rumour at twelve or thirteen, a rumour in a girl's high school about a forbidden book … with "good" parts about explicit sex.'[23] It was not a book they were supposed to read. Hiding it from her teachers, Brand was transformed by the experience of the book, which she never read again as an adult and whose factual details were lost to her, remembering the characters in silhouettes, but 'a kind of anxiety, a kind of exquisite agony I looked forward to having some day.'[24] What kind of a book is it that one forgets the details of but of which one merely retains a burning sensation? What kind of reading is it? She felt 'as if I had been led into another skin, a woman's, a man's.'[25] It changed her from the girl she had been a moment ago before reading it. The girls shared one copy between them, focusing on different paragraphs, different pages, different sentences, keeping it hidden by covering it in brown paper, 'as my grandmother had covered the avocadoes, to ripen'.[26] She read holding her breath, 'the narrative interpolated into the humid air of a going-home-after-school afternoon'.[27] She imagines a strange afterlife of this reading, scattered all over the world: 'I like to think of us now, eight or so women then girls, each in a different part of the world, each in possession of a different paragraph of *Lady Chatterley's Lover*, a different line now perhaps interrupted, intercut by how we chose to live our lives, how we chose to interpret Lawrence.'[28]

Identification with characters, however, remained fluid and unpredictable, especially along gender lines. Even though all the secret readers were girls, it remained hard to know who identified with the lady and who identified with the gamekeeper, as the gendering of the book, Brand felt – the gendering of any book, could not possibly be 'seamless'.[29] She and her classmates heard echoes of the conversations about culture, class, technology, and sexuality going around them in Lawrence's book. 'We', she writes, 'on an island at the bottom of the New World, we too were representatives of the primitive.'[30]

Unexpected acts of reading shaped Brand's subjectivity, and shattered it. If *The Black Napoleon* brought strange, lost, and invisible pieces of a puzzle together for her, *Lady Chatterley's Lover* threw her in the middle of an alien world and revealed cracked mirrors. The novel had started its life for its young readers in the New World outside its covers, as a rumour. But the readers 'had begun outside of the book also, the colonial consciousness, the female consciousness'. Seeking to identify, they were 'flung apart ... disintegrated ... abstracted', and emerged after turning the novel 'into a more complex, more fluid sense of desire'.[31] What had started as a child's desire for sweets finally matured into the agonizing desire of adulthood through Lawrence's ecstatic novel.

Material possession was unpredictable. Her uncle, the one who had forbidden her to touch *The Black Napoleon*, eventually led her keep the book. She never shared it with anyone. Once, while trying to run away from home, she 'tied a belt around it along with the rest of my books, going I don't know where'. She took no clothes, no shoes, 'just books and three dollars'.[32] But she never possessed a copy of *Lady Chatterley's Lover*, only sharing a copy with the other girls, just taking a few lines for herself.

Brand writes unforgettably about the physical impact of books: 'Books leave gestures in the body; a certain way of moving, of turning, a certain closing of the eyes, a way of leaving, hesitations. Books leaves certain sounds, a certain pacing; mostly they leave the elusive, which is all the story.'[33] She thinks she has been writing these two books ever since, imagining them all over again. She cannot quote a single line from either of them; she knows that she remembers them only in her body. They revealed desire to her as a intricate, nuanced complex, of body and history, pain and ecstasy, perhaps because 'the canonical locations of light and dark, male, female, master, slave were broken or interrupted in both books'.[34] From the accident of the initial discovery to the mute but intensely bodily nature of their lifelong impact, these books, through their dangerous play of bodies, desire, and history, shattered and remade the education of the poet and opened up risky, bumpy paths far beyond her strategically deployed colonial education.

Omnipresent and inescapable as they are in the West Indies, English literature and European history took on radically different afterlives in the island, shaping writerly growth and fierce artistic polemic – but always getting reinvented. Between *The Black Napoleon* and *Lady Chatterley's Lover*, Brand shows the fierce expanse of this range. Canonical English novels have also played conflicted roles in the writerly self-making of Jamaica Kincaid. Love and fury have fought each other, points out Denise Decaires Narain, as Kincaid felt 'forced to imbibe the cultural values and "civil" sensibility associated with Charlotte Bronte and others'.[35] Narratives of self-making, particularly the European genre of the *Bildungsroman*, take on a different, deeply tormented life in the colony, as Kincaid's own fiction reveals. And she writes back to foundational European texts just as sharply. Her lyrical polemic, *A Small Place*, a hybrid of a letter, a memoir, and a travelogue, Kei Miller has argued, can be read as an indirect reply to Christopher Columbus' first letter, announcing the results of his first voyage in 1492 that took him to the Americas. With the indigenous version unavailable in the fifteenth century, Kincaid's text offers 'the indigenous account on how to properly see the Caribbean'.[36] There is irony then, Miller, points out, that Kincaid himself becomes the tourist in her later work, *Among Flowers*, demonstrating behaviour that she criticized in her earlier text, 'not bothering to learn the names of the local people who are there to serve her, and seeing Nepal as a place where she might go to extract things (flowers) for her own consumption back home'.[37]

The eminent Victorian

Responses to British literary texts make for a tumultuous *Bildung* for Caribbean writers. For Dionne Brand, a book on the Haitian Revolution and D.H. Lawrence's class-shattering story of passion melt into each other, and the European travelogue and the *Bildungsroman* provoke Jamaica Kincaid to rewrite these genres with polemical passion. Something more complex, I think, happens with an older figure, C.L.R. James – something that looks more traditional on the surface, but which reveals an ironic reworking of English social ideology through hidden and unpredictable relationships between Victorian literature and cricket, and the re-enactment of this relationship in the colony.

Elements of the *Bildungsroman* in James' memoir of his early years, *Beyond a Boundary* raise fundamental questions about colonial selfhood and its relationship with the construction of the self in modern European imagination, which the genre defines and celebrates. It is also a fundamental question for my project, as self-making between colonial education on one hand, and experimental and polemical acts of reading is central to the story I have been trying to tell. In what way must the postcolonial *Bildungsroman* revise the trajectory of its European counterpart? Is its existence an affirmation of European selfhood in the colony, or a radical redrawing of that selfhood? Later writers like Jamaica Kincaid and Tsitsi Dangarembga would pose that question not only in terms of racial and postcolonial identity but also of gender, as the classical European *Bildungsroman* was not only White but also male. The *Bildung* in *Beyond a Boundary*, not a novel but with the temporal structure and progression of an autobiography, invites these questions about personhood that are invariably refracted through James own education and reading, particularly of Victorian novels. In their commemoration of the fiftieth year of the book, David Featherstone, Christopher Gair, Christian *Høgsbjerg*, and Andrew Smith read traces of the Dickensian *Bildungsroman* on *Beyond a Boundary*, particularly of the stubborn and unwilling protagonist who ignores everyone's advice to have their own chastening yet ultimately rewarding journeys. 'James's self-representation', they write, 'constructs an almost quintessentially Dickensian hero: as a child, he displays talent and is rewarded with success in the form of the free exhibition to the Queen's Royal College.'[38] James himself, however, recalls the short-lived nature of this initial success, quickly followed by 'breaches of discipline' that turned his scholastic career into 'one long nightmare' for him, his family, and his teachers, eventually getting entangled in a disastrous 'web of lies, forged letters, borrowed clothes, and borrowed money'.[39]

The 'breaches of discipline' that came to mark his relationship with colonial education also set out a strong autodidactic strain that shaped an intense engagement with English literature that led to complex and unexpected results. Between the failure and the re-engagement,

Beyond a Boundary shapes a rich and polemical response to European ideas of personhood. James' use of the autobiography, Consuelo Lopez Springfield has suggested, springs from a desire to challenge racist notions of personhood put forward by Thomas Carlyle's biographer, J.A. Froude, who said about the West Indies: 'There are no people here, with a purpose and character of their own.'[40] Reading Western literature entails engaging with these different genres, and the implicit or explicit ways in which the genres embody racist or imperialist ideology and practice. This has enabled a rewriting of these genres by Caribbean writers – as Kincaid has done to the genres of the travelogue and even that of the letter. It is illuminating to see James craft a similar response to both the genres of the autobiography and the *Bildungsroman*.

But like his Indian contemporary Nirad C. Chaudhuri, whom I read later in this book, James remains a somewhat divisive figure. While the radical socialism of his later life is clearly established, the phase of his early life as captured in *Beyond a Boundary* is seen by many as more traditionally shaped by the norms of imperialism. Particularly, some feel that there is a real contradiction between his love for cricket and his 'avowed politics',[41] and that his love for cricket seems 'politically "disfiguring" – a mutation'.[42] Later critics have also pointed out the ways in which James, in his enthusiasm for the game, fails to make its many exclusions visible.[43] However, what makes *Beyond a Boundary* such a unique book is that it is the account of an earlier, more traditional phase of a life that is recalled and crafted from a later phase that has experienced an immersion in radical socialism and anti-imperial thought. The apparent traditionalism of James' early positions in this book, particularly the way they are presented here with the benefit of political hindsight, is far less transparent than it may look on surface.

Even so, it is hard to miss that political radicalism came to James through his later life experiences, travel, and reading, following an early life shaped, as he has said himself, by the influence of Victorian fiction, cricket, and religious Puritanism – all of which came from his Barbadian background shaped by British colonialism. 'C.L.R. James came quite late to revolutionary politics,' opens Frank Rosengarten's book on the revolutionary James, *Urban Revolutionary: C.L.R. James and the Struggle for a New Society*. Even though rebellious as a child, Rosengarten points out, James did not, on the whole, stray from the path set by his parents. It is also revealing that 'whenever he looked back to his formative years, from his birth in 1901 to his departure for London in 1932, James tended to stress the literary side of his education'.[44] Strands of rebellion came out in his fascination with calypso singers and their 'ribald ditties',[45] for which his mother had a Black middle class disdain and moral suspicion. But the parental influence was far stronger, such as his mother's reading habits, which shaped James' reading in his formative years. 'She was a reader,' he writes, 'one of the most tireless I have ever known. Usually it was novels, any novel.'[46] James goes on to list Scott, Thackeray, Dickens, Hall Caine, Stevenson, Mrs Henry Wood, Charlotte Bronte, Charlotte Braeme, Shakespeare, Balzac, Nathaniel Hawthorne, Mrs. E.D.E.N. Southworth, Fenimore Cooper, Nat Gould, Charles Garvice, and Victoria Cross, forbidden by his mother but read 'just the same'.[47] If a ravishing appetite for books came from his mother, his father's legacy was literary judgement: 'My mother's taste in novels was indiscriminate, but I learnt discrimination from my father.'[48] Even though the latter was 'no reader', except for books linked to his teaching, but as a man of education, he had a sense of what the classics were. They were served by an itinerant bookseller who came around once a month with a huge pack on his shoulders, which had many magazines, and 'sixpenny copies of the classics' – which is where James' father would pick out a copy of books such as Dickens' *The Pickwick Papers* and insist that his son read it. 'And so', writes James, 'I began to have my own collection of books as well as my own bat and balls.'[49] It looks forward to, in some ways, the literary anthology V.S. Naipaul would start to put together for himself, shaped by the choices made by his father Seepersad. However, James' collection, more driven by his strong Victorianism behind his making, would have greater coherence and integrity than the relative eclecticism of the body of texts constructed by Naipaul. In the meantime, the magazines were also where James started to read articles about cricket, and its great figures of the day.

It was in the course of following his mother's indefatigable and chaotic reading that the young James came to develop an odd but intense relationship with a Victorian classic, *Vanity Fair*. He got hold of an old copy his mother had, one with a red cover. He first read it at the age of eight, and the book became 'my Homer and my bible'.[50] Whenever he finished a new book, he returned to *Vanity Fair*, reading it from the beginning to the end. 'For years', he writes, 'I had no notion that it was a classical novel. I read it because I wanted to.'[51] Even though he outlines his deep and lasting preoccupation with the novel, James barely says anything particular about the book, or even why it drew him so. 'What drew me to it? I don't know, a phrase which will appear often in this book.'[52] The earliest books that drew him when he had to while his time away on the windowsill, 'were biblical', including many stories from the Bible, religious pamphlets, a large book called *The Throne of the House of David.* This biblical shadow on his consciousness can be traced to the Anglican influence on Barbadians in the nineteenth century, which shaped James' mother. 'If James parents had been Roman Catholics', Selwyn Cudjoe writes, 'James would not have been heir to such a literary influence', as at that time the lay members of the Roman Catholic Church were forbidden to read the Bible.[53]

James' 'reading', he recalls, 'was chiefly in the Old Testament and I may have caught, too, some of the stern attitude to life which was all around me, tempered, but only tempered, by family kindness'.[54] He feels he might have recognized 'the same rhythms and the same moralism' in *Vanity Fair*. Its social context – 'the lords and ladies and much of the life described' – was something of which that he, 'a West Indian boy of eight', had no idea. This instinctive identification with an alien cultural world is deeply intriguing, and yet in the colonial and the postcolonial world, where metropolitan texts travel easily as part of culture and curriculum, this entry into the inner rhythm of such texts without little knowledge or familiarity with their contextual reality is a known occurrence. Such instances of 'ignorant' yet passionate engagement with metropolitan texts, when coming from individuals of unique imaginative ability, create new and unexpected orders of meaning. The peculiar passion James brought to his relentlessly repetitive reading of this one book becomes very evident: 'By the time I was fourteen I must have read the book over twenty times and I used to confound boys at the school by telling them to open it anywhere, read a few words and I would finish the passage, if not in the exact words at least close enough.'[55]

But even for the imaginative and passionate reader, engagement with literature from the metropolis comes at the expense of alienation from one's immediate environment and community. His preoccupation with Victorian literature, cricket, and Puritanism, James feels, led him to become 'a British intellectual long before I was ten, already an alien in my own environment among my own people, even my own family'.[56] Paradoxically, however, the roots of this alienation were already implicit in his background and family legacy, and particularly the training he received, directly, and indirectly, from his parents. Coming from a West Indian family who became completely free in 1833, James, speaking for the BBC in 1933 on the centennial of the abolition of slavery in Trinidad, outlined an ancestral narrative 'not only one of exploitation and degradation, but also of survival, resourcefulness, and occasional good fortune'.[57] As he described in this talk, education and religious training became defining values of his family. While his father was a native Trinidadian, his mother came from Barbados and was deeply attached to the teachings of the Anglican Church. As Selwyn Cudjoe has explained, the Africans who came from Barbados in the nineteenth century to work in the Tacarigua, Tunapuna and Arouca area, particularly on the sugar estates, 'brought with them particularly strong forms of Anglican tradition, including the use of the Book of Common Prayer and the Bible',[58] and accordingly the Barbadian parents were firm with their children's religious upbringing and church-going habits. It was his father Robert James' diligent tutoring that helped the ten-year-old boy win a scholarship in 1911, to the Queen's Royal College (QRC), where the curriculum was designed by Englishmen, and where James would absorb the basic elements of a British public school education for the next eight years. Bolstered by a family emphasis on education and Christian values, James entered and experienced, through his formative years, the world of the Victorian and Edwardian public school, where, as Ian Baucom has argued, headmasters made 'Cricket the first C in a revised trivium of Cricket, Classics, and Christianity'.[59]

In most visible ways, therefore, James reflected the values he received from his values and the institutional education to which he was incorporated. The early interpellation by Victorian literature, the English sport, and Anglican Puritanism feels inevitable in this light. Even so, mischief and rebellion were never fully absent. There was his fascination with calypso and 'Port-of-Spain's lowlife',[60] and for some reason, James felt that he had strayed from the path his family had marked for him, one of religious and educational conformism that would bring predictable success. The writer Louise Cripps, with whom James had been intimate in London in the 1930s, recalled how James described his wayward nature: "'My family had such high hopes of me," he said. "And suddenly I stepped out of the role they had set for me." … "I even stole small things sometimes just for the heck of it, just for the risk and the adventure.'"[61] But notwithstanding these small acts of rebellion, his love for his mother and his admiration for the discipline and ambition of his father, among other things, made him follow the course they set for him. Robert Alexander James, in some ways, was to become the father to C.L.R. that Seepersad would become to the young V.S. Naipaul a couple of decades later in Trinidad; there is a kind of polymath ambition to both fathers that gave a touch of eclecticism to the literary self-formation of both writers. 'James wrote enthusiastically of his father', states Frank Rosengarten, 'as a largely self-taught polymath who excelled as a long-distance runner, cricket player, newspaper reporter, church organist and preacher, schoolteacher and principal, and shorthand specialist.'[62]

Education, however, was of supreme importance in James' Black middle-class family, and it was as a teacher that James' father truly excelled. He taught in several primary schools throughout Trinidad after graduating from the Government Training College, and he took special pride in his job. As Selwyn Cudjoe points out, he was particularly good at producing college exhibition winners, and he successfully trained his son to be one as well. But his influence went far beyond that as he encouraged several other aspects of James' intellectual life, particularly the liberal and the performative arts, particularly debating and Western classical music, both of which he practised and performed himself. The inevitable combination of family background, parental guidance, and institutional atmosphere ensured a deep commitment to a kind of an education that became a deeply driven intellectual self-making which, however, often departed from curricular and classroom structure. Cudjoe quotes Besson, James' classmate at QRC recalling James 'reading history and literature, that is, in he classroom … instead of doing the class work he would actually be reading'![63] James' immersion in European humanities again ran in occasional defiance to curricular education, as 'he would read the masters' textbooks and he used to read Shakespeare and books which were entirely out of the curriculum'.[64] Often, he did so under difficult conditions, as when he 'used to come up to our house and we used to study by candlelight or lamplight, because in those days there was no electricity'.[65]

Be that as it may, it is clear that James came out of QRC formed as a Victorian. 'I began to study Latin and French, then Greek, and much else,' he writes, 'I learnt and obeyed and taught a code, the English public-school code.'[66] But even though he spent several years teaching English and history at the QRC before teaching at the Government Training College, he was, as George Lamming put it, 'A Victorian with a rebel seed'.[67] Lamming goes on to outline the complex class experience within which James dwelled as part of his growing up, particularly through his immersion in local cricket: 'James was growing up a middle-class boy, a schoolmaster's son, but he was looking out the window at working-class boys playing cricket. They were not five hundred miles away. This reciprocal influence across the class lines was permanent and continuing.' Quoting Lamming, Grant Farred goes on to point to the reality and the thickness of the glass pane that separated the young James from the local boys playing cricket. This separation, Farred argues, limited James' identity as an organic intellectual rooted in his community, as his presence there was always defined by this distance. This distance accounted for the conflict between his political commitment and 'his physical and psychic remove' all his life, complicating his identity as a marginalized colonial intellectual committed to the cause of socialism.[68] Such are the contradictions that make James such a fascinating figure who continues to evoke divided responses.

A middle-class life and an immersion into the codes of the English public school, the Anglican Church, and British literature doubtless limited his awareness of his colonized condition. He would only see this limitation later, with the benefit of political hindsight. 'It was only long years,' he wrote, 'that I understood the limitation on spirit, vision and self-respect which was imposed on us by the fact that our masters, our curriculum, our code of morals, *everything* began from the basis that Britain was the source of all light and leading, and our business was to admire, imitate, learn, our criterion of success was to have succeeded in approaching that distant ideal – to attain it was, of course, impossible.'[69] At school, the masters and the boys accepted this alike; the former simply knew this to be their duty, while James himself looked at England as 'the beacon that beckoned' him on.[70]

In some ways, James was primed for an education in the European humanities as that defined the English public school curriculum even before he entered QRC, which, he writes, 'fed' one of his two great obsessions, English literature (the other one being cricket). Through his eight years at the school, he read the Greek and Latin classics, mathematics, French and English languages and literatures, English and European history. It was here that he discovered that Thackeray had written thirty-six books other than *Vanity Fair*, and started reading them, two volumes at a time, reading them 'for twenty years after', stopping only after he came to England, after which he only read him sporadically. He also discovered and read a range of other novelists, Dickens, George Eliot, and others, poet's in Matthew Arnold's selections – Shelley, Keats, Byron, Milton, and Spenser. In the public library he discovered more writers, such as Fielding, and he discovered criticism: the writings of Hazlitt, Lamb and Coleridge, Saintsbury and Gosse, the speeches of Burke, and much more. His engagement with literature, intense as it was, was more critical than he might have realized at that time. Part of his rebellious instinct, Christian Høgsbjerg has argued, might have come from his reading of English literature, and particularly, of Victorian writers critical of Victorianism.[71]

James was acutely aware of the gulf between him and his immediate social reality that was created by his upbringing, particularly his education and his immersion in English literature. And yet this gulf is the pervasive and inescapable reality for the colonial and postcolonial thinker growing up on the fringes of empire, once they are drawn into the fold of an education in the Western humanities, in which they participate both structurally and idiosyncratically, as James did. 'My theme,' James describes *Beyond a Boundary* in 1957, 'is my upbringing with English literature, cricket and puritanism. These are the three fundamental characteristics of English middle-class society. I shall show first of all that, precisely because they were not native to the West Indies, they assumed a reality for me that placed me in violent contrast with the people among whom I lived.'[72] The language of English literature permeated deep into his sensibility, to the point, as Christian Høgsbjerg shows, references to its memorable phrases flood *Beyond a Boundary*, from William Shakespeare ('All the World's a Stage', 'Patient Merit', 'The Most Unkindest Cut', 'Wherefore Are These Things Hid?' 'The Art and Practice Part'), John Milton ('To Interpose a Little Ease'), Thomas Hardy ("Return of the Native"), Rupert Brooke ('In That Rich Earth'), and C.P. Snow ('The Light and the Dark'), among many others.[73] However, there were certain writers who left defining imprints on James' worldview as a writer and a human being, the most significant among them, the four Williams as Frank Rosengarten has pointed out: Shakespeare, Wordsworth, Hazlitt, and Thackeray. If Shakespeare gave him a range of characters from kings to beggars, covering the entire human spectrum, Hazlitt was the epitome of the man of letters and his achievements, Wordsworth revealed the power of common speech transformed into poetic eloquence, and Thackeray illuminated the world of aristocratic pretence and its fallibilities, particularly in *Vanity Fair*, the work that had an obsessive resonance for James.

There is no doubt that English literature, particularly that of the nineteenth century, and especially that from the Victorian age, was a shaping influence on James, with the latter commingling powerfully with Puritanical values. But James was also crafting a larger programme of aesthetic education for himself that went beyond Victorian or even English literature. This included French authors such as Gautier, Hugo, Lamartine, and Balzac. More important, however, is the unique affinity the young James felt with the worldview of the ancient Greeks, which, I think, allowed him to transcend the mind-body hierarchy erected by the European Enlightenment and allowed the aesthetics of art to define and permeate what for him was to become the aesthetic of sports. 'When I read', he writes, 'that the Greeks educated their young people on poetry, gymnastics and music I feel I know what that means.'[74] He saw in the Greeks the intense thoughtfulness about their games that he brought to his own relation with cricket: 'I did not merely play cricket. I studied it. I analysed strokes, I studied types, I read its history.'[75] Crucially, he saw in his love for cricket a powerful and immersive amateurism that had opened up horizons of beauty and possibility in sports for the ancient Greeks: 'It was in that way, I am confident, that the Greeks educated themselves on games with their records and traditions orally transmitted from generation to generation. Amateur though I am, I see signs of it in Greek literature, but you must have gone through the thing yourself to understand them.'[76] That amateur immersion in sports can rival any professional engagement in its fullness and intensity was something James would see in the ancient Greeks, and this in turn shaped his own amateur involvement in sports and thinking about cricket, as well as the play of amateurism and professionalism in the life of the game – and in the literary sensibility that places it at the centre. Indeed, in his own reading of the aesthetics of sport, and the coupling of cricket and literature, he reveals a persuasive plebeian sensibility that lays the foundation of his socialism, limited as it is by his Victorian middle-class identity.

In a striking chapter of the book titled 'What is Art?', James ruminates on the artistic potential of sport. It is a kind of thinking rarely pursued around sport, not even by the great cricket writer Neville Cardus who wrote about both cricket and music but did not see the artistic identity of the game in the conscious way that James did: 'It is an art and we have to compare it with the other arts.'[77] Specifically, he compares it with dramatic art. In cricket, 'two individuals are pitted against each other in a conflict that is strictly personal but no less representative of a social group'.[78] This representational nature of the game is what James sees as continuous with literature, music, and drama: 'The dramatist, the novelist, the choreographer, must *strive* to make his individual character symbolical of a larger whole.'[79] He remains deeply aware of the raw aesthetic power of the game that ranges from his childhood observation of Matthew Bondsman outside his Tunapuna window to the legendary performances by W.G. Grace, and the reawakened meanings of the artistic terms 'classical' and 'romantic' in the realm of cricket, as with the batting style of Leary Constantine.[80] But it is the representation of a larger whole – be it a community, a society, or a nation – is something that James identifies as the most definitive feature of both art and sport.

James combines the intensity of an aesthete's eyes with the submerged social conscience of a colonial observer in his discussion of the continuities between art and sport, particularly between drama and cricket. Arguing for the structural perfection of cricket as a dramatic spectacle, he defines it as a spectacle made of a series of individual, isolated episodes that are self-contained in their own right: 'Each has its beginning, the ball bowled; its middle, the stroke played; its end, runs, no runs, dismissal.'[81] The structural unity is precious to the spectator, who is able to distinguish the uncertainty of the game from mere anarchy: 'It would not be glorious if it were not so firmly anchored in the certainties which must attend all successful drama.'[82] In addition, cricket offers 'tactile values', which, as James points out, is considered essential to forms of visual arts such as painting. Cricket is a genuine art form because, 'without the intervention of any artist the spectator at cricket extracts the significance of movement and of tactile values.'[83] What is essential to such movement and tactile value is something all cricket enthusiasts know by the name of 'style'. It is the place of style in cricket that makes lovers of the game 'accustomed in cricket to speak of beauty' even though 'critics of art are contemptuous of the word'.[84] It is impossible for someone without a true aesthetic sense to identify movement, structure, and spectacle in cricket in these terms – but it is equally impossible for someone without an almost primitive immersion in the game. It is impossible to think of anyone in whom these two qualities have had this rarest of unities as they had in James.

But even so, I feel James' most original and striking contribution to the unlikely comparison of art and sport goes beyond his formal attention to the game and reads its strange social implications in the colony. It becomes particularly evident in the way he identifies social ideology in fiction and sees their continued life in sport. There are aspects of the relationship between England and the colonies that are only perceptible in this continuity, and only an eclectic reader like James, reading literature and cricket alike, can perceive it. In Thackeray's *Vanity Fair*, he identifies elements of middle-class British Puritanism of the nineteenth century. Did this ideology transfer to the colonies? 'The West Indian masses', he writes, 'did not care a damn about this', being the kind of people who 'stamped and yelled and expressed themselves fully in anger and joy then, as they do to this day, whether they are in Bridgetown or Birmingham'.[85] But not only did they know the code but they were careful about observing it when it came to sport, and any lapse from it, particularly by English cricketers, was strongly condemned by the islanders. It was not only the English masters of the colonial schools, but the cricketers and anyone involved with the game who 'held tightly to the code as example and as mark of differentiation'.[86] While James the reader was alert to the Victorian values energizing English fiction, it was only James the cricketer and astute observer of the game who could see the colonial afterlife of these values in the social behaviour structured and inspired by the latter.

There was no doubt that he could do so because the code came to mean something to him, through its manifestations in literature and cricket, and in the Victorian subjecthood that was instilled in him. Probably because it was a value instilled in him by his colonial education – both institutional and autodidactic – that it eventually ran its course. James recalls 1938 as a year that he associated with the meaninglessness the code came to signify for him. For him, the code lost its value after his experience of Labour politics in England, but also by his reading of 'debunking autobiographies of the twenties by Robert Graves, Siegfried Sassoon and others'.[87] The code which for him originates in Victorian fiction and finds colonial afterlife in cricket runs its course through his reading of disenchanted First World War poets and the direct experience of English politics. This is a fascinating trajectory, at once unique and representative – of the imaginative colonial thinker for whom social realities of the imperial metropolis arrive in textual and literary form long before they can be experienced in a material or immediate way. The uniqueness of James' experience lies in his identification of the code in cricket, for him an embodied experience in the colony since childhood, a repository of English ideology otherwise unsustainable in the West Indies.

One of the most intriguing features of James' reading of English literature is the closeness with which it comes to correspond with the traditional literary canon that was beginning to shape in England very much around the same time James was reading in Trinidad. 'James' youthful reading', Claire Westall points out, 'maps the canon of English Literature, even as it still functions today, but takes place as this canon is solidifying – that is, as the discipline of English literature is taking root in England, particularly via the Leavisites at Cambridge University.'[88] What do we make of this? That James was deeply interpellated by the Matthew Arnoldian idea of culture that played a decisive role in the early formation of the English literary canon and academic literary studies? It is difficult to imagine James' reading pattern as separable from these canon-shaping ideas, but this should not prevent us from seeing the reflexive analysis James brings to the development of the Arnoldian idea of culture and development in English society (though in his reading Thomas would eventually emerge as more significant than Matthew), as well as on its colonial periphery in the West Indies.

It is a unique awareness, articulated through the intersection of cultural discourses that are rarely brought together.

The most crucial part of *Beyond the Boundary* that reveals James' perceptive reading of Victorian ideology between the unexpectedly twinned venues of literature and cricket is the chapter 'Prolegomena to W.G.'. To understand the Victorian import of the character of W.G. Grace, James turns to literature, to figures who precedes the Victorian period, such as the early Dickens and William Hazlitt. He has great admiration for Hazlitt, his identity as an intellectual, and his admiration for classical education, and his fine embodiment of 'the age that among its other creations produced the game of cricket'.[89] The game was made by a motley group – the yeoman farmer, the gamekeeper, the potter, the tinker, the Nottingham coalminer, the Yorkshire factory hand, with financial contribution from rich and idle noblemen, and all of them, by 1837, 'had evolved a highly complicated game with all the typical characteristics of a national art form'.[90] But it was the Victorian middle class, the social group rapidly accumulating wealth in the nineteenth century, which converted cricket into a national institution. This was also the class that read, loved, and worshipped Charles Dickens, who, however, according to James, 'saw Victorian England with the eyes of a pre-Victorian'.[91] Much as they loved Dickens, the Victorians wanted to look ahead and sought a culture of their own, which they eventually came to find in the work of three men: Thomas Arnold, the headmaster of Rugby, Thomas Hughes, author of *Tom Brown's Schooldays*, and in W.G. Grace: 'these three men, more than all others, created Victorianism'.[92] Haunted by England and the world being cracked open by social revolution, Arnold 'aimed to create a body of education for men of the upper classes who would resist the crimes of Toryism and the greed and vulgarity of industrialists on the one hand, and the socialistic claims of the oppressed but uneducated masses on the other'.[93] The union of the church and the state, he felt, would help to achieve this goal, and he shaped Rugby after this vision, and his methods spread to many schools throughout England. As the English ruling classes came to accept Arnold's vision and methods, far-reaching transformations took place in culture and education. But this is where James makes a striking observation, one only he could make, about the ruling classes, who, according to him, separated Thomas Arnold's vision from the 'cultivation of the intellect and substituted for it organized games, with cricket at the head of the curriculum'.[94] Such is how expressions as 'a straight bat' and 'it isn't cricket' came to be 'the watchwords of manners and virtue and the guardians of freedom and power'.[95] The role of the playing fields in the formation of the Victorian schoolboy in Hughes' popular novel, *Tom Brown's Schooldays*. It is against the backdrop of the formative power of sports, particularly cricket, in Victorian England, that the wider significance of W.G. Grace can be fully understood.

James' understanding of cricket has been faulted by later Marxist critics for its failure to fully take into account the exclusions through which the game works. That may very well be the case. But his perceptive analysis of the Victorian ideology and its cultural formation, from its material roots to its idealistic aspirations, between literature, sports, and the public school, should give us a meaningful pause. To simply call James a West Indian Victorian – which he doubtless was, in some ways – would be to miss the unique perspective he brings to this Victorianism from the colonial periphery, and the socio-political hindsight he brought to it from his decades of radical socialism and anti-colonial activism. It is with this hindsight that *Beyond a Boundary* his account of his early years of growth under English social and religious values, literature, and cricket was written. The trajectory of colonial subject-formation and the making of the professional reader-critic that would entail are all the more remarkable in this early account because of the writer's striking and radical departure from them later in his life.

A deceptive cosmopolitanism

That is what makes *Beyond a Boundary* such an intriguing book – that it is the recollection of something of a British Victorian childhood and education by a thinker from a period of his life when he had definitively embraced a radical socialist and anti-colonial identity. The latter offers a reflexive awareness of an early life shaped deeply by English educational, religious, and literary ideologies, but instead of demonizing it, reads this life as real and substantial, with genuine empathy. A keen socialist understanding enables him to see the dissemination of Arnoldian ideology of social cohesion through the codes of cricket, also made possible by his unique immersion in the game. His Barbadian background, inherited through his mother, was to a great measure, influential behind his Victorian values and Puritanism, even though he never directly discusses it beyond outlining the personal influence of his mother. But if the complex entanglements of race, empire, and forced migration create unpredictable relationships with imperial culture in the West Indies, no figure has been quite as divisive as the influential one of V.S. Naipaul, James' fellow Trinidadian and younger by three decades. Naipaul's formation as a novelist and a non-fiction writer is a complex, intriguing, and sometimes mysterious process, and the deep political problems he posed – mostly through his non-fiction and controversial media utterances throughout his life – are also partially driven by the intricate forces and the gaping lacunae that he faced in his education, growing up, and by his the reality of his family history.

Naipaul's boyhood is marked by the strong contrast between a deep, impulsive attraction to the idea of writing and an eclectic familial-cultural background that felt eons away from the individualism of modern Romantic creativity, to which he felt drawn in ways he could not justify. 'I was eleven, no more, when the wish came to me to be a writer'; thus he opens his personal account, 'Reading and Writing', 'and then very soon it was a settled ambition.'[96] At the same time, he could recognize that it was rather a romance with an idea than any real relationship with it, even in rudimentary form: 'the ambition to be a writer was for many years a kind of sham. I liked to be given a fountain pen and a bottle of Waterman[97] ink and new ruled exercise books (with margins), but I had no wish or need to write anything; not even letters: there was no one to write them to.'[98] He did not, in fact, show any of the traditional early markers of a life of literary creativity: 'I didn't make up and tell stories at home. And although I liked new books as physical objects, I wasn't much of a reader.'[99] The oddity of his own 'ambition' to be a writer, presumably on hindsight, becomes all to clear to the writer. But the incongruence of this desire was the result of his peculiar colonial and family predicament, as he would soon come to realize in a tentative, childish way.

School and the literary education it sought to offer felt curiously empty. Naipaul recalls the headmaster, Mr. Worm, reading from *Twenty Thousand Leagues Under the Sea* to them in the fifth standard, but even though Jules Verne was a writer boys were expected to like, listening to Mr. Worm read was a vacant experience for the young Naipaul: 'I understood every word that was being spoken, but I followed nothing.'[100] But at the same time, the idea of being a writer continued to grow in him, and Naipaul came to realize it as 'a private idea, and a curiously ennobling one',[101] and while it was significantly detached from the chaotically disintegrating communal life of their Hindu extended family, it was keenly shaped by the bits and scraps of texts his father introduced to him.

Naipaul's father Seepersad, whose shaping influence on him has been widely known, appeared to combine the roles played by C.L.R.

James' parents – bringing together the avid but eclectic reading habits of James' mother with something of his father's training intent, though expressly in the field of writing. Naipaul identified his father as an autodidact – a 'self-educated man' who had made himself a journalist. Following no pedagogic discipline, he read in his own way, 'many books at once, finishing not for the story or the argument in any book but for the special qualities or character of the writer'.[102] He would call his son and read out a few pages he'd particularly enjoyed. And it was in what Naipaul saw as 'this unlikely way – considering the background: the racially mixed colonial school, the Asian inwardness at home – I had begun to put together an English literary anthology of my own'.[103] It was a collection of texts that reflected its imperial character, with a bulging Victorian middle: speeches from *Julius Caesar*, early excerpts from *Oliver Twist, Nicholas Nickleby, David Copperfield*, pages from *The Mill on the Floss* and *The Heroes* by Charles Kingsley, a romantic Malay tale by Joseph Conrad, a couple of tales from Lamb's *Tales of Shakespeare*, stories by O. Henry and Maupassant, a couple of 'cynical' pages from Aldous Huxley's *Jesting Pilate* and something similar from J.R. Ackerley's *Hindoo Holiday*, a few pages from Somerset Maugham.

But most of these texts would only come to him in fragments. When he actually approached the books, anything beyond what had been read out to him felt too difficult. 'What I already knew was magical; what I tried to read on my own was very far away.'[104] The fragments made a dent in his mind inasmuch as they were given to him personally by his father; by themselves, they meant nothing. And the gulf was between the provincialism of the colonial periphery and the cosmopolitanism only available to the imperial writer, whether in England or across the empire. The books were inaccessible in their texture and worldview alike: 'The language was too hard; I lost my way in social or historical detail … I couldn't pretend to be Maugham in London or Huxley or Ackerley in India.'[105] This alienation between text, tradition, and place, an inevitable one for the colonial or postcolonial reader on the margins of empire, was a particularly defining one for Naipaul. It troubled the beginning of his relationship with Western literary form, leading to generative results, but it also scarred his relationship with the metropolitan west, the non-west, and the reality of migrancy in a damaging way to politically disastrous results that would later appear in his non-fiction and travel writing. Central to this was what happened to his father, and the racial and communal violence around his ancestral community in Trinidad. In his memoirs, however, Naipaul only records the vast cultural distance between his writerly ambitions and the alienness such ambitions posed before the reality of his immediate context: 'I wished to be a writer. But together with the wish there had come the knowledge that the literature that had given me the wish came from another world, far away from our own.'[106]

Later readers and scholars of Naipaul have helped to bring to surface troubling aspects of the writer's experience with family and community that the writer has articulated elsewhere, such as in his letters to his wife, Patricia Hale. His father's failures and frustrations as writer and community member, and the racial animosity against Hindus in post-independence Trinidad were prime reasons. For Sanjay Krishnan, writing in 2020, 'Naipaul's traumatic experience of racial tension in Trinidad in 1956 and his belated discovery of his father's humiliation and decline' become important points of departure for the understanding of his work – no doubt, particularly, of the writer's troubling political and ideological trajectories in his non-fiction that has been so openly disdainful of the postcolonial world.[107] The violence of decolonization that led to the oppression of the minorities – Trinidadian Hindus in this case – as an exercise of Black nationalism arguably corrupted Naipaul's vision of a postcolonial world and the ability of decolonized nations to thrive in peace and prosperity.

The Hindu Indian part of his Trinidadian identity was both real and mythical to the young Naipaul, as much part of an immediate reality as of an impossible past. 'Only forty of fifty years out of India' in all of their extended family, the colonial life around them was drawing them in, making their Indian past, as Naipaul would say in a slightly different context, 'fraudulent'. But even in this community, the performance of Ramlila, based on the Hindu epic *Ramayana*, was significant, and a memorable event for the young Naipaul. He recollects it in vivid and sensory detail, even as he recognizes that 'everything in that Ramlila had been transported from India in the memories of people'.[108] And even though it was 'crude' as theatre, Naipaul felt that he 'understood more and felt more' than the very first films he saw, *The Prince and the Pauper* and *Sixty Glorious Years* – with which he never really had an idea what he'd been watching. The Ramlila, on the other hand, gave an embodied reality to what he already knew of *The Ramayana*, the story of which was deeply felt and widely known within the Hindu community of Trinidad. 'I didn't have to be taught it,' he writes, 'the story of Rama's unjust banishment to the dangerous forest was like something I had always known.'[109]

The experience of Ramlila, fragmented and transplanted as it was, would leave a lasting impression on the young Naipaul and would, in unpredictable ways, become a part of the literary anthology he was building for himself. The troubling but productive tension between the textual and the performative, Western and Indian that would haunt him soon as a young writer clearly had something to do with his experience of Ramlila, as it also had to do with his experience of early Hollywood films. But even this 'little rural Indian world', the disintegrating memories of an India lost to his ancestors, were to be left behind soon when Naipaul's father got a job on the local newspaper, and they had to go and live in the city, after which Naipaul 'never saw another Ramlila'.[110]

Life in the city, following the severance from the primitive memory of ancestral, faraway India, was also a forced entry into colonial ideology, particularly an imperially structured curriculum, classroom, and career trajectory with its rewards and incentives. Like James before him, he also found his way into an exhibition class, but 'cramming hard all the way, learning everything by heart, living with abstractions, having a grasp of very little, was like entering a cinema sometime after the film had started and getting only scattered pointers to the story'.[111] This is a very representative colonial experience, of inevitable insertion into the narrative of metropolitan modernity through the ideological chute of education, accompanied by a perpetual sense of belatedness on one hand, and deferral and unfinishedness on the other. The colonial subject was trapped in an intense, dedicated path to development: 'all but nineteen months of those twelve years were spent in blind, driven kind of colonial studying'.[112]

An insular island life was but a childhood illusion; insertion into the *Bildung* of modernity was the stark awakening to the imperial power that moulded that modernity. 'Very soon', he writes, 'I got to know that there was a further world outside, of which our colonial world was only a shadow. This outer world – England principally, but also United States and Canada – ruled us in every way'.[113] This world enabled material life on the islands, making the ideological structure inevitable, sending them governors and administrators, cheap preserved foods that had become essentials there, pills and tonics and other medicine. Their coins and nickels gave values to the dollars and cents on the islands. It shaped mental, imaginative, and ideological life on the islands by sending textbooks in grammar and mathematics, films and newspapers, book series such as the Everyman Library, Penguin Books, Collins Classics – through which his teacher had acquired his Jules Verne, and his father, his eclectic, private anthology. Just as importantly, it structured learning on the island by sending examination models and question papers.

But the books that arrived from the metropolis continued to be inaccessible to the boy. His educational canon was shaped by texts whose contextual reality were remote and alien – the classic alienation experienced by students in the colonial and postcolonial world alike, where the educational apparatus remains largely structured by empire and its legacy. He could not enter the books 'on his own', he writes, as 'he didn't have the imaginative key'.[114] Important as it is to note Naipaul's emphasis on imagination, possibly identifiable to his (perhaps yet unconscious) indebtedness to an aesthetic culture shaped by the European Enlightenment and Romanticism, just as debilitating is his lack of social and contextual knowledge around these texts: 'Such social knowledge as I had – a faint remembered village India and a mixed colonial world seen from the outside – didn't help with the literature of the metropolis. I was two worlds away,'[115] It is this gulf between his existing, albeit fragmentary knowledge and the more fully shaped social reality evoked by Western metropolitan literature that would also trouble him later with regard to the formal anchoring of the genre of the novel as well as in the internal aspiration of some of his key fictional characters. The cultural politics of publishing and education of both colonial and postcolonial Trinidad, Gail Low points out, shapes the instincts of self-making in *A House for Mr. Biswas*, which is 'literally crammed full of printed texts: magazines, journals, and above all, books'.[116] They are as eclectic and as diverse as possible within the colony's inheritance of the contemporary educational and publishing infrastructure: textbooks, self-help books, literary classics including Charles Dickens, T.S. Eliot, W.H. Auden, Marcus Aurelius, William Shakespeare, along with Samuel Smiles and Élie Halévy, British educational primers and grammar textbooks such as Nelson's *Royal Readers* and Nesfield's *Grammar*, David and Alexander Bell's *Standard Elocutionist* along with books for the local market such as Nelson's *West Indian Readers*, Blackie's *Tropical Readers* as well as how-to-do manuals such as Cecil Hunt's *How to Write a Book*. Canonical and curricular Western texts are positioned against the nostalgic imagination around older Hindu texts such as the *Ramayana*, Sanskrit verses, and other religious texts. But in the world of Mr Biswas, Low reminds us, 'English texts are endowed with an educational mystique that signals modernity.'[117] Elements of this aspiration as well as this anxiety are clearly traceable in Naipaul's early life and in his habit of building reading anthologies for himself.

Though Naipaul added a few more books to his 'anthology' by the time he completed secondary school – texts from continental Europe such as *Tartuffe*, *Cyrano de Bergerac*, and *Lazarillo de Tormes* – it was an education where he felt, 'he couldn't truly call myself a reader'. He did not have 'the capacity to lose myself in a book'.[118] He had inherited from his father only a sporadic, fleeting way of reading. Nor were his school essays exceptional; 'they were', he felt, 'only crammer's work'.[119] There was a great deal of personal idiosyncrasy in this wandering, distracted, failing narrative of reading, also a good bit of his eclectic, autodidactic father. But there was also, no doubt, the curiously disembodying influence of the imperial metropolis that owned so much of material, educational, and imaginative life in a tiny peripheral island, felt acutely by the child of indentured labourers from a distant land. The metropolis gave him the stirring of a romantic desire but withheld all the paraphernalia available to a metropolitan subject. The miracle was that he still continued to think of himself as a writer. The disjuncture between his inherited and inhabited reality and the alienness of his ambition was debilitating, but also, in a curious way, the initiator of a new, unheard of story. It was the possibility of this story to which he clung desperately when he sought to turn his hard-earned (by years of colonial cramming) scholarship to England – the chance to 'go at the government's expense to any university or place of higher education in the British Empire' – to the proverbial artistic journey to the metropolis to carve his growth, fulfilment, and arrival as a writer.

The journey from the colonial periphery to the imperial metropolis in search of intellectual, artistic, or educational fulfilment – to inhabit the modernity that makes all of it possible – marks the lives of several figures I read in this book, particularly those from India and the Caribbean. It Naipaul's case, however, it is complicated further by the doubleness of his removal and displacement, which gives him a stranger disembodiment. 'To be an Indian from Trinidad, then', he writes, 'is to be unlikely an exotic. It is also to be a little fraudulent.'[120] While the disorienting spatial roots have enabled Naipaul to create unique fictional universes, it has also pushed him to become a commentator on vast swathes of the non-western world that has elicited polarizing responses from British and American critics on one hand, and those from Caribbean, South Asian, Arab, African, and Latin American writers and thinkers on the other. The former group has offered praise to him as an oracle on the non-western world, and the latter has frequently condemned him for affirming Western prejudices about these places. Writing in 1993, with Naipaul at the height of his powers, Rob Nixon addresses this complicated problem within Naipaul's oeuvre, particularly in his non-fiction and the provocative persona he has consistently projected in his media engagements and public utterances. Nixon argues that while his significant reputation as a novelist has enabled the condition within which he has carved his image as 'an interpreter of the postcolonial world', Naipaul has moved far beyond that initial literary condition and has, 'in those border regions where British and American belles-lettres meet popularized political thought – he is treated as a mandarin possessing a penetrating, analytic understanding of Third World. In short, he has grown into an "expert".[121]

Does Naipaul's analysis of the postcolonial world indicate expertise, or a gadfly amateur with an provocative origin and trajectory? Does he inherit multiple traditions or does he inherit none, embodying the deterritorialized, 'fraudulent' identity that he has sometimes accepted, perhaps a little too easily? In a provocatively titled chapter of his book on Naipaul, 'The License of Exile', Nixon examines the liberating implications of the notion of exile, particularly as those that have come to consolidate Naipaul's status as an 'expert' commentator on the postcolonial world. A certain rootlessness has been associated with Naipaul's freedom from the weight of traditions; his carving of unique literary universes has been traced to his own 'homelessness' – perhaps most importantly, a certain 'melancholy modernity' and alienation has elevated his status as a major writer by deepening a mystical aura around him. But Nixon believes that it is possible to turn things around and look at them in a different way – 'not Vidia the exiled victim of historical mischance, but Vidia the beneficiary of a narrative of dislocation that ultimately bolsters the myth of his detachment'.[122]

Part of the force behind the empowering aura of his supposedly exilic status is, as Nixon argues, the fact that the idea of the literary exile is itself an elevated one, enhanced by high modernism, and driven by the emergence of the Western metropolis as the coveted centre of global artistic culture, shaping trajectories of migration towards it. By removing himself from a national tradition, Naipaul has 'linked himself to an aesthetic one'.[123] But this was not always the case. Naipaul's earliest anxieties had to do with the lack of social and national traditions of writing being available to him, to the point where even originality became an 'ambiguous virtue', as 'to be wholly original was to be wholly isolated'.[124] His fear, at that point, was that 'his thematic attachment to marginalized societies had destined him to become a marginal writer'.[125] But soon, he got around this problem of marginality by affiliating himself with the figure of Joseph Conrad, who had powerfully combined modernist exile with a global trajectory to create a magnetic figure of the deterritorialized, universal writer with intimate knowledge of non-Western societies. It is this identity that Naipaul has embraced convincingly in his fiction, subsequently becoming, through his non-fiction and travel writing, the expert commentator on these societies – 'as one of the wretched of the South exiled in the North, he is treated as qualified to speak as a "universal man" in whom all vectors of geographical bias are perfectly canceled'.[126]

Naipaul's understanding of colonialism and its aftermath is simultaneously acute and deeply problematic. In Sanjay Krishnan's persuasive argument, it is conditioned by both family and history – by his father's marginalization and humiliation in the local community and by Naipaul's own experience of the rhetoric of violence and exclusion in postcolonial Trinidad. Rob Nixon, on the other hand, points out how certain strategic affiliations and disaffiliations have given the writer, particularly in the Anglo-American world, a position of an impartial outsider, yet originating from the postcolonial world, and hence the west's favoured analyst of this world, who has consistently offered conclusions that have met Western approval. Such conclusions have become overwhelming enough to shadow the unique perception about colonialism and cultural responses to it that Naipaul is actually capable of offering. While his educational journey, particularly his experience of colonial education in Trinidad, recalls that of his predecessor, C.L.R. James, for me, he also bears striking resemblance to another figure I examine in this book, Nirad C. Chaudhuri. Both Naipaul and Chaudhuri repeatedly frustrate the progressivist political impulse of postcolonial studies, both appearing to celebrate the cultural hegemony of the British Empire that has thoroughly nurtured their education. I think Chaudhuri shows a greater sense of irony and mischief about this apparent narrative of celebration, and greater empathy and understanding of the culture of the colonized – famously captured in the dedication to his *Autobiography of an Unknown Indian,* discussed in the following chapter. But it says much about Naipaul's understanding of the reality of English culture across the British Empire when he chose, in 1963, to pair his review of James' *Beyond a Boundary* with Chaudhuri's *Autobiography,* calling them 'part of the cultural boomerang from the former colonies, delayed and still imperfectly understood'.[127] But as Rob Nixon, who points to this review, writes, Naipaul lets this valuable moment slide in his career, and subsequently, does 'little to further our understanding of the cultural boomerang,' or, perhaps even more crucially, 'to return his own circumstances to that considerable phenomenon'.[128]

Naipaul's failure to provide an empathetic account of Third World cultures, Nixon goes on to argue, is embodied in his situation of such cultures between two vectors of description – 'primitive' on one extreme, and 'mimic' on the other, the former implying the 'pure natives', and the latter, those who ape metropolitan values – reserving equal scorn for both categories. In deploying these categories, Naipaul falls into the old imperialist scheme of progressive temporality, which Dipesh Chakrabarty would later define as historicism. As Nixon points out, Naipaul's 'use of "primitive" and "simple society" argues for a conception of postcolonial societies as stagnant due, in large part, to their isolation from history'.[129] It is an irony that comes full circle when we read Naipaul's utterances in conjunction to Jamaica Kincaid's impassioned polemic about Antigua's 'smallness', its exclusion from history and modernity, or Dionne Brand's accidental childhood discovery of a historical account of the Haitian Revolution and her lifelong, tormented pursuit of the invisible history of the Black diaspora. Caribbean trajectories of homelessness can elevate one writer to an empowering universality while keeping another in a perpetual quest for the oxymoron of diasporic roots – or, as with James' Barbadian legacy, transform the religious and educational legacy of Empire in a seamless manner. That is what makes their self-crafted journeys through literature and history particularly fascinating and unpredictable, and their relationship with British colonial education riven with rich and illuminating paradoxes.

Chapter 5

THE LIGHT AND SHADOW OF EMPIRE

He opened his suitcase, took out a book, and tossing it over to me said, 'Here's something I have been reading in the train.' It was Amiel's *Journal Intime* in Mrs. Humphrey Ward's translation. Pankaj explained that he had borrowed it from the Bengali assistant station-master of Tangi junction, whose acquaintance he had made while waiting for his train on the lonely platform of that half-wild place. Whatever remarkable things might have seen in its later history – I believe it came to possess a very large airfield in the Second World War – the meeting on its platform between a potential lender of Amiel's journal in the person of the assistant station-master and potential borrower in the person of Pankaj and the offhand completion of the transaction must be reckoned as the most queerly memorable event.[1]

— Nirad C. Chaudhuri, *Autobiography of an Unknown Indian*

How did Indians respond to Western education under British rule? Particularly, what was their response to the humanistic, and especially the literary education that occupied a place of central importance in the administrative vision of the British Empire? Few subjects have drawn as much debate and disagreement in South Asian postcolonial studies – perhaps because few feel more influential in the very making of the postcolonial subject. The early Foucaldian years of postcolonial studies – particularly following Edward Said's arguments about the discursive structure of imperialism and Louis Althusser's identification of education as a totalizing, hegemonic force – Gauri Viswanathan's work on English education in nineteenth-century India as soft imperialism felt deeply convincing. Rosinka Chaudhuri, on the other hand, has been a consistent critic of Viswanathan's argument of English as 'masks of conquest'; she has argued for the agency and willingness of Indians in taking what they 'found good and liked best' from Western education, particularly in nineteenth-century Bengal, the hub of British colonial administration.[2] From Sanjay Seth we have received insights about the radically different subjectivities posited by pre-modern and colonial education in India, indeed, about the limitation of imagining the very epistemological category of subjectivity within pre-colonial education.

These are crucial historical debates that have, over the last few decades, helped us see contours of educational development for the postcolonial Indian subject and the curricular locations and trajectories of literary study, as well as the formation of a modern literary sensibility and public sphere in colonial India. The questions, much less the answers, are far from being settled – if indeed they can ever be. I draw from these studies, or more importantly, from the conflicts between them. But my particular goal is to read certain individuals who imbibed European culture and education wilfully and yet in modes of jagged disobedience from the imperial mission of European humanities in the colony, and the postcolonial sphere that has been its inescapable legacy. Taking place either in the absence of institutional education or in a seriously conflicted relation with it, the learning of these individuals has been primarily driven by the autodidactic instinct, which in turn has shaped an amateurism in their writing that I see at once as deviant, dissident, and unexpectedly productive. I seek to ask a few questions: in what sense can they be called amateurs? Against what contextual measure of professional aptitude? And more importantly – what is the connection between their deviant amateurism and the unique, often provocative nature of their appeal as popular literary intellectuals?

If, in the late 1970s, Edward Said revealed the deep complicities between European knowledge and the discursive construction of the orient, the 1980s were the key decade when the historical development of literary study and the project of criticism in England came to be understood through their structural and ideological collaboration with British rule in the colonies, particularly India. Chris Baldick's influential book, *The Social Mission of English Criticism*, traced the importance of literary criticism in organizing and reflecting on public life and the nation on the whole, going back to the figure of Matthew Arnold as the trailblazer of this narrative. With the power of both priesthood and aristocracy on the wane, and the fear of the working classes as philistine barbarians at the gates of universities and other institutions, English literature came to be established as a permanent part of British education, driven by the need to manage three obstreperous but unavoidable constituencies – the working class, women, and empire. Terry Eagleton's popular book, *Literary Theory: An Introduction*, also published in 1983, as well as *Criticism and Ideology* and *The Function of Criticism* (published in 1976 and 1984, respectively), also took aggressively Althusserian positions on the emergence of literary study in late-nineteenth- and early-twentieth-century England, reading it as a project of domestic social control and ideological interpellation in the colonies. And in 1989, Said's student and subsequent colleague at Columbia, Gauri Viswanathan, would publish the book that would for many define the relationship of British colonialism and the literary humanities, *Masks of Conquest*, foregrounding the hegemonic project of English literary study in colonial India. Thomas Babington Macaulay and his infamous Minute, declaring the inferiority and insignificance of oriental learning next to Western knowledge, leading to the aim of creating the brown mimic man – Brown in flesh but White in soul – became the sourcebook, not just of colonial mimicry, but the entire making of the Anglophone postcolonial subject.

According to Rajeswari Sunder Rajan, there were two key purposes to this education, which, in her introduction to her 1992 collection, *The Lie of the Land*, she distinguished as the 'instrumental' and the 'integrative', pointing out that Macaulay's Minute seemed unaware of any possibility of contradiction between the two.[3] This distinction enables her to make an argument for a more ambivalent acceptance of English education by native elites of this time. These elites readily accepted and even demanded English education for its 'instrumental' purpose, as a path to employment in the colonial bureaucracy. But they variously negotiated the second, 'interpretative' purpose of that education, whether through direct opposition to Western education's trespass on indigenous religions, or through subtler 'forms of appropriation and a subversion of the values that were intended to mould them as subjects'.[4] What is particularly interesting to my project is the manner in which 'the English book remained uncontaminated by the material practices of colonialism'.[5] As a consequence, English literature, rather than being indicted for its association with British imperialism, became 'a repository of abstract and universal values freely available to the colonized as much as to the colonizer'.[6]

Critical university studies in India have also read administrative control as the driving mechanism behind key curricular and pedagogic initiatives in British India that the independent nation has allowed to continue uninterrupted all the way to the present. An influential voice here belongs to Andre Beteille, who has traced the centrality of examinations, which creates a culture of rote-learning, to the British government's need to train and certify clerks in massive numbers to staff the imperial administration. While this remains a deeply persuasive argument given the pervasiveness of both rote-learning and the continued demand for government clerical jobs, Sanjay Seth has offered important correctives to this line of argument in his book, *Subject Lessons*. Seth admits to the widely accepted reality of Indians merely using Western education for instrumental purposes, essentially, to the goal of securing a government job. But he also argues that it is misleading to interpret this as the 'failure' of Western education, or even to talk about the 'intent' behind such an education. He goes on to illustrate the radically different, disruptively plural subjectivities of pre-colonial India and their incompatibility with the kind of modern subjecthood Western education sought to create. 'If the Indian student was bending things his own way', Seth writes, 'was the failure of subjectivity occurring because another subjectivity was intervening – an indigenous one?'.[7] Eventually, he argues that the very notion of 'subjectivity' becomes inadequate as an epistemological category in understanding this conflict. Learning habits perceived as mechanical and unimaginative, such as that of rote-learning, for instance, appear rooted in bodily forms of learning as those shaped by memory, not merely of the liturgical learning of religion, but also of secular knowledges of poetry and arithmetic.

Seth takes the question of intent to a whole other place, where the essential incompatibility of colonial and pre-colonial modes of education makes 'intent' irrelevant and meaningless. From another end altogether, Rosinka Chaudhuri challenges the dominant argument about ideological control exercised through Western education. Like Sunder Rajan, she also argues for far greater agency on behalf of the colonial subject who willed this education. Perhaps even more importantly, she traces the origins of Western educational institution in India decades before Macaulay's Minute, notably in the establishment of Hindu College in Calcutta in 1817. 'The colonial Indian desire for English literature, however', she writes, 'was a conflicted impulse that was deeply imbricated also in the creation of India's powerful modern regional languages; in each of these languages, a movement towards the consumption and creation of world literature mediated through English manifested itself creatively and critically from the nineteenth century onward.'[8]

In an earlier work, *Gentlemen Poets in Colonial Bengal*, Chaudhuri offered a critique of Homi Bhabha's theory of colonial mimic men who enacted the Macaulayian dream, as such a theory undermined the agency of colonized Indians, many of whom where active and vocal in their desire for an English education. Notable examples, for her, include the social reformer Rammohun Roy and the English-language poet Henry Derozio. In her more recent work, she mentions Chief

Justice Sr Edward Hyde East's statement: 'Many Hindus were desirous of forming an establishment for the education of their children in a liberal manner as practiced by Europeans of condition.' And in fact, the Bengalis 'wrestled with the authorities' to build Hindu College with their own funds, nearly two decades before Macaulay's Minute. Nor was this an exception, as many wealthy Indians contributed to establish many other private schools to implement similar education during this period.

This conflicted desire for English and European education created some of the earliest exponents of colonial and postcolonial literature. These are figures who illustrate critical agency in assimilating Western culture against the argument of its programmatic dissemination among a passive or resistant population. There is no doubt that the latter also existed – as for instance articulated in Seth's argument about Indians' fulfilment of personal desires through vernaculars and their use of English education merely for instrumental purposes – but they certainly do not tell the whole story. Some of the most memorable instances of assimilation of Western culture, in fact, does not happen within institutional spaces, but takes place along trajectories of autodidactism; the resultant process is often patchy, inconsistent, and flawed. But when carried out by deeply imaginative individuals, it is this amateur assimilation of, and engagement with, Western humanities that creates the most influential model of the postcolonial reader and writer. Whatever the larger reach, impact, or success of the colonial education system, the most interesting and memorable assimilation of Western humanities happened outside this system, or at least at contrarian angles to it.

Ephemeral insights from a brief life

Seth points out that for the British administrators, one of the implicit goals of English education was to turn the native away from idolatrous Hinduism. 'It is my firm belief that', he quotes Macaulay as writing in 1836, 'if our plans of education are followed up, there will not be a single idolater in respectable classes in Bengal thirty years hence.'[9] And after Western education had corroded their idolatrous beliefs, they would eventually be on the path to readiness for the word of God. While Western education did turn certain sections of Hindu society away from polytheistic religious practice, the monotheistic sects and institutions that came into being as a result, such as the Brahmo Samaj and later the Arya Samaj, did not necessarily become pathways to conversion to Christianity, rather turning into final religious and communal destinations themselves. The Dutts of Rambagan in north Calcutta, a family of well-placed colonial officials deeply absorbed in Western education and literary culture, were something of an exception to this dominant religious pattern. Toru Dutt's father, Govind Chunder Dutt, converted to Christianity along with his whole family – his wife, Kshetramani Dutt, and the three children: the daughters Aru and Toru, and a son, Abju.

'These Dutt families', wrote Mrs Barton, the widow of the missionary J. Barton, 'were the backbone and the mainstay of the Christian Church and congregation which was in Cornwallis Square.'[10] While socio-economically privileged – Govind, as well as his father, had held significant positions in the British colonial government – this was a family fated for great personal tragedy. All three children died young of tuberculosis – Toru died in 1877 at the age of twenty-one. Toru's short life reflects a certain social isolation and detachment from Calcutta society, partly due to their religious conversion, which naturally distanced them from all ritual and communal dimensions of that society and the ties that came with them. This isolation partially accounted for the immersion in books that shaped her nature and daily life. While she received no institutional education, beyond a short stint at a boarding school in France and a lecture series in Cambridge, she was educated at home by her father and a Christian private tutor, Babu Sahib Chunder Banerjee. In addition to Bengali, Toru learned English, French, and Sanskrit, and studied music for a while in London. When Toru was thirteen, the family travelled to Europe, downcast after a great tragedy – the death of Toru's elder brother, Abju, at fourteen. They spent a year in France and three years in England, in London and Cambridge, where she met Mary Martin, the daughter of John Martin, a vicar in the university town – a meeting that was to turn into a lifelong friendship. The Dutts returned to Calcutta when Toru was seventeen, where she would spend the remaining four years of her life, leaving behind a significant body of prose and poetry.

While there has been significant critical attention on Toru Dutt's poetry and unfinished novels in French and English, I want to turn to her thoughts on her reading life as it emerges in her series of letters and the couple of brief essays and responses she published. Together, they reveal an account of self-learning, at once privileged and constricted – a kind of a colonial counterpart to the limited and rarefied life of the 'educated man's daughter' as envisioned by Virginia Woolf.[11] Primarily through her letters, written to her friends and cousins, we get an account of a private literary education put together by her father and herself, through a steady supply of books, both French and English, the learning of Sanskrit, as well as traditional songs and stories in Bengali from her mother. This hybrid education, unusual for a girl of the time, finds imaginative expression in her poems and fiction. Her letters, which contain her sporadic attempts to record her reading experience, reveal the fragility and superficiality that might be expected of a teenage girl, but which also curiously evokes the weight of a much longer life that she never had. Her involvement in European literature, along with the inheritance of ancient Indian tales from her mother, indicates a fused sensibility, which, even though extinguished before a fuller maturity, leaves a valuable map for the future development of the Indian writer in English.

I'm particularly interested in the process of her assimilation of knowledge, adventurous and diffident, sustained and fleeting at the same time, where books, reading, and writing, along with a few bookish friendships, come to define an isolated life that slowly and invisibly, start to lose to energy, growing frail through a corrosive consumption. It is the story of the making of a unique self under a set of conditions both curiously enriching and adverse, an indefatigable will that produces writing as expansively as it consumes books, in spite of the slow destruction of the ailment. Conducted in the close company of a loving father but far outside the structure of institutions that were making and remaking the men of her times – the educated man's sons in Woolf's formulation – it is a life, curiously like Woolf's, privileged by class but constricted by gender at the same time, alienated by Christian affiliation in a primarily Hindu society, and cut too short by a terminal illness. Even though her learning happened almost entirely outside institutions, reading was an integral part of her daily life, and almost no letter – written to her friend Mary Martin, her cousins, and a few to the French writer Clarisse Bader (whom she translated) – concludes without some mention of what she has been reading at that time, and a sense, howsoever fleeting, of exploration and discovery, albeit articulated in the amateur language of a teenage self-learner. It is a learning journey conducted sometimes through accident and chance access, through the vagaries of location, one where her father is sometimes her companion. As she writes in a letter to Mary Martin:

Papa and I are going to begin Sanskrit in December. Papa says as there is no good opportunity to learn German now, we had better take up Sanskrit instead of doing nothing. I am very glad of this.

> I should so like to read the glorious epics, the Ramayana and the
> Mahabharata, in the original. I shall be quite a Sanskrit pundit, when
> I revisit old Cambridge![12]

Her engagement with Sanskrit too was that of a deeply engaged amateur. She collaborated with her cousin, the famous economic historian RC Dutt, in learning the language. While he went on to magisterially and with supreme ease translate the entire epic, the *Mahabharata*, into English verse that nobody now reads, she took episodes from it – Sita, Savitri, etc. – and turned them into translucent gems of poems that found instant fame when published posthumously by her father in 1875 as *Ancient Ballads and Legends of Hindustan*, which have survived and are still read.

In his book *Life and Letters of Toru Dutt*, Harihar Das describes Edmund Gosse's enthusiasm about Dutt's writing, particularly her poetry, who felt that she turned to writing in European languages 'despairing of an audience in her own language'.[13] The death of her only sister, Aru, from phthisis at the age of twenty, Das goes on to say, isolated Dutt further, leaving her engrossed with reading and writing. Even though her engagement with literature happened outside of institutions, it was shaped by the places where she spent time and their relation to her reading. Her relationship with French suffered after her departure from Europe; but even so, Das points out that she never lost sight of that on which she had set her heart. It was shortly after her return to Calcutta from Europe, when she was barely eighteen, that she published her first essay, on Leconte de Lisle, in the December 1874 issue of *Bengal Magazine*.

For Edmund Gosse, that essay had as its subject 'a writer with whom she had a sympathy which is very easy to comprehend'.[14] The title of the essay is intriguing: 'An Eurasian Poet'. It evokes, Dutt says at the outset, 'the hackneyed subject of Derozio'. But the subject of this essay is not Derozio, nor is it T.B. Lawrence, 'nor the hundred others who have written a great deal, and not a line worth remembering'. It is not also one of the Bengali poets who wrote in English, for they cannot be described as 'Eurasian poets', rather as 'pure Indian or Asiatic poets writing in an European language'.[15] But then, who can actually be described as a 'Eurasian poet'?

'He is,' she goes on to write, 'a poet born in the Mauritius – a Creole, and his name is, – I wonder if ever you have heard it, – Leconte de Lisle.' Dutt's reasons for calling de Lisle 'Eurasian', and her very decision to focus on his poetry, while not without its problems, intriguingly anticipate later critical discourse about hybridity. The Francophonie scholar Anjali Prabhu has referred to the range of terms associated with hybridity, terms such as 'diaspora, métissage, creolization, transculturation', and Mauritius has indeed been read extensively as a site of such hybridity by scholars such as Prabhu and Francoise Lionnet. And yet, Dutt's vocabulary is sometimes troubling, if only due to the kind of hierarchy she constructs between Europe and Asia, as well as within Asia, that is possibly symptomatic of her time: 'Is it not a wonder that a Creole from the Mauritius, should beat all our Indian and East Indian poets, and acquire a celebrity in the civilized world which they have yet to attain?'[16] Her detection of de Lisle's poetic strengths is also an evocation of the usual weaknesses of Asiatic poets writing in European languages: 'The faults generally attributed to all Asiatic or half-caste poets writing in the languages of Europe, are weakness, languor, conventionalism, and imitation.'[17] Dutt's detection of the faults of nineteenth-century Indian poets writing in English resonates remarkably with post-independence Indian poets' reservations about their predecessors, such as that articulated by P. Lal in the 1950s. As opposed to that, Dutt finds Lisle 'wonderfully vigorous, and very often thoroughly original'. Crucially, he has the ability to extract poetry out of the 'meanest objects'. Dutt goes on to invoke two influential poetic figures from nineteenth-century Europe to convey a sense of Lisle's poetic achievement. She quotes a phrase from William Wordsworth – 'The vision and the faculty divine' – to capture Lisle's ability to transform banalities into poetry. And then she quotes a long passage from what Charles Baudelaire wrote about Lisle's poetry, elaborating the excellence of his poetic techniques that become rich vehicles of the 'absolute rule over his idea' that Lisle possesses.

It feels significant that the most substantial text of literary criticism Dutt has left behind – 2–3 pages of analysis followed by several pages of English translation of the writer's verse and prose – focuses on a French-Mauritian poet of the Parnassian movement, which, though French in origin, quickly became transnational in scope and influence. Just as interesting is the fact that she was writing about him in *Bengal Magazine* in 1874, to a readership she knew was unlikely to be familiar with his name, much less his poetry. 'I wonder if ever you have heard it' – she wrote while introducing her subject to her readers. Her claim to both agency and responsibility as a commentator is limited, and she draws attention to it herself, not hesitating to name purely personal preference as the core of her judgement, which she passes on texts without reading them: 'He has some heavy pieces on religion, which

I have never read, and which I do not care to read for two excellent reasons, – firstly, they seem very dull, and secondly, they appear to embody views like those of M. Renan.'[18]

Dutt's autodidactic education is entirely shaped by what she cares to read. With no curriculum before her, nothing she does 'not care to read' ever comes in the way. As might be expected from such a reading practice, what is 'interesting' and what is 'stale' become determining factors, and the institutional and communal isolation of this amateur education becomes its greatest freedom. 'I am now reading,' she writes to Mary Martin in a letter dated 9 May 1974, '*Histoire de la Révolution française*, by Mignet. It is very interesting, as you may well conceive, but I find the subject rather stale, for I have read three or four histories of the Revolution, including Carlyle's.'[19] A story by Erckmann-Chatrian, *Les Deux Frères* is 'very interesting' – indeed, they are 'always healthy and amusing'. She also likes Shakespeare 'immensely', and has 'read all his plays except five'. Canonized moments of European literature and history – such as Shakespeare and the French Revolution – occupy her in the course of her reading life, but her attachment to them, or the lack of it, is always personal and subjective, unmediated by pedagogic structures, and for the most part, untouched by larger critical conversations around them.

Libraries, naturally, play a large role in this life of reading where pleasure and instruction always meet on terms of equality. In a letter to Mary Martin dated 21 September 1874, she writes: 'We get the volumes from the Calcutta Public Library, of which Papa is a shareholder – we can get as many books as we like at a time and keep them as long as it pleases us.' As it happens, the library does not have too many French works, which she likes to read more than works in English, 'but the volumes of Revues des Deux Mondes make ample compensation for this defect'. She also writes about 'a tale recently published from the pen of Victor Hugo – Quatre-vingt-treize … a very interesting work and treats of the French Revolution of 1793'. She likes the book 'exceedingly' and finds that 'some parts of it are highly poetical'. Though it is a large book in three volumes, she 'never got tired in getting through it'. She has also been reading 'a criticism of his poems 'Les Châtiments from the Revue', and feels that she 'should like to see the poem itself very much', as the extracts she read from it were 'sublime'.

Returning to Calcutta from her four-year sojourn in Europe, Dutt became physically distant from her archive of European literature, particularly books in French, which remained close to her heart but were harder to get hold of in nineteenth-century Bengal with the frequency and abundance she liked. If her reading was eclectic and arbitrary, further lacunae were created by the perpetually belated arrival of Western literature in the colony, particularly in its material form, the physical text. However, it is here that her social privilege ends up providing access to texts, especially in French, that are far from either curricular or popular reading around her in Calcutta – even though it is a delayed access. In her letter dated 23 April 1875, she writes: 'The books we sent for from England have at last come to hand; there are only two more to come.'[20] These include the book we already know she's been waiting for: 'Les Châtiments, by Victor Hugo, a book which I have been longing to see; the poems therein are very beautiful.' The shipment has an eclectic list of books: Victor Hugo's *Les Châtiments and Napoléon le Petit*, books by Taine, Saintine, Marmet, Sandeau, two volumes of Charles Nodier's *Contes*, and a simple scientific account of the human and animal bodies, *Histoire d'une bouchée de pain* by Jean Macé, which is 'so simply told, and so well explained, that it is most interesting reading.'[21]

While it is clear that books provide her daily company and nourishment, indeed, the comfort of a loving presence, it is hard to get more than a rudimentary sense of the nature of her engagement with individual texts. Her response is fleeting and amateurish, and basic responses such as 'like', 'love', 'interesting', 'stale', make up a charming but superficial social conversation in her letters – responses which, by themselves, do little to indicate the depth and seriousness of her reading archive. Take, for instance, the following passage from her letter to Mary Martin dated 8 November 1875, on Victorian novels:

> I am glad you like *Mill on the Floss*; I like it very much. Have you read any of Thackeray's? I like his books immensely. Esmond is the best, and *Newcomes* and *Pendennis* are excellent. His books make me laugh, cry, smile, look grave, by turns; after having finished one of his books, one remains thoughtful for an hour afterwards. *Vanity Fair* too is very good.[22]

She chronicles responses that are spontaneously human: 'made me laugh, cry, smile, look grave, by turns'; they are mostly about what the books did to her, how they made her feel. Very rarely do we get a sense of their content, elements of style and narrative, characters – elements essential to any sustained discussion of literary texts. On rare occasions there is some response to the style, particularly of poetry, but even that response is limited, for the most part, to generic adjectives such as 'beautiful' or at the most 'sublime'. The overarching impression we get is that of a life shaped by books, rather than an account of particular books themselves. But that is perhaps what is expected from letters between friends, particularly of this age, where books make up a purely personal thing, outside of any curricular or professional concern.

That Martin's friendship is precious to Dutt is understood tenderly by the latter's father as well. Father and daughter celebrate the warmth and love, the 'kind affection' in Martin's letters to her friend in Calcutta, and Govind Dutt says something that indicate the isolation of this Christian, Europeanized family in nineteenth-century Calcutta. "'Let us return to England; where in Calcutta will you get such warm-hearted friends, Toru?" "Where indeed," say I.' For Dutt, life in Europe, writes Malvika Karlekar, 'signified a freedom away from the constraints of the restricted life of a Christian bhadramahila', implying the unlikely, indeed, the ironic identification of a *bhadramahila,* a Bengali lady from polite society, as Christian.[23] Toru goes on to write, in the same letter: 'How swift Time passes.' It is a strangely wistful letter that melts into an ominous melancholy: 'now I am getting quite old, twenty and some odd two months, and with such an old-fashioned face that English ladies take me for thirty! I wonder if I shall live to be thirty.'[24]

Father and daughter lead a life of quiet solitude in Calcutta, which is deepened whenever they go to spend time in their garden house in Baugmaree. The quietness of their life makes for a rich reading life:

> The reason why I can go through a book so fast is very plain and simple; it is simply owing to our quiet and retired mode of life; the time we would have had to give to dinner, lunch, breakfast, croquet, lawn-tennis, or picnic parties, is wholly given up to reading; and then I was always a book-worm, even when I was quite a child.[25]

The lack of social activity, a consequence of temperament, personality, and the relative communal isolation of the family in Bengali-Hindu society, combined with a father's strange and anachronistic desire to educate his daughters and expose them to both cosmopolitan and indigenous culture, creates this life of delicious, throbbing loneliness where books and correspondence with a few distant friends shape a unique sensibility. The account of the reading life is immediately followed by a more detailed experience of reading, this time of novels in French and English.

> No, I am not above novels; why, *Les Misérables* is a novel, but I have not read the one you mention. *Her dearest Foe.* Have you read

> Black's *A Princess of Thule* or *A Daughter of Heth*? They are both very
> readable and rather well-written novels. *Far from the Madding Crowd*
> is a very powerfully written novel by a Mr Hardy. It reminds me in
> places of George Eliot's *Adam Bede*.

'Readable and rather well-written' – that's about how specific Dutt's
responses to books usually gets. The comparison between the personal
experiences of reading *Far from the Madding Crowd* and *Adam Bede*
offers an added dimension here, something we don't get very often in
her letters. What we are rather likelier to get is a direct articulation of the
affective experience of reading, which takes her to certain conclusions
about texts. Take this letter written to Mary Martin in the last year of
her life, 1877:

> Have you read *Daniel Deronda*, George Eliot's last novel? I was
> reading an abstract and review of it in one of the numbers of the
> *Revuue de Deux Mondes*. It seems interesting, in an abstract; but in
> the original there is too much about Jews and their religion, and the
> author philosophizes it in a meaner [*sic*] which, I dare say, she herself
> thinks highly of, but which is very tiresome to the reader. The book
> would have been better if it were more condensed, for the author
> displays high dramatic powers in portions of it.[26]

Dutt's response to books helps to situate her as a unique figure in
the contemporary climate of Western education in India. Her father,
Western-educated himself, is one of the Indians, as Rosinka Chaudhuri
has argued, actively wished Western education for their children.
Conversion to Christianity put them in some isolation from their
original social context, and in any case, the education of a girl, that too
in a family damaged by great tragedy, was not destined to be something
conducted easily in an institutional space, a meaningful freedom
from which was also made possible by the family's social status. The
transnational life of quiet, leisurely autodidactism, albeit plagued by
death and illness in the family, shaped Dutt's literary life, as it shaped her
keen, mostly self-acquired interest in literature, though with supportive
parents behind her. It probably explains why the volume and scope
of her reading – remarkable in someone so young – is not matched
anywhere by any sustained attempt to analyse or even discuss them past
the arbitrariness of personal preference. This is evident in her essay on
Leconte de Lisle as well as her letters to Mary Martin, where her reading
figures constantly. But these fleeting, superficial, and purely subjective

responses nonetheless record a remarkable *Bildung*, which is admittedly impossible for us to read outside the shadow of her untimely death. But that is, I hope, not the only reason that I sense, in her amateur account of reading, a curious vulnerability amidst the privileges she had. While well-off and supported by loving parents, she comes across as a figure who is isolated, a little lonely, deeply valuing the few friendships she has – and surrounded closely by the profound experience and awareness of human mortality. In addition to her body of work in French, she is canonized as a pioneer of Indian writing in English, but she is, I think, even more fascinating as a Western-educated Indian from the nineteenth century. A woman – a 'Christian bhadramahila' in Karlekar's evocative description, a fiercely private learner, never professionalized in her education, and dead at twenty-one, she offers a memorable illustration of a transient, amateur but deeply engaged life in letters.

The provincial polymath

How was Toru Dutt seen by writers who immediately followed her – particularly by Bengali writers who wrote in English? An intriguing account comes from Nirad C. Chaudhuri. 'In a Bengali magazine subscribed to by my mother,' Chaudhuri wrote in *The Autobiography of an Unknown Indian*, 'there had appeared in 1901 an illustration showing two Bengali girls in the late Victorian English dress.'[27] The photo created curiosity in the family, and some confusion too, 'for they, though dressed like English girls, did not look English'. Chaudhuri's mother explained that the older girl was Toru Dutt, 'the young poetess who was the only Indian whose English verse was recognized as poetry in England'. Though Chaudhuri's mother identified the sisters incorrectly – Toru was the younger of the two sisters – she identified the rest correctly, that they were the daughters of Govinda Dutt of Rambagan, and they had both died young. In fact, the illustration accompanied a Bengali poem mourning their death. In 1901, Chaudhuri would be four years old, and he was unable to read the poem or any other writing accompanying the illustration. 'But', he wrote, 'I felt very proud that a Bengali girl had secured a place in English literature. My brother also felt proud. So did our parents.'[28]

In his introduction to his evocative book of literary history, *Partial Recall*, the poet Arvind Krishna Mehrotra describes his previous work, *Towards a History of Indian Literature in English*, as ending with 'the examples of writers who, when they looked in the mirror in the hallway, saw more than their own smiling faces staring back at them.' He goes on to outline a persuasive genealogy: 'I. Allan Sealy saw Henry Derozio, Nirad Chaudhuri saw Toru Dutt, Salman Rushdie saw G.V. Desani.'[29] Mehrotra's identification of a lineage of Indian-English writing is both prescient and rich with historical hindsight. But Nirad C. Chaudhuri, born twenty years after Dutt's untimely death, would have to work much harder to attain the cosmopolitanism and transnational appeal he saw, even as a child, Dutt as occupying. Indeed, it was a space that she came to inhabit far more easily than Chaudhuri could have, by dint of her metropolitan location within the colonial capital of Calcutta and far greater proximity to European culture, thanks to the nature of her family heritage.

Chaudhuri's relation to this Eurocentric transnationalism could not be more different. Writing about the place of his birth, Kishoreganj in colonial Bengal, he describes it as a country town but offers the caveat that the place is nothing like an English country town, which he knows only from books and illustrations, 'these being my only sources of knowledge about England, since I have never been there, nor in fact anywhere outside my own country'.[30] He wrote these lines in his first book, published when he was fifty-four; he would make his first trip outside of India at the age of fifty-seven, to travel to England and continental Europe. But in many ways, a key element of his whole life till that point was the preparation for this very trip, which would culminate in his life in Oxford, where he would settle for the last two decades of his life and where he would die at the age of one hundred and two.

The intellectual identity Chaudhuri carved for himself – anticipated in a charmingly eclectic, ambitious, and somewhat confused student life in his youth – contains the seeds of this transnational journey towards the imperial epicentre of cosmopolitan knowledge near one of the ancient universities. Even at that age, he suppressed an inclination to be 'an orientalist' feeling 'that to confine myself solely to Indian studies at this stage would be a great mistake', as that would not only distance himself from 'world currents' but would confine him to 'the second-rate in scholarly technique'. The call of scholarly cosmopolitanism that had Europe as its unmistakable core warned him against the danger of remaining provincial. 'I had', he wrote, 'already picked up a notion of the difference between the "note of the centre" and the "provincial note" from Matthew Arnold, and wanted to be trained only in the best and hardest of schools and tested by the highest of standards.'[31]

Unlike Dutt who inherited a colonial world of close proximity to European and Christian culture, Chaudhuri made a long trek from a remote and peripheral town, first to the city of Calcutta, and then much later, through circuitous routes, to Europe, and particularly to England. Aware of origins he considers provincial, Chaudhuri longs to both imagine and inhabit a larger world with a passionate intensity that evokes the teenage boy, Apu, from the Bengali novelist Bibhutibhushan Bandopadhay's modernist *Bildungsroman, Aparajito*, who, in the cinematic version created by Satyajit Ray, hugs a globe as his most precious possession as he leaves behind a life of poverty in his village with his mother to study in Calcutta. The irony of the poor, rustic student hugging a globe as he sets outside his village for the first time in his life defines his entire aspiration to travel, learn, read, and write – a reality that echoes with Chaudhuri's trek to the metropolis (including several other striking historical parallels between his life and that of both Apu and his creator, Bibhutibhushan, who was to become a close friend of Chaudhuri), even though his milieu, while provincial, is far from Apu's abject rural poverty. What is important, however, is the way this discrepant aspiration for the cosmopolitan shapes the character and texture of an intellectual identity, particularly that of the polymath Chaudhuri ended up becoming, one that represents the eclectic and the amateur rather than the focused and the professional. It was in fact the aspiration to be intellectually cosmopolitan, from within a peripheral location, which pushed a peculiar kind of colonial subject towards the idiosyncrasies of autodidactism and amateur learning rather than towards the curricular grids of institutional education. If Dutt's amateur self-making was shaped by the transient frailty of her life as young and socially isolated, albeit culturally privileged woman, Chaudhuri's ambitions of amateur learning embody a different dimension of colonial relationship to European humanities – that of the sustained and painstaking attempt to inhabit this knowledge from within a peripheral and provincial space. Headed to the capital of British India just like Apu, Chaudhuri too, is destined to learn far more from the library than from university lectures, as the institutional curriculum could not help him navigate the vast distance between his own peripheral location and his desire to embrace the world.

In his autobiography, Chaudhuri describes a funny social experience that becomes an intriguing revelation of the provincial subject's relation with metropolitan knowledge and life. It is a relation of longing as much as of confusion. This happened in the hostel of the Oxford Mission in Calcutta, where Chaudhuri was a student-resident, as was Pankaj Siddhanta, the young man with whom Chaudhuri would become friends there. Their first meeting started with a smiling request by Siddhanta to be allowed to look around Chaudhuri's room, quickly followed by the Siddhanta 'handling whatever objects on the table or on the shelves took his fancy'.[32] Randomly picking up a bottle of Burroughs Welcomes' Hazeline Snow, he asked if he could put some on his face, following which, he 'made liberal use of the cream'.[33] Soon after, searching through Chaudhuri's possessions, he discovered a pot of jam, and in response to his query, was told by Chaudhuri that it was something to eat – though not with rice as Siddhanta thought, but with bread, or even by itself. 'He helped himself, and after that asked if he could take a spoonful or two more. I had no objection.' But then he spotted something else a bottle of German mineral water that Chaudhuri had been taking for medicinal purposes. Not convinced by Chaudhuri's caveat that it was 'a medicinal water which is very unpleasant to take', Siddhanta took a liberal quantity of it as well, then, according to Chaudhuri, 'soon got a demonstration of my truthfulness, although the cost was mine, for he made the room very messy'.[34] To get rid of the taste, he took another spoonful of the jam before leaving Chaudhuri's room.

Odd as this initial encounter was, it was also strangely intimate and revealed a certain inquisitiveness in Siddhanta about things that appeared new and promising – which sometimes led to disastrous discoveries. That this incident is not a trivial metaphor for his scholarly curiosity is captured by Chaudhuri when he writes, in the very next paragraph: 'For with all his oddity, Pankaj was dreadfully earnest in the pursuit of intellectual truth.'[35] But it was a pursuit that was at least as eclectic as it was earnest, and full of an idiosyncratic courage that often became counter-productive, as with his critique of a history lecture in college, full of 'sentimentality and superficiality about Indian civilization', which got him badly lampooned, not the least because he was not a student of history, and hence far from an expert on the subject. On another occasion, during a chance meeting with Chaudhuri in Kishoreganj, he opened his suitcase and revealed what he had been reading in the train – Amiel's *Journal Intime* in Mrs Humphrey Ward's translation, borrowed from the assistant station master of Tangi junction. 'Whatever remarkable things Tangi might have seen in its later history.' Chaudhuri writes, 'the meeting on its platform between a potential lender of Amiel's journal in the person of the assistant station-master and potential borrower in the person of Pankaj and the offhand completion of the transaction must be reckoned as the most queerly memorable event'.[36]

The idiosyncratic and arbitrary pursuit of knowledge that connects these various figures – the fictional Apu as well as real-life characters such as Chaudhuri and his friend Pankaj Siddhanta – reveals a mode of the colonial acquisition of European knowledge that undoes the binary between the resistant, indigenous subjectivity and Macaulayian mimicry – between the professionalized Anglophone subject intended by the British Empire and the orientalists who rejected the Western curriculum. The scholarly lives of Chaudhuri and Siddhanta, and that of the fictional Apu indicate that such amateur and accidental – albeit intense – pursuers of European thought were more common than one might expect. They remain imaginative, individual aberrations to the dominant narratives of colonial assimilation of European knowledge.

Chaudhuri, who was born in Kishorganj in 1897 and died in Oxford in 1999, is justly celebrated as one of the most provocative, insightful, and entertaining Indian essayists of the twentieth century, whose popularity among English and Bengali readers is only matched by the invective he has inspired with incendiary comments on everything from colonial history to the place of Muslims in modern India. He sits at an uneasy angle to almost every narrative of postcolonial writing, most blatantly to the liberatory image of the empire writing back, and he has proved embarrassingly difficult to integrate into the progressivist political vision of postcolonial criticism. His long life and late start as a writer (at fifty-four) make him a strange sort of anachronism, not only in the historical but also in a political and aesthetic sense. His Anglophilia occasionally conjures an older model of the colonial mimic man; socially and intellectually, he shares biographical space with the Bengali liberal middle class, but throughout his writing life he seemed to survive on the prickly delight of disrupting almost every value and belief upheld by this social group. Tempted by the illusion of his pro-Hindu, Sanskritic sensibility, Hindu nationalist groups occasionally tried to court him, only to meet with the same frustration that he inspired in the liberal and progressive segment of the Indian middle class. At the heart of these infuriating anomalies, I would suggest, is a way of perceiving the world. This is the way of the engaged amateur, of an eccentric talent who trained himself to read cultural phenomena through the inspired and eclectic self-making of the autodidact. His powerful and seductive idiosyncrasies kept him at some distance from the paradigms of institutional knowledge and, hence, from the recognizable markers of progressive and reactionary worldviews, yet at the same time he appeared to flirt with the reactionary and the progressive alike, and to draw the wrong kind of attention from them both.

Though born in Kishorganj, Chaudhuri studied in Calcutta, often leading the life of the migrant student that belonged to the fictional Apu. Following college, he worked in the lower ranks of British administration, as a clerk in the city's military-accounts department. That, in fact, was to be his closest brush with the Macaulayan class of mimic men, the stereotypically effete figure known as the 'babu', who, in the popular colonial imagination, implied 'a native clerk who writes in English'.[37] But Chaudhuri's reading habits quickly pushed him farther away from this professional track than towards it. In 1922, a two-month leave to study the rule books and accounts manuals used by the department was deliciously squandered reading the English classics, notably Matthew Arnold. His obsession with Arnold's poem 'The Scholar Gipsy', about the mythical figure of a wandering English student who joined a band of gypsies, seems to have provided the final push to quit his job and lead the life of the bohemian scholar. Family financial responsibilities delayed the plunge by a few years, but he finally gave up his job in 1926 and, for the next decade and a half, wandered through the uncertain, semiregular world of literary journalism, broadcasting, editorial stints, and ghostwriting that barely kept the family of five (he and his wife Amiya had three sons during this period) from poverty in Calcutta. A measure of stability was earned in 1937 when he was appointed secretary of the lawyer and nationalist leader Sarat Chandra Bose.

But Arnold's poem had made a lasting mark, and Chaudhuri would remain something of a scholar gypsy for much of his life. He did, however, a long stint with All India Radio in Delhi through the decades following independence; but it was not until his mature years that his books would give him the distinction and the fully independent life that were finally due to him. *The Autobiography of an Unknown Indian* and *A Passage to England*, two of his most successful books, were to meet with great acclaim in England and with an equal measure of hostility in India, including from the government. A contract with the publishers Weidenfeld and Nicholson to write a book on Hinduism took him to England in 1970, and he eventually settled in Oxford, the happy roaming ground of the scholar gypsy who had prompted his defection from a life of clerical administration to the uncertainties of literary life nearly half a century earlier in Calcutta. He spent the next two decades of his life in Oxford, till he died there, in 1999, at the age of one hundred and two.

Chaudhuri's life was as idiosyncratic as it was long, and just as controversial. But it provides a powerful alternative narrative, taking shape through late colonial and eventually postcolonial India, about the amateur commentator on cultural phenomena, about the relation between provincialism and autodidactism, and, finally, the emergence of an influential model of the public intellectual enabled by this provincial genealogy. His Anglophilia, most memorable in his travelogue *A Passage to England* but also obvious in much else he has written, evokes one of the most famously theorized indigenous bourgeois subjects of colonial-discourse analysis – the class of mimic men identified by Homi Bhabha in Thomas Macaulay's dream for English-educated Indians who would become the administrative and ideological link between the British and native populations. Chaudhuri's alliance to this tradition is interesting, in the end, partly because of his startling deviation from it.

The curricular and institutional nature of English education, however, was key in the planned development of the colonial mimic men, and Nirad C. Chaudhuri's relation to this education brings his intellectual idiosyncrasy to light. His experience with the institutions of colonial education and bureaucracy is more one of failure than one of success; he emerges from their material and ideological infrastructure not as a professional but as something of an intriguing amateur, a shape he retains all his life in spite – or perhaps because – of the versatile nature of his eclectically acquired erudition.

Chaudhuri is, in fact, the perfect example of the popular intellectual whose scholarly and political 'flaws' and discursive oddities win him a wide audience, through admiration and antipathy alike. Blame for such seductive, alternately provocative and endearing faults must fall to the polymath sensibility, which is driven by his colonially inflected cosmopolitanism, essentially provincial in its origin and texture. Ian Almond's veneration for Chaudhuri's erudition illustrates this mix. Admiring Chaudhuri's 'reference-peppered prose', Almond reminds us that Chaudhuri is 'the Bengali who has not simply read the biography of Napoleon, but also that of his valet; or who can describe the village communities and practices of Mymensingh in terms borrowed from classical Greek – *polis, nomos, metoikoi*'. But this cosmopolitanism, Eurocentric as it might be, is made distinct and memorable by the accent of provincialism that undercuts it: 'hidden beneath all the references to Bernheim's *Lehrbuch* and Zola's *La terre* lies the subaltern voice of Chaudhuri's East Bengali, speaking the language almost completely excluded from the *Autobiography*, a language not even conceded the tradesman's entrance of a footnote or a parenthesis'.[38] The various dialects of East Bengali, associated with the eastern part of undivided Bengal (now Bangladesh), have suffered the prejudice of being less urbane and sophisticated than the dialects spoken in the

Western districts (including Calcutta), a consequence of the large-scale migration from east to west of people uprooted by religion and politics.

A provincial genealogy, among other things, hinders a smooth insertion into the metropolitan institutions of colonial higher education. Autodidactism, therefore, becomes the most visible form of provincial self-making. In Chaudhuri's case, this autodidactism is inseparable from what Ruvani Ranasinha has called 'self-Westernization', which exemplifies 'the process of affiliation in an extreme form: identification through culture', where the colonised replace filiative (that is, by descent) connections to indigenous cultural traditions, with affiliations to the social and political culture of the colonising power'.[39] However, as Ranasinha also points out, Chaudhuri was painfully aware that self-translation had severe limits. In the absence of blood ties to imperial culture that settler colonials could claim, his identification with that culture was abstract and could only happen on the level of ideas.

'We stand nowhere in relation to England,' Chaudhuri writes, '[i]f we give up things like literature. Neither the racehorse, nor cricket and football, nor even whisky, on which greater reliance is often placed, can be an adequate substitute.' He is acutely aware of the absence of blood ties that link settler Australians and New Zealanders, even Americans, to the English 'manor or farm'.[40] At the same time, he shows an intriguing indifference towards more popular and widespread ties that exist between England and other colonies in the Global South, such as sports. The force with which he claims literature as the *sole* medium of affiliation with England, rejecting other colonial links that live on elsewhere, indicates a clear identification with the group Rosinka Chaudhuri has called the gentlemen poets of colonial Bengal and their strong desire for an English – and especially humanist – education. But in Chaudhuri's case, it also indicates the autodidact's freewheeling claim of a colonial legacy, the historical verisimilitude of which is often patchy, simultaneously delightful and disturbing.

Chaudhuri's desire for an affiliation with the European humanistic tradition places him on an ambitious course of irregular self-learning. 'I never became a scholar,' he writes, '[b]ut every true scholar will forgive me, for he knows as well as I do that the greater part of his métier is the capacity for experiencing the emotion of scholarship'.[41] Passionate and idiosyncratic, this emotion of scholarship is inspired by a desire to embrace the world, reminiscent of Apu's feeling in *Aparajito*. Apu moves back and forth whimsically between history, drama, astronomy, poetry, botany, and every discipline he stumbles on. His friend Pranab, who is a far more organized scholar, reprimands him for his promiscuity and indiscipline as a reader: 'Dur? O ki pora? Tomar to pora noy, pora pora khela' ('Come on, you call that studying? What you do is not studying; it is making a sport of it!').[42] Around the same time, another young man, who had also arrived in the city from the provinces and also enrolled in a city college, was pursuing an agenda of eclectic autodidactism. Had Apu been alive in real time, they might have run into each other, perhaps in the bookstores fringing the pavements of College Street or in the Bowbazar sweetshops.

Nirad C. Chaudhuri is this young man alive in history. He comes from a more privileged background than Apu, but they both arrive in Calcutta from outside the city – Chaudhuri from the country town of Kishorganj and Apu from Nischindipur, a village in the southern part of West Bengal. And both are students in a peripheral and precarious way. There are moments of interaction with memorable teachers, and occasionally a riveting lecture grabs their attention, but they spend most of their time reading on their own, earnestly but patchily, occasionally trying to impose structure but failing more often than not, setting themselves afloat in a scholarly flânerie that defies the curricular grids of college education. The proverbial image of this defiance is that of a student lounging in the back of the lecture hall, reading a book for pleasure while the tedious and uninspiring lecturer drones on. That exact image is captured in the novel *Aparajito*, as well as in Chaudhuri's *Autobiography*. Apu is caught in the back of the lecture hall with a book that is not welcome in a class on logic – Francis Turner Palgrave's *Golden Treasury*. The professor is not amused. After a moment of public humiliation, Apu slips out through the back door to head to the library, where he chats with the staff and borrows a volume of Edward Gibbon's history of Rome. And in his autobiography, Chaudhuri records a similar indifference to the lectures at Calcutta University, making exceptions for just a handful of professors. 'As for the rest', he writes, 'I paid no attention whatever to what they said and sat on one of the back-benches, either reading a book of my choice, or scribbling, or thinking my own thoughts.' If there is an institution to which the autodidact has a debt, it is the library. 'It was another institution, the Imperial Library, to which I owe nearly all my higher education.'[43] The library offers an archive of knowledge and a realm of possibilities that seem limitless; at the same time, it creates a space of apparently unlimited freedom for the intellect.

By fleeing the classroom, Apu and Chaudhuri try to escape the bureaucratized tedium of the colonial higher education system, whose ideological consequences they embody as well as disrupt. They continue their quest for a wider, more exciting world in a European humanist tradition, whether in Gibbon's history or Palgrave's poetry anthology. But they do it as undisciplined interlopers, in an eclectic and intermittent way that derives from their background as provincial aspirants to cosmopolitan knowledge represented to them by this humanist tradition. But this engagement with humanities scholarship is not only a historical exigency for Chaudhuri as a colonial literary intellectual but also an essential part of his *Bildung*, of his development into a writer of unique charm as opposed to a rigorous professional scholar.

The subject that truly consumes both these figures – the fictional and the historical – is history. In fact, Apu and Chaudhuri admire some of the same historians – Gibbon, Theodor Mommsen, and James Bryce are among their favourites. The autodidact's hunger for knowledge drives Apu's reading of history, and he romanticizes the subject much as he romanticizes poetry, approaching its figures with the same empathy he feels for literary characters. For Chaudhuri, however, historiography must aspire towards a pure objectivity that has the epistemological authority of scientific knowledge. This objectivity is universal and transcends the vagaries of time and place. 'Who would think of judging the world by standards either Indian or European? It must take its stand on broader human grounds.'[44] Partisan scholarship, unfortunately practised by many eminent historians, at best is 'pre-eminently readable and possess[es] all the charms of a pamphlet' and, at worst, presents a distorted picture of history and demonstrates the 'uncultured man's bondage to the eschatology of political dogma'.[45] Nationalist use of history, whether in nineteenth-century Germany or in anticolonial India, was to him a betrayal of the objective reason of history. Such a humanism rests its faith in the authority of scientific reason that has been associated with the values derived from the European Enlightenment. The rush of enthusiasm over the scientific authority of a system of knowledge now understood to shape structures of power and ideology perhaps looks more suspicious than ever in a colonial subject living and learning under the shadow of imperial rule.

Chaudhuri's commitment to British and European historiography of the eighteenth and the nineteenth centuries now appears particularly ironic next to the historiographic critiques made by present-day postcolonial historians such as Dipesh Chakrabarty and Priya Satia. 'Historicism', Chakrabarty wrote in 2000, 'enabled European domination of the world in the nineteenth century'.[46] Historicism, in such a formulation, is the teleological philosophy of history that reads historical progress as a necessary passage from savagery to civilization.

European colonial domination of non-Western territories, in this vision, is an essential precondition of this passage. And in her 2020 book, *Time's Monster*, Priya Satia, setting out to explain the process of imperial decision-making through which historicism enabled this domination, pointed out that since the eighteenth century, the study of history in Britain had been rooted in the narrative of the making of 'great men' and their political ambition. It followed naturally that 'the rule of historians coincided with the era of British imperialism'.[47] Seeking to study 'the sway of a particular historical imagination in the unfolding of empire', Satia goes on to reveal that it wasn't till after the end of the Second World War and during the period of decolonization that historical imagination started to be claimed against the established powers by the very 'victims of modern history'.[48] Nirad C. Chaudhuri, reading in the early decades of the twentieth century in an India gathering intense anticolonial storm, was celebrating the eighteenth- and nineteenth-century ascendancy of British historical imagination and with it, this historicism's complicity with the project of imperialism.

But Chaudhuri has evoked a lot more than *suspicion*, which is in fact a mild word for the vitriolic emotions that have been poured on him – if only for his provocative take on the cultural relation between the empire and its colony, of which his most infamous articulation is the dedication to his autobiography, the irony of which has gone unnoticed for the most part:

TO THE MEMORY OF THE

BRITISH EMPIRE IN INDIA

WHICH CONFERRED SUBJECTHOOD ON US

BUT WITHHELD CITIZENSHIP

TO WHICH YET

EVERY ONE OF US THREW OUT THE CHALLENGE:

CIVIS BRITANNICUS SUM

BECAUSE

ALL THAT WAS GOOD AND LIVING

WITHIN US

WAS MADE, SHAPED, AND QUICKENED

BY THE SAME BRITISH RULE

Aspirations to a universal humanism shaped by a faith in a scientific model of history make this well-known Anglophile a target of postcolonial theorists, many of whom embody the anti-humanist scepticism of poststructuralist thought. And the critics are not wrong. This humanist vision, it becomes clear, underlies a version of cosmopolitanism that is far more limited than Chaudhuri claims it to be. Pallavi Rastogi has argued that Chaudhuri's work is shaped by the dialectic of two mutually contradictory models of cosmopolitanism – the 'metropolitan cosmopolitanism' that privileges England as the centre of the world and the 'cosmopolitan cosmopolitanism' that undercuts the former with a sense of fantasy and irony. According to Rastogi, 'It is this dialectic inter-play of "discrepant cosmopolitanisms" that allows a nuanced reading of *A Passage to England* to emerge'.[49] 'Even though cosmo-cosmopolitanism emphasizes egalitarianism', Rastogi reminds us, 'in Chaudhuri's cosmology, India is often represented as small, provincial, and stifling while England connotes an all-encompassing vastness, vigor, and above all cultural antiquity, always subsuming the world in its grasp'.[50]

But the failure to attain the objectivity he fetishizes is in some ways Chaudhuri's most triumphant success. At the outset of 'Initiation into Scholarship', a chapter of his autobiography, Chaudhuri warns us that 'this chapter has certainly been presumptuously titled, for I never became a scholar'.[51] What prompts the presumption is the feeling that he has experienced 'the emotion of scholarship'. This emotion, he knows, is the very life of scholarship. Everything Chaudhuri writes, in this book and elsewhere, trembles with this emotion; it is his hallmark and appeal as a public intellectual. While his idealization of scientific reason in historiography might imply an aspiration to scholarly professionalism, the reality of his intellectual habits and activities implies something quite different, something more playful, rather immature and romantic. 'I hardly know,' he writes, 'what made me read Stubbs week after week, month after month, when I could not understand three-quarters of him.' The provincial autodidact is driven not by the conventions of professional scholarship but by an amateurish excitement experienced in the act of reading, even before he quite comes to understand the material. For while such texts withhold comprehension, he knows, they give him something else, something less tangible, perhaps, but more valuable. 'I should have been driven away by Stubbs after breaking my teeth on him,' he writes, 'and if I was not, even after breaking my teeth, it was to be explained only by the taste of the emotion of scholarship I found in the book'.[52]

Something in Chaudhuri's amateur aspiration as a polymath evokes an older worldview that held on to some of its waning strength during his student days: 'The compulsion of our humanist culture of the nineteenth century was still strong.' He recognizes, however, that students like him and his brother were among the last products of this culture. 'It was', he writes, 'almost the last proddings of this compulsion which made my brother, when he had just entered the degree class of Calcutta University in 1914, buy Comte's *Positivism*, Mill's works, and some of Huxley's essays.'[53] He knew, as did some of his peers, that their aspiration was more utopian than real, since the great age of the polymath had passed. Frequently, they 'discussed the relative merits of the encyclopaedic or polymathic mind and the mind of the specialist', identifying Leibniz and Goethe as the great encyclopaedic minds at the end of the seventeenth and the eighteenth centuries, respectively, and recognizing that the emergence of the specialist had eroded the conditions of the polymath's existence by the end of the nineteenth century. But it was the polymath they loved and wanted to become, even if they knew that it was not to be, not anymore. For them, the magic word was *synthesis*.[54] The concept, they felt, was epitomized not only by the Hindu way of life but also, more immediately, by the presence in their midst of a figure who represented encyclopaedic learning – Brajendranath Seal, who held the George V Chair in Philosophy at Calcutta University. Seal awoke in Chaudhuri and his fellow students the admiration due to the polymath, fast becoming an anachronism, and, on Chaudhuri's candid admission, some jealousy as well.

Nevertheless, Chaudhuri emulated the polymath, to curious effect. 'I could pass from physics to Sanskrit literature or from novels to astronomy with an agility which seemed like volatility to those who did not know me well.' The chequered social response to his restless encyclopaedic aspirations predicts the immediate and long-term consequences of this mode of scholarship. Those who did not like him called him 'Jack of all trades, master of none'. To them, he knew that he 'appeared like a squid or octopus in the world of knowledge'.[55] Indeed, throughout his life, the intellectual idiosyncrasies that amused his personal acquaintances also endeared him to the non-specialist reader looking for narrative gratification; at the same time, they put him at odds with institutional norms of scholarship. For all his interest in large structures such as origins and histories of people and cultural phenomena, Chaudhuri retained, throughout his life, a quirky and mischievous interest in concrete trivia. Much of this is the kind of knowledge that might help one win a television game show rather than get scholarly citations. Knowledge of this kind delighted both the writer and the man, and it provides the novelistic texture to his social analysis, sometimes (though not always) at the expense of sociological rigour.

The odd angle between academic scholarship and delightful trivia comes to life in Chaudhuri's encounter with the academic Meenakshi Mukherjee. Mukherjee was at work on a monograph on Jane Austen when she visited Chaudhuri in Oxford in 1989. As part of her research she had been spending time at the British Museum, reading bestselling eighteenth-century novels that Austen mentioned in her own novels. The idea was to get a sense of what Austen was reading, the kind of knowledge, most would agree, that is still valued in academic literary scholarship. Chaudhuri had little interest in this sort of thing. An avid reader of Austen all his life, he was fascinated instead by arcana such as 'the details of Darcy's clothing on specific occasions …, the meaning of certain colours of British heraldry, the distance between Hunsford and Longbourne, the number of horses used for drawing different kinds of carriages'.[56] Mukherjee had to undergo an extempore test in esoteric Austen trivia before the ninety-two-year-old Chaudhuri, and she confesses that she 'barely managed a B grade'. The most esoteric 'fact' was 'the size of Fanny Price's room in the attic in Mansfield Park', which, the bewildered Mukherjee recalls, 'had something to do with the space taken up by Fanny's bookshelf which he calculated by locating the original edition of each book mentioned and adding up their dimensions'.

I will not deny that the collection of such arcane – sometimes absurd – details is on one level an expression of Chaudhuri's sense of humour. But the humour is not irreverence, and nor do the trivia trivialize the archive. In a way, this arcana genuinely reflects Chaudhuri's preferred mode of reading cultural phenomena, which is more anecdotal and novelistic than faithful to institutional paradigms of scholarly research. Small surprise that the successful academic Mukherjee scored a poor B on Chaudhuri's test. Perhaps it is a hint why, nearly seventy years earlier, Chaudhuri himself had failed his MA examination. 'The great adventure came to nothing,' Chaudhuri recollects. 'I failed to pass my M.A. examination.'[57]

It is a significant failure not only in terms of Chaudhuri's personal career but also symbolically for the figure of the Bengali intellectual enrolled in the great colonial institution of higher education, the University of Calcutta. It is not a coincidence that this failure embodies Chaudhuri's disavowal of affinity with perhaps the most famous Bengali mimic man of English literature, Hurree Babu of Rudyard Kipling's *Kim*, who is eager to establish his intellectual credentials as 'an M.A. of Calcutta University'.[58] Hurree Babu is keen on institutional education and wants to impress its importance on Kim. He is convinced that 'going to school' is the only way Kim can get an education derived from the best in the classical European humanist tradition. Chaudhuri's failure signifies his inability to professionalize himself as a scholar (and possibly as an academic, as his youthful ambitions implied), as well as the failure of the university to interpellate him into the ideological enterprise of the British Empire. The more popular image of Chaudhuri as a lifelong Anglophile misses the significance of his failure at this venue of colonial learning, all the more spectacular after his success at the BA examination, where he stood first. Even as he aspired to the utopian intellectual ideals of European humanism and the scientific epistemology of the Enlightenment – which doubtlessly shaped him to a great extent – the institution failed to produce him as a subject after the pragmatic vision of colonial pedagogy, one who might be a capable ideological and professional agent of empire, such as the Indian civil servant who was part of the Macaulayan dream.

Academic failure, therefore, augured his success as an engaged amateur. Nothing in his autobiography suggests a sense of betrayal or even surprise at his failure to pass the MA examination. Towards the end of the section titled 'Academic Failure', he makes it clear that he came to understand the cause of his failure: the eclectic nature of his developing scholarly identity, which, no matter how striking, lacked consistency and did not amount to any real command of any subject. 'Thus, although I came to acquire a deep knowledge in certain aspects of certain subjects very unusual in a student of my age, taking it all in all, I did not succeed in having an even grounding in any subject.'[59]

But why, in the first place, did he try so hard to achieve something that could not really be achieved? To possess that remarkable anachronism, the encyclopaedic mind? Doubtless it was, as he narrates so vividly, the still-living compulsion of the 'humanistic culture of the nineteenth century' that urged him towards this utopian goal.[60] But there was, I would suggest, another impulse more peculiar to his personal history. This is the passion for intellectual self-making that is unique to the scholar who undertakes the arduous and exciting trek from the province to the metropolis. Coming to the metropolitan centre of learning and culture from a small, peripheral place, Chaudhuri had in him a scale of ambition and a dreaminess of vision that urged him towards a utopian intellectual goal. The dream of cosmopolitanism conceived in the provincial periphery promised to come to life only through the eclectic routes of amateur and autodidactic learning.

Chaudhuri in Calcutta is a more confident and empowered figure than the fictional Apu who roamed the city around the same time. Yet Chaudhuri reveals something of Apu's spirit of provincial cosmopolitanism throughout his student life in the city. There is, for instance, the episode when he sits in the hostel of the Oxford Mission, lost in reading about naval range finders in the *Encylopaedia Britannica*. It is a scene from a play rich with colonial ironies: urging the eager learner to shut his book and come out to play is the superintendent of the hostel, the Harrow-and-Cambridge-educated priest Carlos Edward Prior. Having arrived in the colony from the privileged centres of learning in imperial Britain, the priest is playful and humane. 'If you read when you ought to play,' he says as he shuts the book and drags Chaudhuri out of the room by his arm, 'I won't let you have the Encyclopaedia at all.'[61] This kind and affectionate man cannot understand the fervour and intensity of the provincial subject's self-making, a project that might strain a boy's childhood with the heavy demands of an ambitious, utopian *Bildung*, an anxious attempt at *becoming* cosmopolitan. Anxiously, too, the young Chaudhuri tells Prior that he wants to learn Latin, to which 'he replied that he would not mind my learning Latin when I was two inches taller, but for the moment I must come and play'.[62] Physical growth, one suspects, is the least important part of growing up for the young Chaudhuri. This is yet another moment when Chaudhuri, small and frail all his life, comes teasingly close to the (in)famous stereotype of the Bengali 'babu' as an effeminate aspirant to English education. While in Bengali *babu* simply implies the equivalent of *Mister* or *Esquire*, for the English in late-nineteenth-century India, a babu is a negative stereotype, a disturbing regional version of the mimic man, a loquacious, unsporting practitioner of Western education who is as superficially obsequious as he is secretly subversive, a potential anti-colonial nationalist and a threat to empire.

Clearly, the provincial polymath of late colonial Bengal invites tantalizing comparisons with the Bengali babu – a title which Nirad-babu wore with the composure it has always possessed in the Bengali language. But his adolescent quest for world knowledge is unique and passionate, and makes him far more than a mimic man. He is the boy who would rather spend his growing years collecting arcane knowledge about a broad range of subjects in the true spirit of the passionate amateur. For such a spirit, the *Encylopaedia Britannica* is the happiest romping ground. The encyclopaedia offers free range for the young and restless scholarly amateur and promises knowledge of the wide world that can turn the provincial subject into a cosmopolitan scholar. In the process, the aspirant might even become the carrier of eclectic knowledge, sometimes of surprise historical relevance. 'Thus it happened that in August 1914 I was able to surprise my acquaintances by chattering about the German

General Staff, General Brialmont and his fortifications, artillery and aeroplanes.'[63] The frail Bengali delights in his theoretical command of military affairs even though he is not to be found anywhere near a real battlefield – and his family delights in it too. The perversely precocious knowledge gave great pleasure to an old uncle of his, who declared that he was happy someone in the family was using the volumes of the encyclopaedia, even if his son, for whom they were intended, was not.

Encyclopaedias are key for the amateur, both as modality and metaphor. 'Perhaps in the whole course of my life,' Chaudhuri wrote in his autobiography, 'I have learnt nothing but the cartography of learning.'[64] The youthful instinct that sought recreational absorption in encyclopaedias stayed with him all his life, as evident in his exchange with Meenakshi Mukherjee at the age of ninety-two. He identifies a contradiction deepening within himself even in the early years of his attempt at becoming a scholar. On one hand, he was drawn to 'wide views, sweeping generalizations, and comprehensions of wholes which were continually expanding into bigger and vaguer wholes', but at the same time, he sensed an undeniable attraction of 'specialized scholarship and its methods'. It is this doubleness of his instinct that, he feels, came in the success of his development as a professional or academic scholar. It is clear, as he identifies above, that he has a kind of meta-fascination with the processes of learning, knowledge and scholarship, but his actual temperament remains too mischievous, too eclectic, and too deeply idiosyncratic for the subordination of the self to the archive and methodology that professional disciplinary trajectories require. His irregular, and eventually frustrated engagement with the British colonial education system shaped the unique character of his personal relationship with European humanistic culture that absorbed him so deeply. He shared that absorption with his youthful predecessor Toru Dutt. But while Dutt, living the life of a teenage Christian girl in a westernized family a few decades before him, dwelled outside institutions entirely, Chaudhuri was the provincial youth who came to the colonial capital to seek curricular instruction, only to deviate from it in the most spectacular way. His death in the last years of the twentieth century symbolizes the end of a prolonged period of Bengali modernity and renaissance – captured in the words of the historian Dipesh Chakrabarty, who wrote in a different context in 2004: 'The long Bengali nineteenth is perhaps finally dying.' While Dutt lived her short life in this long nineteenth century, Chaudhuri, with his literary career that started at the age of fifty-four, brought that century close to the threshold of the twenty-first.

Prison houses of boredom: the postcolonial university, the culture of examinations, and the delights of amateurism

The sheer inertia of colonial reality far beyond decolonization is evident in the way the university lecture hall experiences of Nirad C. Chaudhuri and the fictional Apu continues to resonate with succeeding generations of students in Indian universities, particularly those structured on the colonial, affiliated-college model. This is the recognizable moment of boredom or disconnection in the classroom. With the uninspiring voice at the podium droning away the lecture in a monotone – perhaps reading from brittle, yellow notes – and a group in front busy taking notes that they hope will help them crack the exams, the imaginative student sits at the back, disconnected from it all. Chaudhuri sits there, not paying attention to his professors but for a few, 'reading a book of my choice, or scribbling, or thinking my own thoughts', while Apu, after being rebuked another book 'out of syllabus', Palgrave's *The Golden Treasury*, slips out of class unnoticed and makes his way to the library, a place that also claims Chaudhuri's loyalty. The negligence of the curricular lecture for reading of one's choice says as much about the university system set up by the British as it does by the kind of individuals who practised it.

'The educational system of British India', Chaudhuri writes in the *Autobiography*, 'has been accused of being only a machine for turning out clerks and officials.'[65] While he argues that this was certainly not the intention of those who set it up, he points to the mistakes they made, which pertained to the reproduction of a foreign system in a country without making any modifications to it. As a result, making something meaningful with this education depended entirely on the personal talent or inclination of individual students, or on an exceptional family culture conducive to true learning. As for the rest, 'they used the system as a man who does not understand the nature and use of live ammunition uses a gun even when he has cartridges, that is to say, only as a cudgel'.[66] But while it is not fair to blame them for this misuse, he argues that it is not fair to blame the system either for people making inadequate use of it.

Sanjay Seth has persuasively argued that 'intent' is the wrong word while trying to understand the rather indifferent results produced by colonial educational policy in India, as is the word 'subjectivity', given the radically incompatible modalities of pre- and post-colonial India. Seen this way, Chaudhuri's vocabulary seems inappropriate. But irrespective of the reality of this mismatch – whether or not it was one of intent – the indifferent and uninspired institution of European humanities in the colonial universities created an academic culture that has continued long past decolonization and continues today. The colonial university, as the historian Sabyasachi Bhattacharya has pointed out, was an institution mainly constructed to 'attribute cognitive authority to Western civilization exclusively' and for passive transmission of knowledge produced in the West to colonized subjects.[67] Students are routinely exposed to a set of texts – often from a canon long dated – but the mode of their engagement with it remains narrow and instrumental, primarily shaped by rote-learning and almost purely driven to satisfy the needs of the examination, which follows predictable patterns year after year. Things promised to change with independence but did not, in spite of some sincere efforts. Even the first prime minister Jawaharlal Nehru's vision for higher education, which shaped the birth of the University Education Commission in 1948 under the leadership of Sarvepalli Radhakrishnan, failed to change the colonial character of Indian universities. It has perpetuated the paradox of exposure to European humanities – radically alien to the lived experience of most students – and a transient relationship to them that, at its best, lasts only as long as examinations need to be cleared. But this is a paradox has also continued to inspire a tradition of contrarian thought in Indian writing in English.

In the title essay of his book *Partial Recall*, an exquisite hybrid of memoir, literary history, and criticism, the poet Arvind Krishna Mehrotra offers a poignant account of his adolescent growth as a poet; in it he narrates stories of his days as a student at the University of Allahabad in 1964. English was his main subject, along with history and economics, but his approach to academic study, even in fields that interested him, appeared oddly instrumental and showed little intellectual passion. His choices of specific fields were shaped by pragmatic criteria: 'because the subject was "scoring", which is to say the examiners were believed to be liberal, awarding high marks to every script they read'. This did bring in some strange disappointments: 'scoring in ancient history was easier said than done, for next thing we learnt was that the marks awarded depended on the length of the answers than what was written in them'. This in return shaped a bizarre kind of instrumentalism, part clerical drudgery, part archival labour: 'Perhaps studying is the wrong word for what we did, for most of our time went in making "notes", an activity he explains soon: 'So making notes in fact meant copying at high speed whole chapters in longhand, the drudgery made worse by the condition of the books.'[68] Following such note-taking, studying simply implied committing vast swathes of this material to memory: 'Quite apart from the hundreds of pages to be crammed, we had dates in history and quotations in English (Graham Hough and Maurice Bowra on the Romantics, A.C. Ward on Shaw) to commit to memory.'[69] It wasn't, of course, merely a brutal labour of rote-learning; there was clever strategizing involved, in the attempt to guess likely exam questions based on the most crucial archive of all, the compendium of test papers from the past:

> We studied selectively of course, like everyone else. There were parts of the syllabus we left out and others we mugged up, depending on the "guess papers' in each subject. To make a guess paper we scrutinized the previous ten years questions, available in inexpensive booklets with flimsy pink of yellow covers on University Road, and after taking into account the hints dropped by teachers and the gossip among students, and after listening to our inner voices, we drew up a list of questions that were likely to be asked.

It becomes clear from Mehrotra's memoirs that his literary education took on a vibrant life exactly at the same time this was going on, and clearly none of that real education was happening at the University of Allahabad, another venerable colonial institution, identified by Andre Beteille as 'a centre of intellectual excellence' along with the University of Calcutta.

Mehrotra also outlines what this academic culture has done for Indian writing, particularly in English – that fragile tradition that aroused suspicion, confusion, and excitement in equal measure. In the introduction to *Partial Recall*, he writes: 'The great betrayal of our literature has been primarily by those who teach in the country's English departments.'[70] This was the 'community whose job was to green the hillsides by planting them with biographies, scholarly editions, selections carrying new introductions, histories, canon-shaping (or canon-breaking) anthologies, readable translations, revaluations, exhaustive bibliographies devoted to individual authors, and critical essays, that, because of the excellence of their prose, become as much a part of the literature as any significant novel or poem'.[71]

Whatever has developed as tradition in this literature has happened in spite of the universities, and primarily because the practitioners traced it themselves, seeing in themselves the images of earlier writers – the way Chaudhuri saw Dutt, Sealy saw Derozio, and Rushdie saw Desani. It is partially in the spirit of correction, no less of sadness and resentment, that Mehrotra offers evocative, often deeply personalized histories of literary texts, figures, and movements – be it a literary and community history of his home city, Allahabad, of his own growth there amidst a network of family, neighbours, friends, and teachers, of poets: Arun Kolatkar primarily, but also Kabir, Toru Dutt, A.K. Ramanujan, Srinivas Rayaprol, Eunice de Souza, Adil Jussawalla, Amit Chaudhuri, and early figures in the Indian-English literary tradition and vernacular writers contemporaneous to them. The account of literary history and the practice of literary criticism offered in two of his books – *Partial Recall* and *Translating an Indian Past* – is far from the amateur practice of both Toru Dutt and Nirad C. Chaudhuri, different as they are from each other. Mehrotra's knowledge of his archive, idiosyncratic and impulsive as it seems often, is far from the polymathic, eclectic mischiefs of Chaudhuri, and is far more substantial and analytical than the transient and superficial comments of Toru Dutt on her daily reading. But it is particularly interesting as it is offered in a spirit that is consciously contrarian to the practice of academic literary study in India, which carries the heavy, rusty legacy of the colonial project and its lifeless engagement of a dated canon put in place as part of the imperialist project. The life of a university lecturer in India goes like this:

> If you were in an English Department, you would open the textbook and, after reading out a Wordsworth poem, spend the remaining forty-five minutes nervously talking about nature and Romantic poetry. At the end of the month you were rewarded for your labours with a cheque. Given the assurance of similar cheques arriving with great regularity over the next many decades, you would be teaching Wordsworth from the same textbook. This was as unvarying as the pink colour of the State Bank of India cheque, except that the salary amount in the cheque would frequently be revised upwards, in inverse proportion to the intellectual labour required of you as a university teacher.[72]

He goes on to outline how he ended up becoming a part of this same system – at the University of Allahabad where he read for his BA and where he soon found himself on the faculty, following a trajectory of accidents:

> I could have missed the ramshackle Indian academic bus altogether. My M.A. degree is from Bombay University, where I failed my Anglo-Saxon paper and almost got a third division, escaping it by the narrowest of margins. With no job prospects anywhere, I returned

to Allahabad, my home town, and not knowing what to do next, I did what people in my situation do. I decided to seek enrolment as a research scholar.[73]

Also requiring a subject for research, Mehrotra arrived at the painter Rabindranath Deb. But within a few months of beginning his research, teaching positions were advertised, and Mehrotra ended up on the faculty. 'There was little reason now for me, after landing the job, to complete my research, little reason to do anything except teach "The Solitary Reaper"'.[74]

That lack of reason, of course, turned out to be a sharply ironic motivator for all the writing Arvind Krishna Mehrotra went on to do subsequently, including his poetry as well as the outlining of the historical consciousness within the living tradition of Indian English writing – an important gesture of undoing the 'great betrayal' of the tradition by the English departments of the country. The contrarian trajectory, his memoir gives me the reason to believe, was indeed egged on by the lifeless machinery of the colonial university and its chronic discouragement of original thought. And well beyond the mid-century experience of Mehrotra, the colonially derived university in India continues to be an entity of dusty, desultory bureaucracy that has inspired acts of deflection from its own track in some of the imaginative readers of literature whose young formative growth happened in its shadows.

A deeply moving account of amateur reading comes from the 1980s, the decade when Pankaj Mishra, after graduating from the University of Allahabad, the same institution that had disenchanted Mehrotra more than twenty years ago, decided to continue a life of autodidactism in the nearby city of Benares. His is, consequently, the autodidactism of a young man who has just completed a perfunctory college degree and feels he is not much better than before, and not any closer, for that indifferent qualification, to the intellectual cosmopolitanism that he seeks so desperately. 'After three idle, bookish years at a provincial university', Mishra writes in an autobiographical essay, '[i]n a decaying old provincial town, I had developed an aversion to the world of careers and jobs which, having no money, I was destined to join'.[75] His autodidactic life in Benares, inactive and indolent on the surface but driven by a feverish intensity beneath, is, in some sense, an attempt to prolong his life as a student, as what seems to lie beyond holds neither promise nor excitement: 'in Benares, with a tiny allowance, I sought nothing more than a continuation of the life I had led as an undergraduate'.

This essay, 'Edmund Wilson in Benares', is an account of four months Mishra spent in Benares in 1988. He was then twenty and recently graduated from the nearby University of Allahabad. In Benares, he rented a room in the dilapidated house of an old, opium-addicted Brahmin musician and spent his days in and around the Benares Hindu University. He was not enrolled there in any capacity, but – naturally drawn to books – he fell into the habit of whiling away most of his daytime hours at the university library, reading the books and periodicals he could find there. 'Edmund Wilson in Benares', primarily, is a chronicle of that reading, of a range of things, but most obsessively, of the works of Edmund Wilson, whom Mishra discovered purely by accident at the stacks. Almost immediately, he became absorbed in Wilson's writing, enough to finish, over the next few months, all of Wilson's books the library had in its collection: 'dust-laden, termite-infested, but beautifully, miraculously present: *The Shores of Light, Classics and Commercials, The Bit Between My Teeth, The Wound and the Bow, Europe without Baedeker, A Window on Russia, A Piece of My Mind.*'[76]

Mishra's essay records a unique intellectual failure: his inability to write an original piece on Edmund Wilson in 1995, the year of Wilson's centenary, which had prompted Mishra to try to write something about the American critic, ideally, an 'exposition of Wilson's key books'.[77] But he could not, he felt, come up with anything original: 'what I wrote seemed to me too much like a reprise of what a lot of other people had already said about him.'[78] It becomes intriguingly clear that if Mishra had succeeded in writing the other piece, we would have never had his essay 'Edmund Wilson in Benares', a product of this very failure. A key reason for his inability to write the essay he had planned about Wilson, Mishra felt, was that he was 'trying to write about him in the way an American or European writer would have'.[79] The essay he produced evokes, slowly but vividly, the meaning and the genealogy of this failure.

An equally important theme in this essay is the city of Benares, especially the university campus, and the atmosphere of violence, corruption, and cynicism that perpetually hung in the air. It was a common enough atmosphere in most of north India in the 1980s, with its economic depression, caste-ridden politics, and widespread disenchantment among educated youth. As Mishra evokes this strange and disturbing environment, the protagonist of the piece emerges: Rajesh, a sometime student at the university but really a political thug of sorts, one who becomes Mishra's friend, and in an equally strange and disturbing way, his mentor and protector in that unstable and volatile atmosphere.

Still, more than anything else, the essay is about reading, and particularly, about engaging with literary criticism. This engagement happens in that unlikely environment of violence and depression, in an ambience where reading seemed an odd and eccentric sort of activity, even in the precincts of a university. Most of all, the essay chronicles the reading of books that seemed absurd in that milieu, books whose discovery were pure accidents, and with which Mishra had little or no prior familiarity. But the thrust of the essay, and its narrative impulse, is provided by the utterly unexpected ways in which the quaint and distant universe of these books enters the quotidian violence of north Indian reality in the 1980s.

At the core of 'Edmund Wilson in Benares' is an unlikely story of autodidactism that, special as it is, is also the product of a curious historical exigency. It contains the vital spirit of a narrative – one that extends beyond these four months and into the larger arc of Mishra's growth as a writer and a thinker – of the development of the provincial intellectual as an autodidact. Such an intellectual experience could come to him only through the odd coupling of sheer serendipity and a ravenous hunger for books. The most meaningful growth of such a provincial intellectual, perhaps the only growth possible, is not as a professional scholar but as an amateur.

Autodidactism it is, however, in every sense of the word: 'I knew little of the social and historical underpinnings to the books I read: I had only a fleeting sense of the artistry and skill to which certain novels owed their greatness.'[80] The irregular and amateurish nature of Mishra's pursuit is shaped not only by the fact that he is doing it alone, outside of an institutional setting – he sits and reads in the library but is not allowed to borrow books as he is not a student – but more strikingly, by the absurd disconnect between his archive of study and his immediate atmosphere: 'For a radically different world existed barely a few hundred metres from where I sat, reading about Santayana.'[81]

The intriguing generic hybridity of Mishra's essay comes alive not only in its immediate texture, but also in the nature of its final achievement: it tells a story just as any memoir or fragment of a *Bildungsroman* might, but seamlessly meshed within this story is a passionate championship of the intellectual as an amateur and an autodidact. What is special about this essay is the utter inseparability of the life-story from this assertion of faith. Faith rests here in the organic power of great literary thought to invite autodidactism, and of the imaginative individual to respond to this invitation. This trajectories of storytelling and the attainment of faith come together in the author's relationship with Rajesh, the former student turned mercenary hooligan, and in the miraculous way Rajesh brings alive, in rural Uttar Pradesh in the 1980s, Edmund Wilson's reading of Gustave Flaubert's representation of the petit-bourgeois world of nineteenth-century France. The absence of scholarly aptitude that defines Mishra as an amateur reader – the lack of the knowledge of 'the social and historical underpinnings' of the books he read – enables a literary humanism that the structure of professional scholarship would have very possibly inhibited. Lack of historical knowledge, and perhaps more acutely, of cultural affiliation prevented Mishra from entering the social context of nineteenth-century France. Unable to enter this world, Mishra instead saw Flaubert's Frédéric Moreau enter late-twentieth-century rural Uttar Pradesh.

For the rest of the essay, Rajesh, Wilson, Mishra, and Frédéric Moreau are intimately entwined together, in the landscape of intermittent poverty, desolation and violence in Uttar Pradesh. The turning point of the narrative comes when Rajesh, who has maintained an attitude of sceptical amusement towards Mishra's obsession with Wilson, takes Mishra with him on a visit to his widowed mother in their village home. Seeing Rajesh's home for the first time, Mishra realizes the sheer poverty and precariousness of his life and that of his mother in a way he had never realized it in the university setting, where Rajesh's bullying leadership had set him apart as some sort of a prominent figure, with a following of its own. The train ride back to Benares is largely silent, but Rajesh breaks that silence to tell Mishra that 'he had read *Sentimental Education*, and that it was a story he knew well. "Yeh meri duniya ki kahani hai. Main in logo ko janta hoon," he said, in Hindi. "It is the story of my world. I know these people well." He gave me a hard look. "Your hero, Edmund Wilson," he added in English, "he also knows them".'[82]

Their lives part and Mishra leaves Benares. He returns two years later for a visit, to hear that Rajesh has become a contract killer: a well-paid profession, but not one where you hope to live for long, as murders tend to be avenged quickly in this world. Mishra never meets Rajesh again, nor does he find out what happened to him in the end. But he discovers Rajesh's last signature in an unexpected place. Going through an old, photo copy of Wilson's essay, 'The Politics of Flaubert', he sees lines marked in Rajesh's hand. Rajesh had underlined in red Wilson's analysis of Flaubert's distaste of the bourgeoisie and his sense of how the corrupting influence of this class threatens to bring about a decline of civilization.

'What did Rajesh', Mishra asks in this essay, 'a student in a provincial Indian university in the late 1980s, have in common with Frédéric

Moreau or any of the doomed members of his generation in this novel of mid-nineteenth century Paris?'.[83] 'Edmund Wilson in Benares' chronicles Mishra's experience of dwelling in this question even as it becomes his attempt to answer it. But no less miraculous for me is the way the question rebounds onto Mishra himself; how Rajesh's life, and its strange entanglement with the lives chronicled by Flaubert and Wilson, grapples with Mishra's own life and takes over his relationship with books. It is the kind of epiphany unique to the experience of the provincial autodidact, for whom books are an attempt to engage with a culture as far removed from his immediate reality as possible. The essay holds within itself the poignant fragment of a life. But it is also a story of a reading that is a startling failure to harness the right apparatus for engagement with criticism. Indeed it is this very failure that holds the genesis of the unexpected amateur engagement with the text.

There is an intriguingly persuasive argument made by J Daniel Elam that in late-colonial India several South-Asian thinkers engaged in a culture of reading that went against the goal of expertise and mastery and became deliberate acts of inconsequence that gestured to a larger, more pervasive act of anti-colonialism going beyond the immediate goal of political independence. 'As an anticolonial practice', Elam writes, 'reading could mark modes of refusal, nonproductivity, inconsequence, inexpertise, and nonauthority' (ix).[84] Such reading had a crucial political function as by opposing the values of British liberalism, 'these recalcitrant ideals were perfect for envisioning a radical egalitarianism rooted in communal reading and collective textual criticism' (x). Bhagat Singh read in prison, facing death, essentially relinquishing goals of mastery. Ambedkar read with the fellowship of suffering in mind, practicing an autodidactism that sought to dismantle 'the telos of mastery and authority' (47). Gandhi's reading was inseparable from his philosophy of perpetual failure, loss, and non-cooperation. And for Lala Har Dayal, reading alone and reading together alike involved a refusal of interpretative authority. In various ways, all these strategies of reading – or un-reading – opposed the Macaulay's project of creating 'mimic men'.

Of all the writers discussed here, it is perhaps Nirad C. Chaudhuri who comes closest to pursuing a programme of reading that, in spite of its passion and intensity, is in many ways, structured for failure, even if he, or any of the others, cannot be linked to the kind of radical anticolonial struggle that defines the figures chosen by Elam. But there is an epistemological failure destined for Chaudhuri's polymath ambition; and then there is real failure in the MA examination, also caused by this ambition. While Toru Dutt was never part of the colonial university, both Mehrotra and Mishra record their frustration and failure with the education offered by public universities that continue the colonial legacy in the decades after independence, which, in turn, become generative of their autodidactic journeys.

It is a failure and frustration with which I have a deep personal connection. A decade after Mishra acquired his indifferent degree in literature in the 'provincial university' in 'a decaying, old, provincial town', I acquired the same in Calcutta, once the capital of British India, and by the end of the twentieth century, on the verge of becoming a decaying, old, provincial city. The residual metropolitan quality of Calcutta in the 1990s gave me a small constellation of charismatic and committed professors in the missionary St. Xavier's College, including the poet P. Lal, a figure much like Mehrotra in his reflexive delineation of an Indian-English literary tradition over several decades. But that island of learning excitement was contained and constricted within the scaffolding of the bureaucratic behemoth, the University of Calcutta – the archetypal colonial university that had provoked, excited, bored, and disappointed a provincial Nirad C. Chaudhuri at the beginning of the century. Reading the accounts of my predecessors at the colonial university in India, I have marvelled at how strikingly similar our experiences were, and what a drearily unchanged narrative it has charted throughout the twentieth century, almost as if decolonization never happened. I cannot say the experience pushed me to a trajectory of amateurism – I did, following my studies in Calcutta, go on to acquire graduate degrees in both literature and creative writing in the United States. But I'd be dishonest if I did not admit that the inescapable indifference and lassitude inspired by the colonially inflected structure of learning and evaluation did not give me an abiding interest in the figure of the amateur purveyor of knowledge who must dwell in the shadowy recesses of this dinosaur institution that thrives into the present day.

Chapter 6

THE VIOLENCE OF HUMANISTIC EDUCATION

… in close touch with a centre and a system of training which
has for centuries produced, and continue to produce, many of the
ablest statesmen, lawyers, publicists, theologians, historians, critics,
writers in prose and verse, men of thought and men of action, of
which the Anglo-Saxon race can boast.
—G.R. Parkin, describing the Rhodes Scholar, in
The Rhodes Scholarship (1913), quoted by Henry Erskine
Cowper, in 'British Education, Public and Private,
and the British Empire 1880–1930'.[1]

What does it mean to read a text from a culture different – and distant –
from your own? The ability to inhabit otherness – and to experience its
dialectical tension with the claim for empathy – resides at the heart of
literature. But literary studies and its attendant culture of pedagogy, in
the recent decades, have worried deeply about the interpretation of a
certain kind of otherness in texts. This is the kind of otherness that has
been historically held in a subordinate relation with the culture of the
interpretative authority – whether that authority be an individual or an
institution. Hence the sensitive cautiousness of a metropolitan reading
of a (post)colonial text – the kind that Gayatri Spivak talks about in
the chapter 'How to read a Culturally different book' in her *Aesthetic
Education in the Age of Globalization*.[2] Spivak's nuanced essay goes
beyond the usual challenges of the Western-metropolitan interpretation
of a postcolonial text, and in its detailed reading of R.K. Narayan's novel
The Guide, invokes questions of vernacularity and subalternity inherent
in the profession of temple dancers that defines the leading female
character. The awareness of cognitive and epistemological limits of
metropolitan cultures of interpretation is writ large in the essay. It is the
necessary and productive worry of a progressive interpretative vision
keen on the difficult task of doing epistemological justice to knowledge
about people and culture lesser known and represented, due to the very

subordinate or marginal relation they have had with the interpretative subjectivity.

Most of the readers I have been discussing in this book have had a problem of a radically different kind. A significant section of the texts they have been reading have come from worlds that are far away from their everyday reality, but which nonetheless positioned themselves as sources of authority. These are worlds that have established themselves as superior to those the readers inhabit with their body and physical memory. The reality of these texts, to them, has thus been both larger and unavoidable on one hand, and difficult to access on the other. It is, for the most part, the world predicated on the hierarchy of the metropolitan and the peripheral, framed by modern European colonialism and its control of the non-European world. The otherness these readers have faced in these texts that come to them pre-loaded with cultural authority, but in the texture of whose immediate reality they have had no personal or inherited connection. A vicarious inheritance is made possible by colonial domination, which has invested them with the cultural authority that becomes evident ever before the reality makes full sense.

Such literature, in the colony, becomes an alien authority – a powerful mythicizer that is, in the end, crucial and inaccessible. Such was V.S. Naipaul's memory of the literature that played an early formative role in his life – that it was 'of peculiar authority; but that literature was also like an alien mythology'.[3] 'There was, for instance', he wrote, 'Wordsworth's notorious poem about the daffodil. A pretty little flower, no doubt; but we had never seen it. Could the poem have any meaning for us?' In the end, it was a reflection, not of the reality of alien flowers, or of the literature they indexed, but of his own society, of its marginality and formlessness: 'It was really an expression of the dissatisfaction of the emptiness of our own formless, unmade society' in Trinidad that was thrown into relief by his distance from a celebrated symbol of English Romantic poetry. But decontextualized, liberated from history, as it were, the social realities within such texts also have a way of finding unexpected resonance with the uninformed but sensitive reader on the provincial margin. Many decades after Naipaul's bewilderment with the daffodil in colonial Trinidad, sitting in 1980s Benares, a young Pankaj Mishra read Edmund Wilson's explication of the soul-destroying social formation of the petit bourgeois in nineteenth-century France as caught in the novels of Gustave Flaubert – and shared it with an even unlikelier autodidact, Rajesh, the college goon, later to turn contract-killer. Nineteenth-century France was distant, remote, and impossible country for these readers dwelling so far in time and place, the names and the contexts unheard of. They made sense of Wilson's interpretation of Flaubert in terms of caste and tribal politics and violence in the Uttar Pradesh around them, touching the heart of the degradation by the petit bourgeois that seemed to straddle societies that looked nothing like one another.

The unpredictable empathies of literature sometimes exceed connections based on personal identity, as they did for Peter Abrahams, who felt he wanted to go to England, the land of the Romantic poets even more than he wanted to visit America, where the Harlem Renaissance had been brought about by Black men and women like him. He had stumbled upon them both, in the manner of the struggling autodidact, and while both had moved him deeply, in the end, he was keener to visit the land of Romantic poetry, the land of the men now dead whose 'songs had pierced the heart of a black boy, a world away, and in another time'.[4] Riveted by the world of nineteenth-century English novels, Sindiwe Magona made up their endings whenever torn and rejected books turned up for her through the generosity of neighbouring White employers but with pages missing. And even when colonial conditions were as nurturing as they could be, there were always glaring gaps in knowledge – as when C.L.R. James read Thackeray's *Vanity Fair* well over a dozen times without any awareness of its classic status. Even reading it with the love and intensity he brought to the book, he could only do so as an amateur, without the scaffolding of the right educational apparatus to support his reading.

The crucial question to ask, however, remains – why were these books there in the first place? Even in the gaping absence of their connection with the lives of people who came across them? What is by now the obvious answer was provided by Chinua Achebe in his 1993 essay, revealingly titled, 'The Education of a British-protected child': 'What we read in the school library at Umuahia were the books English boys would have read in England – *Treasure Island, Tom Brown's School Days, The Prisoner of Zenda, David Copperfield*, etc. They were not about us or people like us, but they were exciting stories.'[5] School and university curricula were a determining force as to what books would be available in the colony. 'In mid-nineteenth century India', writes Alexander Bubb, 'English-language imports and reprints were determined largely by school and university reading lists: set texts for Government schools circa 1852, for example, included *Hamlet, Othello*, and *Macbeth*; *Paradise Lost*; Otway's *Venice Preserved*, Bacon's *Essays*, Johnson's *Rasselas*, and Pope's *Iliad*; Goldsmith, Addison and Adam Smith – the Romantic poets long remained a notable omission.'[6]

The colonial origins of modern British education

By now it is obvious not just of any reader of this book, but indeed to any follower of postcolonial literary and educational history that it was the material and ideological reality of British imperialism that introduced a set of Western, and particularly English texts in the daily life of colonized subjects and kept them as part of their postcolonial legacy – even though the degree of volition with which such subjects wanted these texts varied widely both historically and personally. Ngũgĩ wa Thiong'o has written one of the most passionate of the manifestos against the colonization of African minds through European education, particularly through literary texts in his influential work *Decolonizing the Mind*, with Chinua Achebe celebrating the Africanization of English in his equally influential 'The African Writer and the English Language' – two texts that have defined conflicting dimensions of the role of European languages and literatures in the literary self-formation of Anglophone African nations for several decades. Beyond their crucial difference about the fate of English in Africa, both Achebe and Ngũgĩ agree on the pervasive and defining ideological influence of English texts and literary education on the private lives of individuals and the public lives of nations. The project of colonialism, both argue in different ways, would be incomplete without the soft power of humanistic education in the British colonies in Africa. But even within these colonies, we need to make a distinction for South Africa as it has appeared in this book. The intense and pervasive education deprivations experienced by the Black South African thinkers, writers, and activists that I have discussed were greatly aggravated by the White supremacy of Afrikaner nationalism that was both enclosed and embattled by the British Empire, particularly since the Anglo-Boer wars that set the stage for apartheid. The Afrikaner defeat in the South African War of 1902, previously known as the second Anglo-Boer War, deepened the crisis in Afrikaner identity that sought out White supremacy as a means of a national identity. The Bantu Education Act of 1953, which formalized the educational deprivation of Black South Africans, was the defining legislation of educational apartheid after the victorious National Party assumed power in 1948 and initiated the regime of racial segregation.

It feels deeply ironical that one of the key historical events that energized a long-term change in British educational policies in the nineteenth century was the first Anglo-Boer War of 1870, which the English lost. But historians, literary critics, and educationists have all variously accounted for the pervasive and multifarious ways Britain's global empire shaped and changed the British landscape of education, both domestically and abroad. Henry Erskine Cowper has pointed out that the loudest wake-up call for British education to become more globally competitive was the defeat in the first Anglo-Boer War, which also made them conscious of the poor preparation, training and research of the English next to their European rivals, most notably the Germans. 'The South African War', wrote H.G. Wells, 'laid bare an amazing and terrifying amount of national incompetence. The Empire was not only hustled into a war for which there was no occasion but that was planned with a lack of foresight and conducted with a lack of soundness that dismayed every thoughtful Englishman.'[7] The humiliation in what had seemed like a relatively minor war appeared as an omen for far greater defeats on the global stage: 'For the first time the educated British were enquiring whether all was well with the national system if so small a conquest seemed so great a task.'[8] Universal schooling and universal conscription were seen as great forces through which Germany had found ascendancy. Universal schooling and mass education, both in idea and practice, were to have a wide impact not only within Britain, but across its overseas empire as well. But the very incentive to restructure British education reveals the origin of the initiative as rooted in empire, and particularly to the unique situation in South Africa.

Historians of British education have repeatedly pointed to the colonial origins of change to national education policies in nineteenth-century Britain. 'Missionary societies and British humanitarians in the first half of the 19th century', writes Stephen Jackson, 'developed a powerful ideology of universal education that they applied both to the British working class and to colonial subjects.'[9] While missionaries played the most significant role in the spreading of education in the nineteenth century, the colonial state also started to take initiatives in mass education in the cases of Ireland, the West Indies, and India. Jackson points to the Negro Education Grant that was created by the imperial government after the abolition of slavery in the British Caribbean, set up to promote 'moral and religious education as a means of improving the children of freed people'.[10] State funding came from this grant in the West Indies, Mauritius, and the Cape from the 1830s to the 1840s, when it was abandoned in favour of industrial training.

The humanitarian vision of universal education designed by the missionaries was applicable to imperial subjects globally as a soft pathway to Christian conversion, even though the success of this conversion was uneven across empire. State intervention in Ireland, Jackson indicates, showed the way to the gradual acceptance of universal education in the metropole and in the settler colonies by the 1870s, though the project of mass education in non-White territories was also severely blunted from the mid-nineteenth century following the anti-colonial upheaval across the British Empire that caused racial attitudes to harden. The universality of education as initiated by the British and the White settlers, it has become clear from multiple sources, becomes riven by the question of race and anti-colonialism, and was supported and withdrawn accordingly even after their initiation as ideological support to Christianity and empire. The pattern of establishment of colonial universities in the White settler colonies of Australia, Canada, New Zealand, and South Africa (primarily the Cape Province) is, as such, quite different. Universities in these locations, Tamson Pietsch has shown, 'were not set up by British officials, as in India and later Africa, but rather by self-confident settler elites who saw them as both symbols and disseminators of European civilisation in the colonies'.[11]

These universities were meant to shape the young men who would eventually lead the colonial societies, and to this end, they sought to provide a classical and liberal education, often religious in character, very much in line with the two ancient universities in England. Founded on the universality and superiority of Western knowledge, they established themselves as its local representative, 'proudly proclaiming this position in the neo-gothic buildings they erected and the Latin mottos they adopted'.[12] They were, however, Pietsch reminds us, small and local affairs, at least in their early years, even though they modelled themselves on the capacious model of European universalism. Fashioned by colonial politics and frequently funded by the state, they were small institutions that served the sons of the colonial elite. 'As proud assertions of the maturity of colonial societies', Pietsch argues, 'and, at the same time, anxious agents in the quest to cultivate the culture and character of those who would lead them, in their early years settler universities were very much local institutions that sought to territorialise the structures of universal scholarship and turn them to parochial purposes.'[13]

The three English universities that had defining influences on the formation of institutions across the British Empire were those at Oxford, Cambridge, and London, with slightly different emphases – classics at Oxford, pure mathematics at Cambridge, and a cross-section of arts, languages, and sciences at London. But it was the University of London model, far more cost-efficient than that of Oxbridge, that was the greatest success in settler colonies such as New Zealand and South

Africa – and this was also the definitive influence in India, particularly through its centrality of examinations. Andre Beteille has pointed out that the structure of examinations helped widen the influence of the London model in India; likewise, Pietsch shows that this structure helped colonial nationalists wishing to centralize tertiary education in South Africa. From 1858 onwards, students from different Cape Town institutions could appear at 'higher' examinations set locally by the 'Board of Public Examiners in Literature and Science'.[14] In 1873, this board was converted into the 'University of the Cape of Good Hope', an examining and degree-granting body fashioned after the University of London.

Back in the metropole, the University of London was reconstituted with an imperial role in mind. Cowper quotes Sir Philip Magnus on the imperial role of the university: 'It is marked in this country by the birth of an enlarged sentiment of patriotism, embracing all our colonies and dependencies, which we call imperialism.'[15] The University of London was expected to act in accordance: 'A nation's educational institutions should be vivified by the spirit of the times; and in many ways the new university may be expected to respond to the Imperial idea.'[16] It would be open to 'students from every English speaking country' and would train them to the service of the global British Empire. One of the most manifest structures for the dissemination of British education worldwide was that of the Rhodes Scholarships, through which Oxford played the role of imperial unity. The Canadian-British educationist and later secretary of the Rhodes Trust, G.R. Parkin was an active and ardent champion of British imperialism who saw the scholarships as enabling close touch with a centre that had for many centuries produced scholars and practitioners of the widest range – 'men of thought and men of action, of which the Anglo-Saxon race can boast'.[17] Parkins' work in the active promotion of the cause and unity of empire showed the connection between education and imperialism, which was of course quite directly there in the will of the arch-imperialist Cecil John Rhodes. The will invested in the education of young colonists and at the same time instil into their minds 'the advantage to the colonies, as well as to the United Kingdom, of the retention of the unity of the Empire'.[18] Even though he hadn't attended a British public school himself, Rhodes' philosophy of education was quite attuned to the masculinist character-building vision of empire that came from these elite institutions, including the importance of 'manly outdoor sports' that helped to shape 'the moral force of character'.[19]

It was ironical the way in which the importance of character-training would resurface in the 1920s, with regard to the education of the African administrative class. Lord Lugard would argue that the formation of character was of higher importance in 'African native education than any other single ingredient',[20] and for this the new class had to be trained in residential schools amidst its emphasis on moral instruction. A similar point was made by F.G. Guggisberg, who believed that if character-training was omitted by school education, 'the progress of the African races will inevitably become a series of stumbles and falls'.[21] But in the nineteenth century, the issue of offering mass education to native populations was ridden with issues of racial ideology and conflict, upsetting the earlier humanitarianism of universal education to all imperial subjects. In settler contexts, Stephen Jackson has pointed out, this shaped child separation policies as Western universal education required the eradication of indigenous cultures. At the same time, universal education received little support as Britain scrambled into Africa – or even in the crown colony of India. But even as the colonial governments excluded non-White populations from mass education, indigenous elites came to demand such education in numerous contexts, particularly as they saw that it was a key to material and professional success.

Race, Jackson goes on to show, was a key factor in the belated arrival of mass education in South Africa, and according to the research by C. Soudien, the School Board Act of 1905 provided the first legal definition of race, where 'whites' had educational opportunities superior to those available to indigenous people, 'laying the groundwork for South African apartheid'.[22] Generally in the crown colonies, state-sponsored mass education lagged far behind the development of the settler colonies where local White people initiated successful educational missionaries. As Britain acquired more territories in Africa, education was mostly left to the missionaries, at least till the twentieth century. Colonial officials' occasional involvement in education was predicated on racial dynamics, 'while using the example of India as a "lesson" for Africa'.[23] For instance, in Fiji, the British provided education only for the sons of the local chiefs so that they could act as the intermediary for the colonial state, while ignoring mass education well into the twentieth century.[24] In most other cases, mass education to all was considered a poor investment and was even thought to be dangerous. In India, too, the nationalists adopted the language of universal education, demanding it from the British, even as they lay the groundwork of Indian independence.

Alien, dissident, amateur: colonial readers of western texts

The arrival of Western education in the British colonies turns out to be a far more staggered and uneven process than its imagination as the ideological accompaniment to imperialism allows. Between early missionary ideals of universal education, nineteenth-century conflicts around race, anti-colonialism, and native demand for such education, the policies and investments varied greatly. This is to say nothing of the territorial differences, such as between the settler and the crown colonies – between White settler initiatives for Western education and the eradication of indigenous cultures on one hand, and the tussle over such education between the indigenous elites and the White rulers in the crown colonies on the other. But what was the alchemy of interaction between Western education and non-white native populations once it was instituted among the latter? Beyond the larger historical facts of policy enactment along the British Empire, a sociological understanding of this process through which such education was received is important as a background against which to read the unique practices of amateur reading in the colonies.

Some of the most acute insights into this process have come from Sanjay Seth's work on applicability of Western knowledge systems to non-metropolitan and non-Western contexts brought about by modern European colonialism. In his book *Beyond Reason*, he makes a powerful bid at provincializing what he calls modern Western reason as it is at work in the social sciences, and the universalization of this reason through a historical process marked by global colonialism. His analysis of the imaginative social sciences, including history, anthropology, sociology, political sciences, has echoed deeply with me as I thought through questions about individualism and Romantic creativity, or the novel's rootedness in bourgeois Western modernity – questions which have variously appeared in the doubts and wonderings of the colonial self-makers who sought to connect metropolitan texts with their own artistic and intellectual growth. In fact, for Seth, one of the key historical moments for modern Western knowledge is the celebrated claim by Immanuel Kant that 'the Enlightenment marked "mankind's exit from its self-incurred immaturity"'.[25] The aesthetic modernity rooted in the Enlightenment found its way to the colonies through books and curricula as much as through the scattered, accidental pursuit of knowledge. While acknowledging the plurality of knowledges and disciplines that can be traced to Western modernity, Seth makes the bold claim that the precondition behind such knowledges is strikingly singular. This includes material conditions such as the division of education systems between primary, secondary, and tertiary, and the arrangement of knowledges into disciplines – the latter also foregrounded within a matrix of rewards and punishment by Lewis Gordon in his book *Disciplinary Decadence*. 'It's connotations', Gordon argues, 'over the millennia have shifted considerably to now referring in English to processes of control, at times linked with punishment in one instance and sycophantic allegiance and followers, as in disciples, in another'.[26] But beneath the materiality of disciplinary and pedagogic structures lie more fundamental assumptions about the very nature of knowledge – such as that knowledge is a relation between a subject and an object, that, since Descartes, became a matter of accurate representation in the mind or consciousness. Seth reminds us that 'to conceive knowledge as a subject-object relation, with representation of an independent reality as its essence, is not something obvious or given'.[27]

Seth's arguments about the historic process of the universalization of Western knowledge throw a sharper retrospective light on his earlier work on the Western education of colonial India. There, the 'failure' of the implementation of Western knowledge practices and archives in nineteenth-century India under British colonial policy is established as inappropriately understood, where the word 'failure' implies the realities of both intentionality and subjectivity not quite available in pre-colonial India. A common allegation, for instance, was that Indian students merely used Western knowledge for instrumental purposes – often narrowly with the purpose of getting a government job, dowry, or brighter marriage prospects – while keeping their emotional investment in local and vernacular languages and knowledge. But beyond questions of practical usage and professional association, there was a deeper epistemological disjuncture – if indeed epistemology is a valid category with which to define it. This disjuncture found various practical manifestations. One was the dissatisfaction with the Indian habit of rote-learning, which appears inimical to modern Western model of independent critical thinking, but which Seth demonstrates as embedded in a different subjectivity altogether, one which used memory and bodily/ performative forms of knowledge in both liturgical and secular fields of learning, such as arithmetic and grammar. Similar is the idea of the colonized subject experiencing a moral crisis upon experiencing Western education. Ironically, the experience of this crisis also required a Western imagination of the categories of religion and morality, with belief at the core – when such categories scarcely existed in pre-colonial India.

Seth's work on the reception of Western education in colonial India, however, is a study of larger patterns of knowledge reception across wide cross-sections of society; it is, in that sense, similar to Jonathan Rose's reading of autodidactic patterns across English working-class society, to which I referred earlier in this book. My project differs from both in its focus not so much on larger social patterns but on exceptional individuals and their reading and thinking programmes around the global British Empire. Even though I seek certain patterns in their marginalization in educational systems and their own attempts at autodidactism, it would be difficult to imagine them as individuals representative of a mass culture of reading. Christopher Hilliard's work on the global influence of the Leavises and the *Scrutiny* movement has cast meaningful light on curricular adoption of reading patterns by pointing out that while Leavis' students spread worldwide, including the colonial outposts, on the whole the Leavisite model of reading literature, through methods of 'close reading' or 'practical criticism' never found a significant foothold in the colonial university. The simple reason behind this was the fact that Cambridge was never the model adapted by the colonial university; it was primarily the University of London, and to a lesser degree, that of Oxford. 'University colleges in the empire', writes Hilliard, 'were often formally or informally governed by the federal University of London, not an institution where *Scrutiny* made an unusually deep impact.'[28] While there were colonial universities where Leavis was the 'guiding spirit' – Hilliard refers to Derek Attridge's experience of the University of Natal in the 1960s – such universities were exceptions rather than norms. Hilliard also dismisses as overstated claims about two Nigerian universities – Makarare and Ibadan – having 'Leavisite' English departments.[29] Colonial pedagogy and assessment methods were also shaped by the privileging of scholarship that was central to the Universities of London and Oxford rather than the idea and practice of criticism enshrined in Cambridge, though on rare instances, a conflict between the two created schisms, such as the University of Sydney in the 1960s.[30] The method of assessing knowledge through examinations must have worked better to establish scholarly knowledge than the methods of practical criticism, which could pedagogically demonstrate the kind of critical sensibility that was central to Cambridge.

The effect of these measures fell irregularly on the figures I have read in the chapters above. Native non-white populations were often vocal in their demand for Western education. Rosinka Chaudhuri, as we discussed in the preceding chapter, has demonstrated this convincingly with respect to nineteenth-century Bengal. Nirad C. Chaudhuri would be both an exemplary and idiosyncratic figure in this regard, in the voluminous, eclectic, and encyclopaedic knowledge of European history and literature that he cultivated and sought out on his own, even though his relation with the archetypal institution of colonial learning – the University of Calcutta – was highly irregular, with a first in the BA and failure in the MA. Toru Dutt's family illustrated another trend Sanjay Seth discusses – the Hindu Indian family converted to Christianity, the final goal of Western secular education that happened much more rarely than was expected, with new denominations such as the Arya Samaj and the Brahmo Samaj becoming more popular destinations for westernized Indians breaking away from traditional Hinduism. Both Chaudhuri and Mehrotra several decades after him variously express their frustration and discontent with the mass-examination model of assessment that was in vogue – at the universities at Calcutta and Allahabad, respectively. V.S. Naipaul's curricular experience of English literature in Trinidad also firmly bore the imprint of this British colonial education.

An anti-colonial spirit of gratitude

Provincializing Europe, Dipesh Chakrabarty had concluded, can never be a project of shunning European thought. 'For at the end of European imperialism', writes Chakrabarty, 'European thought is a gift to us all.'[31] Intriguingly, Sanjay Seth too makes it clear that his critique of the universalization of modern Western knowledge is offered on the very terms of that knowledge, and not on that of any of the precolonial knowledge systems that he discusses in *Beyond Reason*. I see the colonial and postcolonial readers in this book as doing something not very different – reading metropolitan Western texts with what Chakrabarty calls 'the anticolonial spirit of gratitude'.[32] They wanted the knowledge, the artistic and intellectual practices of a larger world, and their larger colonial and postcolonial environment ensured that they met texts from the metropolitan west – whether by accident or in the curriculum, in a library, school, college, bookshop, or community centre, or at home given by family or as inheritance from more privileged people, sometimes torn and rejected as garbage. Some of these were already named classics, though that naming might or might not be available to them, as with C.L.R. James' relationship with *Vanity Fair*, or even Peter Abrahams' approach to *Don Quixote*. Did they want to read these particular texts? Are human beings free in the desires they feel? What is the texture of freedom within a larger structure of unfreedom that is sometimes distant and sometimes immediate, sometimes invisible and sometimes felt too painfully? What does it mean to long for modernity in the domain of the intellectual and the artistic, particularly when the close proximity of an overpowering paradigm of that modernity awakens in you, subtly or directly, a desire for it that has foreclosed, or at least pushed to the margins, other ways of being in the world, including those that were once available to you through other traditions?

These questions were felt amidst a wide spectrum of comfort, poverty, pain, aimlessness, and nurturing. If for Dionne Brand the story of the Haitian Revolution was an accidental discovery prompted by a child's sweet tooth, for Toru Dutt French and English novels and poetry were part of a home-crafted pedagogy sometime under the tutelage of a loving father in an affluent, liberal home. If for Nirad C. Chaudhuri books of British history were the gift of a library where he sought refuge from a mechanical-bureaucratic, examination-driven education system, for Peter Abrahams, Romantic poetry and Harlem Renaissance literature came as unexpected gifts in a landscape where a humanist education was denied to him. Their conditions varied widely, and perhaps the only thing that united them was their unusual reading practice, not supported or credentialed by any institutional program, from which they were voluntary or involuntary exiles.

Was there a pattern in the education that dominated the historical landscape around them? Was there a pattern in the education they sought for themselves? Perhaps my real subject in this book is the dissonance between the two – which, I hope, has justified the 'amateur' in the book's title. Was there, indeed, a subliminal pattern in the dissonance between their alienation from established educational programmes and the textual self-making they carved for themselves? Did colonialism provide a material and ideological scaffolding for the dissonances experienced by these highly imaginative and deeply articulate individuals as they etched meandering trajectories of aesthetic education for themselves across the global reach of empire?

This is the making of selves as varied as possible – divergent not only in their contexts but in the particular circumstances of their transience, vulnerability, or sustainability. None is more transient here than the waif-like figure of Toru Dutt, dead from consumption at twenty-one before the nineteenth century was over, while all the others lived much longer lives, some of them still living and working. But self-making in this book also varies widely by ability, ambition, and goal: ranging from the attempts of Sindiwe Magona as a female domestic worker to complete a high-school education to V.S. Naipaul working his way towards a scholarship that would take him to Oxford and closer to his ambition to become a writer. That Magona's brother was a Rhodes Scholar to Oxford throws her own life, with its struggle with motherhood and labour to pointed relief, and tells us something about the particular obstacles women have faced in their projects of self-making.

Taken together, their relationship with these texts seems to connect to an important argument about reading as an ethical practice of self-improvement made recently by John Guillory. 'Reading in modernity', Guillory writes, 'I will argue, belongs to the category of what I will call ethical practice, by which I mean a practice of self-improvement, achieved in and through the experience of pleasure.'[33] Reading as a natural means of self-improvement also becomes, for Guillory, a persuasive case for what he calls 'lay reading', by undoing such reading's identification with mere consumption or entertainment. I see a productive, eternally unresolved tension between the amateur and the professional as essential to literary reading and critical practice that echoes with Guillory's claim that professional reading has never completely alienated the practice of lay reading, in spite of the apparent distance and hostility between the two. Equally importantly, Guillory sees the act of lay reading as situated in the domain of the ethical as it is 'a practice on the self' that is capable of being indefinitely cultivated or refined, in the sense what was called 'self-improvement' in the early modern period.[34] Guillory, however, does not mention Stephen Greenblatt's concept of Renaissance 'self-fashioning' or its relation to what he calls 'self-improvement' in the early modern age. I would insist on the amateur practice of the readers in this book as being pointedly different from Greenblatt's concept, which particularly describes the public construction of identity by noblemen. The figures I read come from various points on the colonial periphery and are distant from the kind of agency and privilege, as well as the social responsibility Renaissance noblemen would possess. Seeded in their self-making, however, is the writer, activist, or intellectual who would, usually decades later, dwell in the public or popular scale, regionally, nationally, or transnationally. But there is scarcely any hint of knowledge of that public identity in the years of tentative *Bildung* on which I focus, nor any idea at all that the flaws and mistakes of the early years will lay the foundation of a highly effective, popular amateurism later on.

Guillory argues for pleasure as the defining mark of the ethical act that is lay reading. It is through pleasure that self-improvement is sought. And I'm in agreement with him when he says that 'lay reading must be defended too', though he remains unsure if such reading can be brought into productive contact with the reading practice of literary scholars. Yet he leaves open the possibility of such a contact when he points to the infinite possibility of improving or renewing the pleasure of reading a text, particularly when such a demand is presented by the lay reader to the professoriate. 'The prevalence of this desire', Guillory writes, 'confronts the literary professoriate with a demand, however difficult it will be to imagine a response to this demand, a new relation to lay readers'.[35] Is it possible for the literary professoriate to have a new relation to lay readers? What kind of a relationship might that be? Would be relationship through which the professoriate would help to enhance the pleasure of lay reading without seeking to subsume them in the community of professional reading? Or would it be a symbiotic relation, in which the professoriate would gain something from lay reading as well?

By Guillory's own argument, lay reading is already a part of professional reading. Derek Attridge, too, has made a related argument, arguing the amateur reader as the precondition of the professional. 'Were it not for the experience of an individual reading, hearing, or seeing a literary work', writes Attridge, 'an experience repeated countless times through history and across geographical spaces and social classes, there would be no libraries of literary works; no literature classes or degrees; no funding for literary research; no call for literary editions, histories, biographies or exegeses; no literary academics, journals, or presses.'[36] Tom Lutz also points to the wide and universal relevance of amateurism as a precondition to professionalism when he writes: 'But people almost always love reading novels or poetry long before they have any professional relation to them. We readers are amateurs before we are anything else. We become critics, at least in part, as a result.'[37]

Lutz goes on to modify his definition of the critic much the way Antonio Gramsci had explained the role of the intellectual – that even though every person is an intellectual, not everyone has the role of an intellectual in society. 'They say everyone's a critic', Lutz writes, 'but they don't mean everyone writes criticism' (49).[38] My book, too, is less about the lay or amateur reader as a general social category than an exceptional group of individuals who read and wrote under variously adverse conditions but with the support of unusual imaginative and creative powers. These are readers whose flaws are generative. But are they outliers to the fullest degree? There is a humanity in their reading, including the fallibility, that is idiosyncratic yet rooted in the common humanity of all practices of reading. Just the way, as Guillory points out, professional reading encloses within itself principles of lay reading, these exceptional readers, too, simultaneously transcend and remain rooted in their respective communities, straddled by various conditions of exclusion and marginalization. The rootedness might be deeper and more obvious with activist-thinkers such as Sindiwe Magona and Es'kia Mphahlele than with a novelist with greater private ambition such as V.S. Naipaul, but it is always there, and manifest throughout the writers' oeuvre no matter where their subsequent location is.

I invoked professional-scholarly debates about reading in the second chapter of this book with the claim that academic cultures of reading have something to take from reading practices of these postcolonial amateurs, and even particularly from their flaws in knowledge. That flawed reading is not just always a becoming, an act on the way of correcting itself, but a practice with its own unique and unexpected rewards. What can professional reading learn from it? It can, perhaps, take a cue from it to move away from a dominant preoccupation with historical context – from the claims of scholarship as Joseph North has put it – to the model of what he has identified as criticism as a programme of aesthetic education. That context 'stinks' and that readers may need a liberation from it has also been claimed by Rita Felski and Bruno Latour. What else? The courage of reading in adversity, the indefatigable will to do so, the ability to inhabit overpowering otherness, the relentless desire to make oneself against all odds – none of these are negligible traits, but none in particular abundance in metropolitan-professional culture of reading today. But the possibility of benefit to professional reading cultures is scarcely the most compelling reason to look at these postcolonial reading practices. They have thrived, and continue to do so, in their own right, and that alone is a good enough reason to take a long look at them, which is what this book has tried to do.

Reading the Other: insights misplaced and unexpected

It is important to reaffirm at the end of this book that in their reading of texts from distant cultures, these colonial and postcolonial readers were sometimes perceptive beyond their own consciousness just as often as they struck what has historically (and often politically) been established as the wrong chord. But it is precisely their ignorance about both their strength and weakness that defines their amateurism. I would like to conclude with an example of each. Take for instance, V.S. Naipaul writing in his memoir-essay, 'Reading and Writing':

> But we read at different times for different things. We take to novels our own ideas of what the novel should be: and those ideas are made by our needs, our education, our background or perhaps our ideas of our background.[39]

Quickly after this candid account of self-motivated and self-directed reading, Naipaul makes an observation that was to be of defining influence on his own novel-writing career:

> It came to me that the great novelists wrote about highly organized societies. I had no such society; I couldn't share the assumptions of the writers; I didn't see my world reflected in theirs. My colonial world was more mixed and secondhand, and more restricted.[40]

It is this sense of historical and cultural inadequacy that would eventually impel Naipaul to shape the fictional world that he did, deriving inspiration from the enigmatic figure of Joseph Conrad whom he mentions in the sentence that immediately follows the passage that I have quoted. What is more important for me at the moment is that he seems to read the tradition of 'great novelists' in accordance with a dominant critical tradition that has only been overturned fairly recently. This is the scholarly tradition of the novel originating in bourgeois Western modernity, in an organized middle-class and print culture in a state of considerable capitalist advancement. The maturity and organization of the society that was the work of Enlightenment modernity was therefore the birthplace of the novel, as has been variously argued by scholars like Ian Watt and Franco Moretti. With the Hindu-Trinidadian society of his origin lacking such maturity and organization, Naipaul felt diffident about his possibility as a novelist. Was this a latent resonance with professional scholarly arguments about the novel that were made in the most pointed way in the middle and the second half of the twentieth century? Or was it a more general response to the dominant zeitgeist about modernity and literary form?

It was only in the second decade of the twenty-first century that the scholar Srinivas Aravamudan would make an argument about the origin of the novel that would overturn the traditional wisdom about its origin in bourgeois Western modernity and go on to show that the novel might have been closer to Naipaul's inherited cultures than conventional wisdom had revealed so far. 'Oriental tales, pseudoethnographies, sexual fantasies, and political utopias', Aravamudan argued, that created speculations about a largely imaginary east, were all variously complicit in the rise of the novel through the antecedent genre of the romance.[41] The domestic bourgeois realism that dominant scholarship has seen as central to the rise of the novel was in fact far more marginal, next to the extravagant genres that shaped Enlightenment orientalism. 'Thus scholars', writes Aravamudan, 'need to reexamine the system of eighteenth-century fictional genres, their circulation, and ways that relative hierarchies have been altered to impose certain outcomes.'[42]

I cannot help but place Naipaul's anxiety about the socio-cultural character of the novel, not only as an aspiring practitioner but also as an amateur reader, next to the radically changing professional-scholarly evaluation about the genre's origins that have continued through his own lifetime. I'm fascinated by the way the vicissitudes in scholarly arguments reflect both Naipaul's own misgivings about his culture's suitability to the novel and the hidden proximity of such cultures, particularly of his Hindu Asian heritage, to the novel that had eluded him during the crucial moments of his self-making. The reality of that hidden adjacency must have returned to him soon, possibly at that moment in London when the streets of Trinidad, left far behind, came back to him, dreamlike, to finally set off his journey as a writer. For professional scholarship, too, things have come full circle as a figure like Naipaul has crucially helped to shape and define the modern postcolonial English novel even as the story of its origin has been persuasively decolonized.

Time brings its own wisdom. Scholarship builds not only on the insights of time but on the edifices of past scholarship, which makes the passage of time loaded with new insights. Belonging and affiliation to a larger community are key markers of professionalism. One of the conditions of the colonial amateurs in my book is their loneliness, particularly at formative moments of their *Bildung*; it is the loneliness that deepens their idiosyncrasy, mark their imaginations as unique. It is also loneliness that makes their relationship with professional scholarship, itself a changeable force, highly irregular and uneven, capable of hidden resonances, absurdities, and other madnesses. Sitting in the libraries of British Calcutta, fleeing the bureaucratized tedium of the classroom in the colonial university, Nirad C. Chaudhuri sought encyclopaedic knowledge, which he knew had already been rendered unprofessional and irrelevant by the rise of the specialist in the nineteenth century.

But he was also in the pursuit of something else, something he felt was more realistically attainable – objectivity in historical scholarship. Historiography must work towards the objectivity of science; partisan historiography, whether from nineteenth-century Germany or anti-colonial India, was for him a betrayal of the objective reason of history. 'Who would', he wrote, 'think of judging the world by standards either Indian or European? It must take its stand on broader human grounds.'[43]

Chaudhuri's quest for a universal, scientific objectivity in historical scholarship stemmed largely from his admiration of British historians, notably, Edward Gibbon, Theodor Mommsen, and James Bryce. It is an admiration that looks deeply ironic next to the critiques of British and European historiography made in the twenty-first century by postcolonial historians like Dipesh Chakrabarty. What Chaudhuri admired as objectivity in historical scholarship now looks suspiciously like historicism, which, according to Chakrabarty, 'enabled European domination of the world in the nineteenth century'.[44] Implicit in this 'objectivity' is the philosophy of progress, which moved from savagery to civilization that European colonial domination helped to facilitate. And Priya Satia, a British historian particularly sensitive to the epistemological sway of imperial power, has pointed out more recently that ever since the eighteenth century, history as a discipline has been as rooted in the narrative of 'great men' and their political ambition as in the pedagogic crafting of more such great men of the future who would drive the ship of British imperialism all across the world. It was therefore inevitable that 'the rule of historians coincided with the era of British imperialism'.[45] Was Chaudhuri's celebration of the 'scientific objectivity' of British historiography the unavoidable fallacy of the autodidact? Or was it perhaps the pro-imperial blind spot of an eccentric reader whose messy amateurism has otherwise thwarted the British project of professionalizing a certain kind of English-educated subject?

One thing remains clear. These readers were not afraid to read culturally different books – to use Gayatri Spivak's phrase from a different context. We may question their freedom and agency to do so, which is a question that must be addressed against the larger background of the colonized subject's demand for Western education. As such, we may be sceptical of their acceptance of, or desire for, the implicit and explicit authority of Western texts and the promise of cosmopolitanism they augured. While aggravated by their alienation from institutional education, their mistakes were also largely rooted in the radical disjuncture between the immediate reality of their lives and the reality contained in the texts they read, distant from them not only in time and place but importantly, in cultural heritage. In this, they were performing the key function of reading literature – the experiencing of radical alterity that shapes the key element of the reading experience. Neither did it prevent them from turning that radical alterity, whenever they could, to a fractured empathy, thus returning to the endless tension of the alien and the familiar that defines the aesthetic experience. But the process involved striking acts of ignorance, of mistakes and misreading – failings that in the fullness of time have revealed themselves to be resonant with larger, invisible truths as well as misapprehensions of historical and political reality.

Their relationship with literature was enclosed by their larger relation with imperialism, and yet the former could never be reduced to the latter, or even to direct polemic or resistance against it. There were unexpected moments of celebration. In the Diocesan Training College in Pietersburg, Peter Abrahams met the 'big, gentle-natured' Afrikaner teacher, Mr Jansen, who not only helped him overcome the 'reserve all non-whites have towards Boers', but introduced him to the beauty of Afrikaans language and literature, a language that, in the twentieth century, came to be identified with the worst of Afrikaner nationalism and apartheid rule.[46] Afrikaans has a complex history in South Africa, notwithstanding its Dutch origin, particularly given the language's early life in the Arabic script and its ownership by indigenous groups as a creolized African language. But throughout the apartheid years, it came to be established, more than anything else, as the language of racial oppression, particularly following its identification as the vehicle of Afrikaner nationalism after the second Anglo-Boer War of 1902. Abrahams had all the reasons of the Black community's suspicion of that language, and yet it was a crucial moment of his *Bildung* when Mr Jansen introduced him to the power of its literature: 'Through him I discovered the rich body of Afrikaner literature and the beauty of the language itself.'[47]

The examples proliferate with each reader. The crucial years of Dionne Brand's self-making as a writer drew together the burning force of two unlikely books – *The Black Napoleon* which chronicled the Haitian Revolution, and D.H. Lawrence's novel of desire, *Lady Chatterley's Lover*, the Englishness of the latter book invisible to the growing girl who was to be a powerful memoirist of diasporic Blackness. With Peter Abrahams again, the English Romantic poets were no less powerful a developmental influence than the poets and chroniclers of the Harlem Renaissance. The latter showed him that poems and songs could be created about Black figures like him, but the English Romantic poets had made 'songs had pierced the heart of a black boy, a world away, and in another time.'[48] And we all know the story of C.L.R. James' great immersion in the world of Victorian novels, most deeply in that of W.M. Thackeray and at its deepest in the unrecognized (to himself) classic of *Vanity Fair*. No matter how closely we identify the Barbadian origin of the Trinidadian James (through his mother's side) and the close links to English culture and the Anglican Church the Barbadian African link brought with it, James' literary Victorianism remains enigmatic next to his later life as a radical Black socialist. And it remains the strangest that he writes *Beyond a Boundary*, with all its mellow recollection of the fondness and attachment to English literary, church, and sports culture precisely from the point of his life when he is deeply immersed in fierce anti-colonial thought and struggle. The relationship between imperialism, culture, celebration, and resistance is never transparent or predictable with the greatest thinkers who bring them together.

These were people who wondered about the absence of people like them in the literature they read, mulling for a moment about the invisibility of the daffodil in the flora around them but immersing themselves in the literature nonetheless, rather than dismissing the culture of the imperialist altogether, as recent zeitgeist would have it. British colonialism brought them deeper into the culture of print modernity that intensified the private culture of reading that seems to be facing a transformational crisis in the global present. In that sense, they are also the last of a breed of transnational readers for whom books were only the way to a wider world, no matter how erratic or misdirected their journeys were. It was perhaps the immersive, bittersweet experience of reading and misreading this alien literature lingering over them like a mythology that finally led them to create literature where people of their skin and culture, and people mixed up in every which way, would play defining roles. It is the important story of the origin and development of postcolonial literature that bears many retellings.

NOTES

Chapter 1

1   Nirad C. Chaudhuri, *The Autobiography of an Unknown Indian* (New York: Macmillan, 1951), 333.

2   Louis Althusser, 'Ideology and Ideological State Apparatuses (Notes Towards and In Investigation)', in *Lenin and Philosophy and Other Essays*, trans Ben Brewster (New York: New York University Press, 2001).

3   Ngũgĩ wa Thiong'o, 'The African Writer and the English Language', in *Colonial Discourse and Post-Colonial Theory: A Reader*, Ed. Patrick Williams and Laura Chrisman (New York: Columbia University Press, 1994), 436.

4   Chris Baldick, *The Social Mission of English Criticism, 1848–1932* (Oxford: Clarendon, 1983), Gauri Viswanathan, *Masks of Conquest: Literary Study and British Rule in India* (New York: Columbia University Press, 1989), Rosinka Chaudhuri, 'Macaulay's Magic Hat: The Colonial Education System and the Canon of World Literature', in *Handbook of Anglophone World Literatures*, Eds. Stefan Helgesson, Birgit Neumann, & Gabriele Rippl (Berlin/Boston: De Gruyter, 2020) 41–53, *Gentlemen Poets in Colonial Bengal: Emergent Nationalism and the Orientalist Project* (Kolkata: Seagull, 2002), Sanjay Seth, *Subject Lessons: The Western Education of Colonial India* (Durham & London: Duke University Press, 2007).

5   Paolo Freire, *Pedagogy of the Oppressed*, trans Myra Bergman Ramos (New York: Bloomsbury Academic, 2000), bell hooks, *Teaching to Transgress: Education as the Practice of Freedom* (London: Routledge, 1994), Gayatri Chakravarty Spivak, *An Aesthetic Education in the Age of Globalization* (Cambridge, MA: Harvard University Press, 2013).

6   Ankhi Mukherjee, *What Is a Classic? Postcolonial Rewriting and Invention of the Canon* (Stanford: Stanford University Press, 2014), 1.

7   V.S. Naipaul, *Literary Occasions: Essays* (New York: Vintage, 2004), 37.

8   Abdulrazak Gurnah, 'Learning to Read', in *Map Reading: The Nobel Lecture and Other Writings* (London: Bloomsbury, 2021), 7.

9   Ibid., 7.

10   Ibid.

11   J.M. Coetzee, 'The Novel in Africa', in *Elizabeth Costello* (New York: Penguin, 2004).

12   Rita Felski, *Hooked: Art and Attachment* (Chicago: University of Chicago Press, 2020).

13   Lauren Berlant, *Cruel Optimism* (Durham & London: Duke University Press, 2011).

14   Amitav Ghosh, 'The March of the Novel through History: The Testimony of My Grandfather's Bookcase; Text of the Arthur Ravencroft Memorial Lecture, delivered at the University of Leeds, 5 March 1997', *Kunapipi* 19 (3), 1997, 3–4.

15 John Guillory, *Cultural Capital: The Problem of Literary Canon Formation* (Chicago: University of Chicago Press, 1993).

16 Ghosh, 'The March of the Novel through History', 5.

17 Marjorie Garber, *Academic Instincts* (Princeton: Princeton University Press, 2001).

18 Ibid., 4.

19 John Guillory, *Professing Criticism: Essays on the Organization of Literary Study* (Chicago: University of Chicago Press, 2022), 50.

20 Ibid.

21 Joseph North, *Literary Criticism: A Political History* (Cambridge, MA: Harvard University Press, 2017).

22 Guillory, *Professing Criticism*, 7.

23 Ibid.

24 Ibid., 9.

25 Merve Emre, 'Has Academia Ruined Literary Criticism?' *The New Yorker*, 16 January 2023.

26 Guillory, *Professing Criticism*, 19.

27 Kenneth Burke, *Performance and Change: An Anatomy of Purpose*, quoted in Guillory, *Professing Criticism*, 29–30.

28 Guillory, *Professing Criticism*, 30.

29 Tobias Skivereen, 'Postcritique and the Problem of the Lay Reader', *NLH: New Literary History* 53 (1), Winter 2022, 164.

30 Guillory, *Professing Criticism*, 12.

31 Garber, *Academic Instincts*, 5.

32 Ibid., 5.

33 Bruce Robbins, *Secular Vocations: Intellectuals, Professionalism, Culture* (London & New York: Verso, 1993), 18.

34 Ibid., 75.

35 Qtd. in Garber, *Academic Instincts*, 15.

36 Ibid.

37 Ibid., 17.

38 Baldick, *The Social Mission of English Criticism, 1848–1932* and Terry Eagleton, 'The Rise of English', in *Literary Theory: An Introduction*, Ed. Eagleton (Minneapolis: University of Minnesota Press, 1996).

39 Baldick, *The Social Mission of English Criticism, 1848–1932*, 34.

40 Ibid., 61.

41 Ibid., 72.

42 Viswanathan, *Masks of Conquest*, 3.

43 Roger Kimball, 'Schiller's Aesthetic Education', *New Criterion*, March 2001.

44 Qtd. in ibid.

45 NA XX, 396/E 163, qtd. in ibid.

46 Gayatri Chakravarty Spivak, 'How to Read a Culturally Different Book', in *An Aesthetic Education in the Age of Globalization*, Ed. Spivak, 73–96 (Cambridge, MA: Harvard University Press, 2013).

47　Simon During, 'The Postcolonial Aesthetic', *PMLA* 129 (3), May 2014, 500.

48　Ibid., 501.

49　Mukherjee, *What Is a Classic*, 4–5.

50　Sanjay Seth, *Beyond Reason: Postcolonial Theory and the Social Sciences* (New York: Oxford University Press, 2021), 15.

51　Jonathan Rose, *The Intellectual Life of the British Working Classes* (New Haven: Yale University Press, 2002), 6.

52　Ibid.

53　Ibid.

54　Ibid., 4–5.

55　Tom Lutz, 'In the Shadow of the Archive', in *The Critic as Amateur*, Eds Saikat Majumdar & Aarthi Vadde (New York: Bloomsbury Academic, 2019), 54.

56　Ibid., 55.

57　Rose, *The Intellectual Life of the British Working Classes*, 1.

58　Regenia Gagnier, *Subjectivities: A History of Self-Representation in Britain, 1832–1920* (New York: Oxford, 1991), 140.

59　Ibid., 140.

60　Ibid.

61　Grant Farred, *What's My Name? Black Vernacular Intellectuals* (Minneapolis: University of Minnesota Press, 2003), 1.

62　Ibid., 4.

63　Ibid., 18.

64　Ibid.

65　Ngũgĩ wa Thiong'o, 'Prophet Mphahlele: Named after Ezekiel', foreword to *Down Second Avenue*, by Es'kia Mphahlele (New York: Penguin Books, 2013), 2.

66　Garber, *Academic Instincts*, 21.

67　Edward W. Said, *Representations of the Intellectual: The 1993 Reith Lectures* (New York: Vintage Books, 1994), 74.

68　Andy Merrifield, *The Amateur: The Pleasures of Doing What You Love* (London: Verso, 2017).

69　Said, *Representations of the Intellectual*, 82–3.

70　Ibid., 83.

71　Emre, 'Has Academia Ruined Literary Criticism?'

72　*New Literary History, Volume 48, Number 1, Winter 2017.*

73　*The Critic as Amateur*, Eds Saikat Majumdar & Aarthi Vadde (New York: Bloomsbury Academic, 2019).

74　Dipesh Chakrabarty, *The Calling of History: Sir Jadunath Sarkar and His Empire of Truth* (Chicago: The University of Chicago Press, 2015), 4–5.

75　Janice Radway, *Reading the Romance: Woman, Patriarchy, and Popular Literature* (Chapel Hill: University of North Caroline Press, 1984), Merve Emre, *Paraliterary: The Making of Bad Readers in Postwar America* (Chicago: University of Chicago Press, 2017).

Chapter 2

1   Sindiwe Magona, *Forced to Grow* (Claremont: David Philip, 1992), 71.

2   Daniel Coleman, *In Bed with the Word: Reading, Spirituality, and Cultural Politics* (Edmonton: University of Alberta Press, 2009), 4.

3   Ibid., 3.

4   Ibid., 7–8.

5   Ibid., 7.

6   Nathan Snazza, *Animate Literacies: Literature, Affect, and the Politics of Humanism* (Durham: Duke University Press, 2019), 17.

7   Partha Chatterjee, *Nation and Its Fragments: Colonial and Postcolonial Histories* (Princeton: Princeton University Press, 1993), 140–3.

8   Snazza, *Animate Literacies*, 131.

9   Louis Althusser, 'Ideology and Ideological State Apparatuses', trans Ben Brewster (https://www.marxists.org/reference/archive/althusser/1970/ideology.htm), first published in *La Pensée*, 1970.

10 Snazza, *Animate Literacies*, 130.

11 Ibid.

12 While as a Subaltern Studies historian Chakrabarty has been keenly aware of the spectral limits of rationalism in historical scholarship, his later book, *The Calling of History: Sir Jadunath Sarkar and His Empire of Truth*, must be acknowledged as his attempt as a present-day historian to seriously engage with an older scholar's commitment to attain objective truth in historical scholarship, after a fashion that has been long discredited (which partly accounts for Sarkar's fall from grace as an academic scholar, as Chakrabarty describes in detail in his book). 'What cannot be missed, though', writes Chakrabarty, 'is the connection that existed between Sir Jadunath's insistence on cultivation of a certain truthfulness on the part of the historian – the demand that the historian make a sincere attempt to rise above his or her own times and interests – and his ideas about historical truth' (*The Calling of History*, 32). The aspiration to this ideal of historical truth entailed continuous self-effacement by the historian: 'A certain cultivation of self-denying ethics in the personhood of the historian, a practice of ascesis, was therefore essential, for without that, the historian could not receive the truth the facts told' (*Calling*, 33). Such a truth-claim, Chakrabarty knows, will sound strange to historians today when scholarly objectivity is understood not so much as metaphysical as procedural, dependent on the methods and processes of professional scholarship in its material form, i.e., journals, presses, and peer review.

13 Dipesh Chakrabarty, *Provincializing Europe: Postcolonial Thought and Historical Difference* (Princeton: Princeton University Press, 2000), particularly the chapter 'Minority Histories, Subaltern Pasts'.

14 See, in addition to Chakrabarty, above, Ranajit Guha, 'The Prose of
    Counter-Insurgency', in *Selected Subaltern Studies*, Ed. Ranajit Guha &
    Gayatri Chakravarty Spivak (Oxford: Oxford University Press, 1988),
    45–84.
15 See, for instance, the association of queerness and failure in the work
    of Jack Halberstam and Heather Love. Jack Halberstam, *The Queer Art
    of Failure* (Durham: Duke University Press, 2011), Heather Love, *Feeling
    Backward: Loss and the Politics of Queer History* (Cambridge, MA:
    Harvard University Press, 2007).
16 Snazza, *Animate Literacies*, 81.
17 Julietta Singh, *Unthinking Mastery: Dehumanism and Decolonial
    Entanglements* (Durham, NC: Duke University Press, 2018), 10.
18 Ibid., 10.
19 Derek Attridge, *J.M. Coetzee and the Ethics of Reading: Literature in the
    Event* (Chicago: University of Chicago Press, 2004).
20 J. Daniel Elam, *World Literature for the Wretched of the Earth* (New York:
    Fordham University Press, 2021), IX–X.
21 Ibid., 9.
22 Gagnier, *Subjectivities*, 148.
23 Daniel Elam, *World Literature for the Wretched of the Earth*, 16.
24 Franco Moretti, 'Conjectures on World Literature', *New Left Review*,
    January/February 2000, https://newleftreview.org/issues/ii1/articles/
    franco-moretti-conjectures-on-world-literature.
25 Joseph North, *Literary Criticism: A Brief Political History* (Cambridge,
    MA: Harvard University Press), 5.
26 Ibid., 1–2.
27 Ibid., 2.
28 Ibid., 7.
29 Priya Satia, *Time's Monsters: How History Makes History* (Cambridge, MA:
    Harvard University Press, 2020).
30 Stephen Best & Sharon Marcus, 'Surface Reading: An Introduction',
    Representations 108 (1), Fall 2009, 2.
31 Ibid., 6.
32 North, *Literary Criticism* 11.
33 Guillory, *Professing Criticism*, 243.
34 Ibid., 246.
35 Ibid., 251.
36 Rita Felski, *The Limits of Critique* (Chicago: University of Chicago Press,
    2015), 20.
37 Ibid., 81–2.
38 Ibid., 38.
39 Best, 'Surface Reading', 12–13.
40 Tobias Skivereen, 'Postcritique and the Problem of the Lay Reader', *NLH:
    New Literary History* 53 (1), Winter 2022, 176.

41 Ibid.
42 Merve Emre, *Paraliterary: The Making of Bad Readers in Postwar America* (Chicago: University of Chicago Press, 2017), 20.
43 Coleman, *In Bed with the Word*, 10.
44 Dionne Brand, *A Map to the Door of No Return: Notes to Belonging* (Toronto: Doubleday Canada, 2001), 182.
45 Ibid., 148.
46 V.S. Naipaul, *Literary Occasions: Essays* (New York: Vintage, 2004), 32.
47 Jamaica Kincaid, *A Small Place* (New York: Farrar, Straus, and Giroux, 1988), 31.
48 Brand, *A Map to the Door of No Return*, 149.
49 Ibid.
50 Coleman, *In Bed with the Word*, 12.
51 Saikat Majumdar, see the abstract of 'The Provincial Polymath: The Curious Cosmopolitanism of Nirad C Chaudhuri', *PMLA* 130 (2), 2015 (https://www.cambridge.org/core/journals/pmla/article/abs/provincial-polymath-the-curious-cosmopolitanism-of-nirad-c-chaudhuri/93957DE8 62335E5A5467C7317C95CEF3).
52 Felski, *The Limits of Critique*.
53 Emre, *Paraliterary*, 8, 10.
54 Ibid., 16–17.
55 Ibid., 47.
56 Ibid., 97.
57 Ibid., 137.
58 Ibid., 179.
59 Ibid., 20.
60 Paul St. Amour, 'Weak Theory, Weak Modernism', *Modernism/Modernity*, 3 (3), 25 August, 28, https://modernismmodernity.org/articles/weak-theory-weak-modernism.
61 Kara Wittman, 'New, Interesting, and Original – The Undergraduate as Amateur', in *The Critic as Amateur*, Eds Saikat Majumdar & Aarthi Vadde (New York: Bloomsbury Academic, 2019), 247.

Chapter 3

1 These racial terms, institutionalized under apartheid legislation, have often been asserted as preferred markers of identity by such writers and activists, as with the figures discussed in this chapter, though the controversies around them have not disappeared. The term 'coloured', descriptive of the mixed-race population in South Africa, is very different from what its historical connotation has been in the United States.
2 Es'kia Mphahlele, *The African Image* (London: Faber, 1974), 66.
3 Ibid., 58.

4   William Bloke Modisane, *Blame Me on History* (Johannesburg & Cape Town: Ad Donker Publishers, 1986), 94.
5   Ibid.
6   Mphahlele, *The African Image*, 60.
7   David Attwell & Derek Attridge, 'Introduction', in *The Cambridge History of South African Literature*, Eds. Attridge & Attwell (Cambridge: Cambridge University Press, 2011), 5.
8   Mphahlele, *The African Image*, 64.
9   Ibid., 90.
10 Ibid.
11 Zoë Wicomb, *You Can't Get Lost in Cape Town* (New York: Feminist Press at the City University of New York, 2000).
12 Njabulo Ndebele, *Fools and Other Stories* (Johannesburg: Pan Macmillan South Africa, 2006).
13 Wicomb, *You Can't Get Lost in Cape Town*, 1.
14 Ibid., 2.
15 Ibid., 9.
16 Sindiwe Magona, *Living, Loving and Lying Awake at Night* (Northampton, MA: Interlink Books, 2009), 37.
17 Ibid., 38.
18 Ibid., 41.
19 Ibid., 42.
20 Ndebele, *Fools and Other Stories*, 156.
21 Modisane, *Blame Me on History*, 309.
22 Ndebele, *Fools*, 90.
23 Hedley Twidle, 'Experiments with Truth: Narrative Nonfiction in South Africa', *Current Writing: Text and Reception in Southern Africa* 31 (2), 2019, 95.
24 Peter Abrahams, *Tell Freedom: Memories of Africa* (New York: Knopf, 1954), 172.
25 Ibid., 174.
26 Ibid., 177.
27 Ibid., 181.
28 Ibid., 189.
29 Ibid.
30 Ibid., 192.
31 Ibid., 218.
32 Ibid., 224–5.
33 Ibid., 225.
34 Ibid.
35 Ibid., 226.
36 Ibid.
37 Qtd in ibid., 230.
38 Ibid.

39 Ibid., 234.
40 Ibid., 253.
41 Ibid., 254.
42 Ibid., 260.
43 Ibid.
44 Ibid., 261.
45 Ibid., 266–7.
46 Ibid., 273.
47 The earliest mission schools were Scottish Presbyterian, then Methodist; the Anglicans followed, and were followed by Catholic missionaries.
48 Ibid., 296.
49 Ibid., 298.
50 Ibid., 343.
51 Ibid., 346.
52 Ibid., 349.
53 Ibid., 351.
54 Ibid., 357.
55 Sindiwe Magona, *To My Children's Children* (Claremont: David Philip, 1990), 90.
56 Ibid., Preface: From a Xhosa Grandmother.
57 Magona, *To My Children's Children*, 26.
58 Ibid., 26–7.
59 Ibid., 27.
60 Ibid., 42.
61 Ibid.
62 Ibid., 49.
63 Ibid., 59.
64 Ibid., 79.
65 Ibid.
66 Sindiwe Magona, *Forced to Grow* (Claremont: David Philip, 1992), 15.
67 Ibid., 18.
68 Ibid., 43.
69 Ibid., 78.
70 Ibid., 80.
71 Ibid., 79.
72 Ibid., 71.
73 Magona, *To My Children's Children*, 89.
74 Ibid., 98.
75 Ibid., 99.
76 Magona, *Forced to Grow*, 43.
77 Ibid., 46.
78 Ibid., 51.
79 Ibid., 183–4.
80 Ibid., 184.

81   Ibid.
82   Ngũgĩ wa Thiong'o, 'Prophet Mphahlele: Named after Ezekiel', foreword
     to *Down Second Avenue*, by Es'kia Mphahlele (New York: Penguin
     Books, 2013), 1.
83   Ibid., 2.
84   Ibid., 3.
85   Ibid., 4.
86   Ibid.
87   Mphahlele, *Down Second Avenue*, 24.
88   Ibid., 36.
89   Ibid., 39.
90   Ibid.
91   Ibid., 72.
92   Ibid., 73.
93   Ibid.
94   Ibid., 107.
95   Ibid.
96   Ibid., 109.
97   Ibid.
98   Ibid., 109.
99   Ibid., 111.
100 Ibid., 112.
101 Ibid.
102 Ibid.
103 Ibid., 118.
104 Ibid., 146.
105 Modisane, *Blame Me on History*, 41.
106 Ibid.
107 Mphahlele, *Down Second Avenue*, 146.
108 Ibid., 147.
109 Mphahlele, *The African Image*, 66.
110 Mphahlele, *Down Second Avenue*, 147.
111 Ibid., 148.
112 Ibid.
113 Ibid., 161.
114 Ibid.
115 Ibid.
116 Ntongela Masilela, 'New African Modernity and the New African
     Movement', in *The Cambridge History of South African Literature*, Eds
     David Attwell & Derek Attridge (Cambridge: Cambridge University
     Press, 2011), 334.
117 Mphahlele, *Down Second Avenue*, 170.
118 Ibid.
119 Ibid., 171.

120 Ibid.

121 Ibid., 173.

122 Ibid.

123 Ibid., 174.

124 Ibid.

125 Ibid.

126 Ibid., 175.

127 Graham Pechey, Foreword to *South African Literature and Culture: Rediscovery of the Ordinary*, by Njabulo Ndebele (Scotsville: University of KwaZulu Natal Press, 2006), 5.

128 Mphahlele, *Down Second Avenue*, 170.

129 Saikat Majumdar, 'The Dailiness and Trauma and Liberation in Zoë Wicomb', in *Prose of the World: Modernism and the Banality of Empire*, Ed. Majumdar (New York: Columbia University Press, 2013), 101–33.

130 Ndebele, *South African Literature and Culture*, 58.

131 Ibid., 68.

132 Ibid.

133 Ibid., 126.

134 Ibid.

135 Ibid., 127.

136 Ibid., 134.

137 Ibid.

138 Lewis Nkosi, *Home and Exile* (London & New York: Longman, 1965), 7.

139 Ibid.

140 Ibid., 8.

141 Ibid.

142 Ntongela Masilela, 'New African Modernity and the New African Movement', in *The Cambridge History of South African Literature*, Eds David Attwell & Derek Attridge (Cambridge: Cambridge University Press, 2011), 335.

143 Nkosi, *Home and Exile*, 13.

144 Ibid.

145 Ibid., 20.

146 Dorothy Driver, 'The Fabulous Fifties: Short Fiction in English', in *The Cambridge History of South African Literature*, Eds David Attwell & Derek Attridge (Cambridge: Cambridge University Press, 2011), 399–400.

147 Ibid., 399.

148 Nkosi, *Home and Exile*, 81.

149 Ibid.

150 Ibid., 82.

151 Ibid.

Chapter 4

1   Dionne Brand, *A Map to the Door of No Return: Notes to Belonging*
     (Toronto: Vintage Canada, 2001), 1.
2   Anjali Prabhu, *Hybridity: Limits, Transformations, Prospects* (Albany:
     SUNY Press, 2007), 12.
3   Brandt, *A Map to the Door of No Return*, 19.
4   Ibid., 137.
5   Ibid., 10.
6   Ibid., 11.
7   George Lamming, *Sovereignty of the Imagination: Conversations III –
     Language and the Politics of Ethnicity* (Philipsburg, St. Martin: House of
     Nehesi, 2009), 4.
8   Ibid., 4.
9   Ibid.
10   Ibid., 5.
11   Jamaica Kincaid, *A Small Place* (New York: Farrar, Straus, & Giroux,
     2000), 79–80.
12   Ibid., 53.
13   Ralph Dalleo & Curdella Forbes, 'Introduction', in *Caribbean Literature
     in Transition, 1920–1970*, Eds Dalleo & Forbes (Cambridge: Cambridge
     University Press, 2020), 2.
14   Ibid., 3.
15   Brand, *A Map to the Door of No Return*, 142.
16   Ibid., 142.
17   Ibid., 143.
18   Ibid.
19   Ibid.
20   Ibid.
21   Ibid.
22   Ibid., 144.
23   Ibid.
24   Ibid.
25   Ibid.
26   Ibid., 145.
27   Ibid.
28   Ibid.
29   Ibid.
30   Ibid., 146.
31   Ibid.
32   Ibid.
33   Ibid.
34   Ibid., 147.

35   Denise deCaires Narain, 'Life Writing, Gender and Caribbean Narrative
     1970–2015: Itinerant Self-Making in the Postcolonial Caribbean', in
     Caribbean Literature in Transition, 1970–2020, Eds Ronald Cummings &
     Alison Donnell (Cambridge: Cambridge University Press, 2020), 76.

36   Kei Miller, 'Here Are the Others: Caribbean Creative Nonfiction', in
     Caribbean Literature in Transition, 1970–2020, Eds Ronald Cummings &
     Alison Donnell (Cambridge: Cambridge University Press, 2020), 158.

37   Ibid., 159.

38   David Featherstone, Christopher Gair, Christian Høgsbjerg, & Andrew
     Smith, 'Introduction: *Beyond a Boundary* at Fifty', in *Marxism,
     Colonialism, and Cricket: C.L.R. James's Beyond a Boundary*, Eds
     Featherstone, Gair, Høgsbjerg, & Smith (Durham & London: Duke
     University Press, 2018), 4.

39   Ibid., 5.

40   Ibid., 10.

41   Ibid., 13.

42   Ibid.

43   Ibid., 14.

44   Frank Rosengarten, *Urbane Revolutionary: C.L.R. James and the Struggle
     for a New Society* (Jackson: University Press of Mississippi, 2008), 9.

45   Ibid., 13.

46   C.L.R. James, *Beyond a Boundary: 50th Anniversary Edition* (Durham:
     Duke University Press, 2013), 16.

47   Ibid., 16.

48   Ibid.

49   Ibid.

50   Ibid., 17.

51   Ibid.

52   Ibid., 16.

53   Selwyn R. Cudjoe, 'C.L.R. James: Plumbing His Caribbean Roots', in
     Marxism, Colonialism, and Cricket: C.L.R. James's Beyond a Boundary,
     Eds Featherstone, Gair, Høgsbjerg, & Smith (Durham & London: Duke
     University Press, 2018), 38.

54   James, *Beyond a Boundary*, 18.

55   Ibid.

56   Ibid.

57   Rosengarten, *Urbane Revolutionary*, 10.

58   Cudjoe, 'C.L.R. James: Plumbing His Caribbean Roots', 37.

59   Ian Baucom, *Out of Place: Englishness, Empire, and the Location of Identity*
     (Princeton: Princeton University Press, 1999), 155.

60   Rosengarten, *Urbane Revolutionary*, 13.

61   Ibid., 13.

62   Ibid.

63   Cudjoe, 'C.L.R. James: Plumbing His Caribbean Roots', 41.

64   Ibid.

65   Ibid.

66   James, *Beyond a Boundary*, 38–9.

67   George Lamming, *The Pleasures of Exile* (Ann Arbor: University of
      Michigan Press, 1992), 151.

68   Farred, *What's My Name?* 109.

69   James, *Beyond a Boundary*, 30.

70   Ibid., 30.

71   Christian Høgsbjerg, 'C.L.R. James's "British Civilization"? Exploring
      the "Dark Unfathomed Caves" of Beyond a Boundary', in *Marxism,
      Colonialism, and Cricket: C.L.R. James's Beyond a Boundary*, Eds
      Featherstone, Gair, Høgsbjerg, & Smith (Durham & London: Duke
      University Press, 2018), 53.

72   Qtd. in ibid.

73   Ibid., 56.

74   James, *Beyond a Boundary*, 32.

75   Ibid.

76   Ibid., 33.

77   Ibid., 196.

78   Ibid.

79   Ibid.

80   Ibid., 131–2.

81   Ibid., 197.

82   Ibid.

83   Ibid., 202.

84   Ibid., 203.

85   Ibid., 40.

86   Ibid.

87   Ibid., 43.

88   Claire Westall, 'C.L.R. James and the Arts of Beyond a Boundary:
      Literary Lessons, Cricketing Aesthetics, and World-Historical Heroes',
      in *Marxism, Colonialism, and Cricket: C.L.R. James's Beyond a Boundary*,
      Eds Featherstone, Gair, Høgsbjerg, & Smith (Durham & London: Duke
      University Press, 2018), 175.

89   James, *Beyond a Boundary*, 160.

90   Ibid.

91   Ibid., 161.

92   Ibid., 162.

93   Ibid.

94   Ibid., 164.

95   Ibid., 165.

96   V.S. Naipaul, 'Reading and Writing: A Personal Account', in *Literary
      Occasions: Essays*, Eds. Naipaul (New York: Vintage, 2003), 1.

97   Ibid.

98   Ibid.
99   Ibid.
100 Ibid., 3.
101 Ibid.
102 Ibid.
103 Ibid.
104 Ibid., 4.
105 Ibid., 3.
106 Ibid.
107 Sanjay Krishnan, *V.S. Naipaul's Journeys: From Periphery to Center* (New York: Columbia University Press, 2020), 31.
108 Naipaul, 'Reading and Writing: A Personal Account', 3.
109 Ibid.
110 Ibid., 5.
111 Ibid., 4.
112 Ibid.
113 Ibid.
114 Ibid., 6.
115 Ibid., 4.
116 Gail Low, '"Read! Learn!": Grobalisation and (G)localization in Caribbean Textbook Publishing', in *The Global Histories of Books: Methods and Practices*, Eds Elleke Boehmer, Rouven Kunstmann, Priyasha Mukhopadhyay, Asha Rogers (New York: Palgrave Macmillan, 2017), 100.
117 Ibid., 101.
118 Ibid., 6.
119 Ibid.
120 Ibid., 33.
121 Rob Nixon, *London Calling: V.S. Naipaul, Postcolonial Mandarin* (New York: Oxford University Press, 1992), 4.
122 Ibid., 18.
123 Ibid., 25.
124 Ibid.
125 Ibid.
126 Ibid., 27.
127 Ibid., 41.
128 Ibid.
129 Ibid., 110.

Chapter 5

1   Nirad C. Chaudhuri, *Autobiography of an Unknown Indian* (New York: Macmillan, 1951), 356–7.

2   As the native elite said to Hyde East in May 1816. Rosinka Chaudhuri, *Gentlemen Poets in Colonial Bengal: Emergent Nationalism and the Orientalist Project* (Kolkata: Seagull, 2002).

3   Rajeswari Sunder Rajan, 'Fixing English: Nation, Language, Subject', in *The Lie of the Land: English Literary Studies in India*, Ed. Rajeswari Sunder Rajan (Delhi: Oxford University Press, 1992), 11.

4   Ibid., 12.

5   Ibid.

6   Ibid.

7   Sanjay Seth, *Subject Lessons: The Western Education of Colonial India* (Durham & London: Duke University Press, 2007), 45.

8   Chaudhuri, 'Macaulay's Magic Hat'.

9   Seth, *Subject Lessons*, 60.

10 Harihar Das, *Life and Letters of Toru Dutt* (London: Oxford University Press, 1921), 10.

11 Virginia Woolf, *Three Guineas* (New York: Harcourt, 1938).

12 *Toru Dutt: Collected Prose and Poetry*, Ed. Chandani Lokugé (Delhi: Oxford University Press, 2006), 254.

13 Das, *Life and Letters of Toru Dutt*, 43.

14 Ibid.

15 Toru Dutt, 'An Eurasian Poet', in *The Bengal Magazine* (December 1874), 189.

16 Ibid., 190.

17 Ibid.

18 Ibid., 191.

19 *Toru Dutt: Collected Prose and Poetry*, 62.

20 Ibid., 238.

21 Ibid.

22 Ibid., 250.

23 Malavika Karlekar, 'An Epistolary Friendship: Toru Dutt Was as European as She Was Bengali', *The Telegraph*, 29 April 2007, https://www.telegraphindia.com/opinion/an-epistolary-friendship-toru-dutt-was-as-european-as-she-was-bengali/cid/1028215.

24 *Toru Dutt: Collected Prose and Poetry*, 277.

25 Ibid.

26 Ibid., 336–7.

27 Chaudhuri, *The Autobiography of an Unknown Indian*, 207.

28 Ibid.

29 Arvind Krishna Mehrotra, *Partial Recall: Essays on Literature and Literary History* (Ranikhet: Permanent Black, 2012), 1.

30 Chaudhuri, *The Autobiography of an Unknown Indian*, 7.

31 Ibid., 391.

32 Ibid., 355.

33 Ibid.

34   Ibid., 355–6.

35   Ibid., 356.

36   Ibid., 357.

37   Mrinalini Sinha quotes this definition of 'babu' from Hobson-Jobson, a glossary of Anglo-Indian words and phrases compiled in the 1880s. Sinha, *Colonial Masculinity: The 'Manly Englishman' and the 'Effeminate Bengali' in the Late Nineteenth Century* (Manchester: Manchester University Press, 1995), 18.

38   Ian Almond, 'Four Ways of Reading Nirad C. Chaudhuri: A Case Study of a Postcolonial Conservative', *Orbis Litterarum* 66 (6), 2011, 2.

39   Ruvani Ranasinha, *South Asian Writers in Twentieth Century Britain: Culture in Transition* (Oxford: Oxford University Press, 2007), 85.

40   Nirad C. Chaudhuri, *A Passage to England* (London: Hogarth, 1989), 16.

41   Chaudhuri, *The Autobiography of an Unknown Indian*, 324.

42   Bibhutibhushan Bandopadhyay, *Aparajito. Upanyas Samagra* (Kolkata: Mitra, 2006), 50 [Translation mine].

43   Chaudhuri, *The Autobiography of an Unknown Indian*, 333.

44   Ibid., 346.

45   Ibid., 335.

46   Chakrabarty, *Provincializing Europe*, 7.

47   Priya Satia, *Time's Monster: How History Makes History* (Cambridge, MA: Harvard University Press, 2020), 1–2.

48   Ibid., 2.

49   Pallavi Rastogi, 'Timeless England Will Remain Hanging in the Air', *Prose Studies: History, Theory, Criticism* 28 (3), 2006, 318–36.

50   Ibid., 320.

51   Chaudhuri, *The Autobiography of an Unknown Indian*, 324.

52   Ibid., 327.

53   Ibid., 329.

54   Ibid., 330.

55   Ibid.

56   Meenakshi Mukherjee, 'We Say Desh: The Other Nirad Babu', in *Nirad C. Chaudhuri, the First Hundred Years: A Celebration*, Ed. Swapan Dasgupta (Delhi: HarperCollins India, 1998), 83.

57   Chaudhuri, *The Autobiography of an Unknown Indian*, 351.

58   Rudyard Kipling, *Kim* (Oxford: Oxford University Press, 1987), 162.

59   Chaudhuri, *The Autobiography of an Unknown Indian*, 352.

60   Ibid., 329.

61   Ibid., 305.

62   Ibid., 304.

63   Ibid., 306.

64   Ibid., 372.

65   Ibid., 160.

66   Ibid.

67 Qtd. in Dipesh Chakrabarty, *The Calling of History: Sir Jadunath Sarkar and His Empire of Truth* (Chicago: The University of Chicago Press, 2015), 38.
68 Mehrotra, *Partial Recall*, 64.
69 Ibid., 67.
70 Ibid., 2.
71 Ibid.
72 Arvind Krishna Mehrotra, *Translating the Indian Past and Other Literary Histories* (Ranikhet: Permanent Black, 2019), 220.
73 Ibid., 221–2.
74 Ibid.
75 Pankaj Mishra, 'Edmund Wilson in Benares', in *The Picador Book of Modern Indian Literature*, Ed. Amit Chaudhuri (London: Picador, 2001), 356.
76 Ibid., 357.
77 Ibid., 370.
78 Ibid.
79 Ibid.
80 Ibid., 358.
81 Ibid., 360.
82 Ibid., 368.
83 Ibid.
84 J. Daniel Elam, *World Literature for the Wretched of the Earth* (New York: Fordham University Press, 2021), ix, x, 47.

Chapter 6

1 Henry Erskine Cowper (1979), 'British Education, Public and Private, and the British Empire 1880–1930' (Ph.D. Dissertation, University of Edinburgh), 288.
2 Gayatri Chakravarty Spivak, 'How to Read a Culturally Different Book', in *An Aesthetic Education in the Age of Globalization*, Ed. Spivak, 73–96 (Cambridge, MA: Harvard University Press, 2013).
3 Naipaul, *Literary Occasions*, 37.
4 Abrahams, *Tell Freedom*, 234.
5 Chinua Achebe, *The Education of a British-Protected Child: Essays* (New York: Knopf, 2009), 17.
6 Alexander Bubb, 'Reading by Chance in a World of Wandering Texts', in *The Global Histories of Books: Methods and Practices*, Eds Elleke Boehmer, Rouven Kunstmann, Priyasha Mukhopadhyay, and Asha Rogers (New York: Palgrave Macmillan, 2017), 84.
7 Henry Erskine Cowper, 'British Education, Public and Private, and the British Empire 1880–1930', 110.

8   Wells, qtd. in ibid., 110.

9   Stephen Jackson, 'Mass Education and the British Empire', *History Compass* (10 January 2022), 2. Jackson refers to further research on the subject: 'May et al. (2016) emphasize these transnational missionary links as applied to indigenous peoples in settler colonial infant schools. Tschurenev's (2019) study of the monitorial system in the early 19th century argues that missionaries applied the same "civilizing" mission to the British working class at home as they did to colonized peoples in India' (3).

10   Swartz, 2019, p. 36, qtd in Jackson, 'Mass Education and the British Empire', 4.

11   Tamson Pietsch, *Empire of Scholars: Universities, Networks and the British Academic World 1850–1939* (Manchester & New York: Manchester University Press, 2013), 5.

12   Ibid.

13   Ibid., 32.

14   Ibid., 20.

15   Cowper, 'British Education, Public and Private, and the British Empire 1880–1930', 116.

16   Ibid.

17   Qtd. in Cowper, 288.

18   Ibid.

19   Ibid., 288–9.

20   Cowper, 'British Education, Public and Private, and the British Empire 1880–1930', 349.

21   Ibid., 350.

22   Jackson, 'Mass Education and the British Empire', 5.

23   Allender, 2016b, cited in ibid.

24   White, 2003, cited in ibid.

25   Sanjay Seth, *Beyond Reason*, 9.

26   Lewis R. Gordon, *Disciplinary Decadence: Living Thought in Trying Times* (London: Routledge, 2006), 11–2.

27   Seth, *Beyond Reason*, 24.

28   Christopher Hilliard, *English as Vocation: The Scrutiny Movement* (Oxford: Oxford University Press, 2012), 217.

29   Ibid., 217–18.

30   Ibid., 223.

31   Chakrabarty, *Provincializing Europe*, 255.

32   Ibid.

33   John Guillory, *Professing Criticism: Essays on the Organization of Literary Study* (Chicago: University of Chicago Press, 2022), 252.

34   Ibid., 253.

35   Ibid., 256–7.

36   Derek Attridge, 'In Praise of Amateurism', in *The Critic as Amateur*, Eds Saikat Majumdar & Aarthi Vadde (New York: Bloomsbury Academic, 2019), 37.

37   Ibid., 49.
38   Tom Lutz, 'In the Shadow of the Archive', in *The Critic as Amateur*, Eds
     Saikat Majumdar & Aarthi Vadde (New York: Bloomsbury Academic,
     2019), 49.
39   Naipaul, *Literary Occasions*, 162.
40   Ibid.
41   Srinivas Aravamudan, *Enlightenment Orientalism: Resisting the Rise of the
     Novel* (Chicago: University of Chicago Press), 4.
42   Ibid., 5–6.
43   Chaudhuri, *The Autobiography of an Unknown Indian*, 346.
44   Chakrabarty, *Provincializing Europe*, 7.
45   Satia, *Time's Monster*, 1–2.
46   Abrahams, *Tell Freedom*, 260.
47   Ibid., 261.
48   Ibid., 234.

BIBLIOGRAPHY

Peter Abrahams, *Tell Freedom: Memories of Africa* (New York: Knopf, 1954).

Chinua Achebe, *The Education of a British-Protected Child: Essays* (New York: Knopf, 2009).

Louis Althusser, 'Ideology and Ideological State Apparatuses (Notes towards and In Investigation)', in *Lenin and Philosophy and Other Essays*, trans Ben Brewster (New York: New York University Press, 2001).

Paul St. Amour, 'Weak Theory, Weak Modernism', *Modernism/Modernity*, 3 (3), 25 August, 28, https://modernismmodernity.org/articles/weak-theory-weak-modernism.

Srinivas Aravamudan, *Enlightenment Orientalism: Resisting the Rise of the Novel* (Chicago: University of Chicago Press, 2011).

Derek Attridge, 'In Praise of Amateurism', in *The Critic as Amateur*, Eds Saikat Majumdar & Aarthi Vadde (New York: Bloomsbury Academic, 2019).

David Attwell & Derek Attridge, 'Introduction', in *The Cambridge History of South African Literature*, Eds Attridge & Attwell (Cambridge: Cambridge University Press, 2011).

Chris Baldick, *The Social Mission of English Criticism, 1848–1932* (Oxford: Clarendon, 1983).

Bibhutibhushan Bandopadhyay, *Aparajito. Upanyas Samagra* (Kolkata: Mitra, 2006).

Ian Baucom, *Out of Place: Englishness, Empire, and the Location of Identity* (Princeton: Princeton University Press, 1999).

Lauren Berlant, *Cruel Optimism* (Durham & London: Duke University Press, 2011).

Stephen Best & Sharon Marcus, 'Surface Reading: An Introduction', *Representations* 108 (1), Fall 2009.

Dionne Brand, *A Map to the Door of No Return: Notes to Belonging* (Toronto: Doubleday Canada, 2001).

Alexander Bubb, 'Reading by Chance in a World of Wandering Texts', in *The Global Histories of Books: Methods and Practices*, Eds Elleke Boehmer, Rouven Kunstmann, Priyasha Mukhopadhyay, & Asha Rogers (New York: Palgrave Macmillan, 2017).

Dipesh Chakrabarty, *Provincializing Europe: Postcolonial Thought and Historical Difference* (Princeton: Princeton University Press, 2000).

Dipesh Chakrabarty, *The Calling of History: Sir Jadunath Sarkar and His Empire of Truth* (Chicago: The University of Chicago Press, 2015).

Partha Chatterjee, *Nation and Its Fragments: Colonial and Postcolonial Histories* (Princeton: Princeton University Press, 1993).

Nirad C. Chaudhuri, *Autobiography of an Unknown Indian* (New York: Macmillan, 1951).

Rosinka Chaudhuri, *Gentlemen Poets in Colonial Bengal: Emergent Nationalism and the Orientalist Project* (Kolkata: Seagull, 2002).

Rosinka Chaudhuri, 'Macaulay's Magic Hat: The Colonial Education System and the Canon of World Literature', in *Handbook of Anglophone World Literatures*, Eds Stefan Helgesson, Birgit Neumann, & Gabriele Rippl (Berlin/Boston: De Gruyter, 2020).

J.M. Coetzee, 'The Novel in Africa', in *Elizabeth Costello*, Ed. Coetzee (New York: Penguin, 2004).

Daniel Coleman, *In Bed with the Word: Reading, Spirituality, and Cultural Politics* (Edmonton: University of Alberta Press, 2009).

Henry Erskine Cowper (1979), 'British Education, Public and Private, and the British Empire 1880–1930' (Ph.D. Dissertation, University of Edinburgh).

Selwyn R. Cudjoe, 'C.L.R. James: Plumbing His Caribbean Roots', in *Marxism, Colonialism, and Cricket: C.L.R. James's Beyond a Boundary*, Eds David Featherstone, Christopher Gair, Christian Høgsbjerg, & Andrew Smith (Durham & London: Duke University Press, 2018).

Ralph Dalleo & Curdella Forbes, 'Introduction', in *Caribbean Literature in Transition, 1920–1970*, Eds Dalleo & Forbes (Cambridge: Cambridge University Press, 2020).

Harihar Das, *Life and Letters of Toru Dutt* (London: Oxford University Press, 1921).

Dorothy Driver, 'The Fabulous Fifties: Short Fiction in English', in *The Cambridge History of South African Literature*, Eds David Attwell & Derek Attridge (Cambridge: Cambridge University Press, 2011).

Simon During, 'The Postcolonial Aesthetic', *PMLA* 129 (3), May 2014.

Toru Dutt, 'An Eurasian Poet', in *The Bengal Magazine* (December 1874), 189.

J. Daniel Elam, *World Literature for the Wretched of the Earth* (New York: Fordham University Press, 2021).

Merve Emre, *Paraliterary: The Making of Bad Readers in Postwar America* (Chicago: University of Chicago Press, 2017).

Merve Emre, 'Has Academia Ruined Literary Criticism?' *The New Yorker*, 16 January 2023.

Grant Farred, *What's My Name? Black Vernacular Intellectuals* (Minneapolis: University of Minnesota Press, 2003).

David Featherstone, Christopher Gair, Christian Høgsbjerg, & Andrew Smith, 'Introduction: *Beyond a Boundary* at Fifty', in *Marxism, Colonialism, and Cricket: C.L.R. James's Beyond a Boundary*, Eds David Featherstone, Christopher Gair, Christian Høgsbjerg, & Andrew Smith (Durham & London: Duke University Press, 2018).

Rita Felski, *The Limits of Critique* (Chicago: University of Chicago Press, 2015).

Rita Felski, *Hooked: Art and Attachment* (Chicago: University of Chicago Press, 2020).

Paolo Freire, *Pedagogy of the Oppressed*, trans Myra Bergman Ramos (New York: Bloomsbury Academic, 2000).

Regenia Gagnier, *Subjectivities: A History of Self-Representation in Britain, 1832–1920* (New York: Oxford, 1991).

Amitav Ghosh, 'The March of the Novel through History: The Testimony of My Grandfather's Bookcase; Text of the Arthur Ravencroft Memorial Lecture, Delivered at the University of Leeds, 5 March 1997', *Kunapipi* 19 (3), 1997.

Lewis R. Gordon, *Disciplinary Decadence: Living Thought in Trying Times* (London: Routledge, 2006).

Ranajit Guha, 'The Prose of Counter-Insurgency', in *Selected Subaltern Studies*, Eds Ranajit Guha & Gayatri Chakravarty Spivak (Oxford: Oxford University Press, 1988).

John Guillory, *Cultural Capital: The Problem of Literary Canon Formation* (Chicago: University of Chicago Press, 1993).

John Guillory, *Professing Criticism: Essays on the Organization of Literary Study* (Chicago: University of Chicago Press, 2022).

Abdulrazak Gurnah, 'Learning to Read', in *Map Reading: The Nobel Lecture and Other Writings*, Ed. Gurnah (London: Bloomsbury, 2021).

Judith Halbestam, *The Queer Art of Failure* (Durham: Duke University Press, 2011).

Christopher Hilliard, *English as Vocation: The Scrutiny Movement* (Oxford: Oxford University Press, 2012).

bell hooks, *Teaching to Transgress: Education as the Practice of Freedom* (London: Routledge, 1994).

Stephen Jackson, 'Mass Education and the British Empire', *History Compass* (10 January 2022).

C.L.R. James, *Beyond a Boundary: 50th Anniversary Edition* (Durham: Duke University Press, 2013).

Malavika Karlekar, 'An Epistolary Friendship: Toru Dutt Was as European as She Was Bengali', *The Telegraph*, 29 April 2007, https://www.telegraphindia.com/opinion/an-epistolary-friendship-toru-dutt-was-as-european-as-she-was-bengali/cid/1028215.

Roger Kimball, 'Schiller's Aesthetic Education', *New Criterion*, March 2001.

Jamaica Kincaid, *A Small Place* (New York: Farrar, Straus, and Giroux, 1988).

Rudyard Kipling, *Kim* (Oxford: Oxford University Press, 1987).

Sanjay Krishnan, *V.S. Naipaul's Journeys: From Periphery to Center* (New York: Columbia University Press, 2020).

George Lamming, *Sovereignty of the Imagination: Conversations III – Language and the Politics of Ethnicity* (Philipsburg, St. Martin: House of Nehesi, 2009).

Heather Love, *Feeling Backward: Loss and the Politics of Queer History* (Cambridge, MA: Harvard University Press, 2007).

Tom Lutz, 'In the Shadow of the Archive', in *The Critic as Amateur*, Eds Saikat Majumdar & Aarthi Vadde (New York: Bloomsbury Academic, 2019).

Sindiwe Magona, *To My Children's Children* (Claremont: David Philip, 1990).

Sindiwe Magona, *Forced to Grow* (Claremont: David Philip, 1992).

Sindiwe Magona, *Living, Loving and Lying Awake at Night* (Northampton, MA: Interlink Books, 2009).

Saikat Majumdar, 'The Dailiness and Trauma and Liberation in Zoë Wicomb', in Majumdar, *Prose of the World: Modernism and the Banality of Empire*, Ed. Manjumdar (New York: Columbia University Press, 2013).

Saikat Majumdar, 'The Provincial Polymath: The Curious Cosmopolitanism of Nirad C Chaudhuri', *PMLA* 130 (2), 2015.

Ntongela Masilela, 'New African Modernity and the New African Movement', in *The Cambridge History of South African Literature*, Eds David Attwell & Derek Attridge (Cambridge: Cambridge University Press, 2011).

Arvind Krishna Mehrotra, *Partial Recall: Essays on Literature and Literary History* (Ranikhet: Permanent Black, 2012).

Arvind Krishna Mehrotra, *Translating the Indian Past and Other Literary Histories* (Ranikhet: Permanent Black, 2019).

Andy Merrifield, *The Amateur: The Pleasures of Doing What You Love* (London: Verso, 2017).

Kei Miller, 'Here Are the Others: Caribbean Creative Nonfiction', in *Caribbean Literature in Transition, 1970–2020*, Eds Ronald Cummings & Alison Donnell (Cambridge: Cambridge University Press, 2020).

Pankaj Mishra, 'Edmund Wilson in Benares', in *The Picador Book of Modern Indian Literature*, Ed. Amit Chaudhuri (London: Picador, 2001).

William Bloke Modisane, *Blame Me on History* (Johannesburg & Cape Town: Ad Donker Publishers, 1986).

Franco Moretti, 'Conjectures on World Literature', *New Left Review*, January/February 2000, https://newleftreview.org/issues/ii1/articles/franco-moretti-conjectures-on-world-literature.

Es'kia Mphahlele, *The African Image* (London: Faber, 1974).

Ankhi Mukherjee, *What Is a Classic? Postcolonial Rewriting and Invention of the Canon* (Stanford: Stanford University Press, 2014).

Meenakshi Mukherjee, 'We Say Desh: The Other Nirad Babu', in *Nirad C. Chaudhuri, the First Hundred Years: A Celebration*, Ed. Swapan Dasgupta (Delhi: HarperCollins India, 1998).

V.S. Naipaul, 'Reading and Writing: A Personal Account', in *Literary Occasions: Essays*, Eds. Naipaul (New York: Vintage, 2003).

Denise deCaires Narain, 'Life Writing, Gender and Caribbean Narrative 1970–2015: Itinerant Self-Making in the Postcolonial Caribbean', in *Caribbean Literature in Transition, 1970–2020*, Eds Ronald Cummings & Alison Donnell (Cambridge: Cambridge University Press, 2020).

Njabulo Ndebele, *Fools and Other Stories* (Johannesburg: Pan Macmillan South Africa, 2006).

Rob Nixon, *London Calling: V.S. Naipaul, Postcolonial Mandarin* (New York: Oxford University Press, 1992).

Lewis Nkosi, *Home and Exile* (London & New York: Longman, 1965).

Joseph North, *Literary Criticism: A Political History* (Cambridge, MA: Harvard University Press, 2017).

Graham Pechey, Foreword to *South African Literature and Culture: Rediscovery of the Ordinary*, by Njabulo Ndebele (Scotsville: University of KwaZulu Natal Press, 2006).

Tamson Pietsch, *Empire of Scholars: Universities, Networks and the British Academic World 1850–1939* (Manchester & New York: Manchester University Press, 2013).

Anjali Prabhu, *Hybridity: Limits, Transformations, Prospects* (Albany: SUNY Press, 2007).

Janice Radway, *Reading the Romance: Woman, Patriarchy, and Popular Literature* (Chapel Hill: University of North Carolina Press, 1984).

Rajeswari Sunder Rajan, 'Fixing English: Nation, Language, Subject', in *The Lie of the Land: English Literary Studies in India*, Ed. Rajeswari Sunder Rajan (Delhi: Oxford University Press, 1992).

Ruvani Ranasinha, *South Asian Writers in Twentieth Century Britain: Culture in Transition* (Oxford: Oxford University Press, 2007).

Pallavi Rastogi, 'Timeless England Will Remain Hanging in the Air', *Prose Studies: History, Theory, Criticism*, 28 March 2006.

Bruce Robbins, *Secular Vocations: Intellectuals, Professionalism, Culture* (London & New York: Verso, 1993).

Jonathan Rose, *The Intellectual Life of the British Working Classes* (New Haven: Yale University Press, 2002).

Frank Rosengarten, *Urbane Revolutionary: C.L.R. James and the Struggle for a New Society* (Jackson: University Press of Mississippi, 2008).

Edward W. Said, *Representations of the Intellectual: The 1993 Reith Lectures* (New York: Vintage Books, 1994).

Priya Satia, *Time's Monster: How History Makes History* (Cambridge, MA: Harvard University Press, 2020).

Julietta Singh, *Unthinking Mastery: Dehumanism and Decolonial Entanglements* (Durham, NC: Duke University Press, 2018).

Mrinalini Sinha, *Colonial Masculinity: The 'Manly Englishman' and the 'Effeminate Bengali' in the Late Nineteenth Century* (Manchester: Manchester University Press, 1995).

Tobias Skivereen, 'Postcritique and the Problem of the Lay Reader', *NLH: New Literary History* 53 (1), Winter 2022.

Nathan Snazza, *Animate Literacies: Literature, Affect, and the Politics of Humanism* (Durham: Duke University Press, 2019).

Gayatri Chakravarty Spivak, 'How to Read a Culturally Different Book', in *An Aesthetic Education in the Age of Globalization*, Ed. Spivak, 73–96 (Cambridge, MA: Harvard University Press, 2013).

Ngũgĩ Wa Thiong'o, 'The African Writer and the English Language', in *Colonial Discourse and Post-Colonial Theory: A Reader*, Eds Patrick Williams & Laura Chrisman (New York: Columbia University Press, 1994).

Ngũgĩ wa Thiong'o, 'Prophet Mphahlele: Named after Ezekiel', in foreword to *Down Second Avenue*, by Es'kia Mphahlele (New York: Penguin Books, 2013).

Hedley Twidle, 'Experiments with Truth: Narrative Nonfiction in South Africa', *Current Writing: Text and Reception in Southern Africa* 31 (2), 2019, 95.

Gauri Viswanathan, *Masks of Conquest: Literary Study and British Rule in India* (New York: Columbia University Press, 1989).

Claire Westall, 'C.L.R. James and the Arts of Beyond a Boundary: Literary Lessons, Cricketing Aesthetics, and World-Historical Heroes', in *Marxism, Colonialism, and Cricket: C.L.R. James's Beyond a Boundary*, Eds David Featherstone, Christopher Gair, Christian Høgsbjerg, & Andrew Smith (Durham & London: Duke University Press, 2018).

Zoë Wicomb, *You Can't Get Lost in Cape Town* (New York: Feminist Press at the City University of New York, 2000).

Kara Wittman, 'New, Interesting, and Original – The Undergraduate as Amateur', in *The Critic as Amateur*, Eds Saikat Majumdar & Aarthi Vadde (New York: Bloomsbury Academic, 2019).

INDEX